PSYCHODYNAMICS, PSYCHOTHERAPY, AND COUNSELING

Collected Papers

of

Rudolf Dreikurs, M.D.

Alfred Adler Institute
of Chicago

Revised Edition 1973
Second Printing 1977
ISBN 0-918560-12-8

Contents

INTRODUCTION

This compilation of papers is designed to present to the students material published over a period of years. We decided to leave the original papers unchanged, to permit the student a glimpse of the way the subjects have been dealt with throughout the years. Repetitions are unavoidable in such a presentation; it would make for smoother reading if an integration of the whole material would have been attempted. But then the characteristic flavor of some of the papers would have been lost. And their publication is not designed for smooth reading but for instruction and study.

It is suggested that the various papers be studied carefully, each by itself, to facilitate the digestion of a rather condensed presentation of many subjects in the field of psychotherapy and counseling.

Chicago, September 1967 Rudolf Driekurs, M.D.

INTRODUCTION TO REVISED EDITION

During the six years that have elapsed since the publication of this book, it has found increasing use as a reference and textbook. In order to serve these purposes more effectively, the original papers are now grouped under topical headings, dated and arranged in order of topicality rather than by historical development. Also added are a number of bibliographic references and a detailed concordance type of index.

Palo Alto, May 1973 Paul J. Kahn

ADLERIAN PSYCHOTHERAPY*

The technique of Psychotherapy, as developed by Alfred Adler and practiced by Adlerian psychologists, can be classified as an uncovering and interpreting form of therapy. A characteristic method of exploration, interpretation and guidance distinguishes it and, like any specific therapy, it has its own theoretic framework.

Man, in this theoretic framework, is perceived as an indivisible social being whose every action has a purpose. This holistic socioteleologic concept characterizes the theory and explains the therapeutic and educational practice of Individual Psychology.

The holistic view of man is reflected in the name, Individual Psychology. It was meant to indicate the indivisibility of man, who is more than the sum total of all his physical, mental and emotional faculties and functions. In contrast to prevalent mechanistic-deterministic theories, Adler recognized man's creative ability, which permits him to set his own goals and determine his own movements. His goals express his total personality, his past, his present and his move toward the future. The teleologic concept implies self-determination. It does not matter whether the individual is aware of his decisions or not. Consciousness is not required for most human functions, be they physical or psychological. Man operates on an economy principle; he is consciously aware only of what he needs or wants to know in detail. He uses his abilities and faculties in

---

* *Progress in Psychotherapy,* F. Fromm-Reichmann and J. L. Moreno (Eds.), N.Y: Grune and Stratton, 1956, 111-118.

line with his intentions. His mind and body, his ability to think and to feel, are at his disposal without the requirement of consciousness, which often would serve rather to impede than to assist him.

Man, as a social being, is primarily motivated by a strong desire to belong. Only within the group can he fulfill himself. All human qualities are then conceived as expressions of social interaction; they indicate movement toward others. Social interest, which permits and stimulates full social interaction, is restricted by feelings of inferiority. The "ironclad logic of social living" presupposes a status of social equality. If the individual feels inadequate or inferior to others, then he doubts his place in the group. Instead of moving toward participation, he defends himself against its demands. Mental, emotional or social maladjustment and dysfunction result from partial or total discouragement. Neurotic symptoms are safeguards; they insure against loss of prestige and against the open admission of antisocial or asocial intentions.

Self-deception about one's intentions is part of normal human experience. Nobody knows himself, nobody can be sure of his motivations and intentions. We need subjectivity to participate in social living; we need a "biased apperception" to move forcefully in a self-chosen direction. Our whole personality is based on the subjective interpretation of life during our formative years. Personality is the result of training which is less stimulated by hereditary and environmental influences than by the child's own interpretations, conclusions and decisions. The basic concept of himself and life, the guiding lines which he has set himself for orientation toward social participation, form a fixed pattern—the life style. The fundamental notions, convictions and logical assumptions underlying the life style from the "private logic" on which the individual operates.

We can distinguish four phases in every uncovering and interpretative form of psychotherapy. They are, (1) Relationship: the establishment and maintenance of a proper therapeutic relationship. (2) Analysis: which implies investigation of dynamics, leading to an understanding of the patient, his personality and his problems. (3) Interpretation: since each school has its own concept of psychodynamics, of personality development and psychopathology, methods of investigation and interpretation show characteristic differences. The Adlerian approach is chiefly distinguished from others in areas (2) and (3). (4) Reorientation and re-education.

While our technique in phases (1) and (4) may be similar to others, our explanation of the effective mechanisms may differ. Particularly our understanding of phase (4) characterizes our general orientation. While these four phases overlap, each deserves special consideration.

(1) Relationship

The proper therapeutic relationship, as we understand it, does not require transference, but a relationship of mutual trust and respect. This is more than mere establishment of contact and rapport. Therapeutic cooperation requires an alignment of goals. When the goals and interests of the patient and therapist clash, no satisfactory relationship can be established. Winning the patient's cooperation for the common task is a prerequisite for any therapy; maintaining it requires constant vigilance. What appears as "resistance" constitutes a discrepancy between the goals of the therapist and those of the patient. In each case, the proper relationship has to be re-established, differences solved, and agreement reached.

This process of maintaining a cooperative relationship, which is in itself of therapeutic value, is part of an educational process. As the patient becomes able to accept the therapist's goals, his own goals undergo a fundamental change. In many instances the patient does not believe he can get well, and his goal of therapy is merely a demonstration of good intentions; or he may want to lose his symptoms without changing his attitudes, without giving up the premises upon which he operates. In either case, the therapist must be able to win at least a temporary agreement as to the immediate procedures.

Since therapy requires close cooperation, this relationship is for many patients the first good human relationship in which the give-and-take of life can be accepted in good grace. Here the patient learns that he can stand friction and clash of interests without disrupting the relationship. An atmosphere of mutual trust and mutual respect characterizes a good therapeutic relationship. The patient needs to feel understood; he needs an anticipation of success. This element of anticipation is essential in a good therapeutic relationship, and is particularly important in moments of relapse, or at times when a plateau is reached.

(2) Psychological Investigation

Our exploration has two objectives: to know the premises on which the patient operates his life style—which requires a study of the past, and of his formative years; and to understand the present area of his field of operation, which will explain his difficulties and his psychopathology.

Most Adlerian therapists do not structure the interviews; the investigation takes place as therapy progresses. I follow a more structured procedure. The initial interview consists of an exploration of the current situation, first of the patient's "subjective situation," and includes his complaints, problems and symptoms, and how he feels and what bothers him. Then we explore his "objective situation," which involves an exploration of the patient's function in the three areas of social living—at work, in his social relationship and in his family—and in his relationship to the opposite sex. After having established the subjective and objective situation of the patient, we link both sets of information with "The Question." We ask the patient what would be different if he were well. The answer to this question explains his complaints and emotional stress in a given situation. It indicates for what purpose the patient is sick, against whom or what his symptoms are directed, and against which social threat or demand he defends himself by being sick. If his condition is of longer duration, we explore the "crisis situation" at the onset of his ailment.

After having established the nature of the present conflict and arrived at a tentative understanding of the dynamics underlying the symptoms and complaints, we explore the patient's personality. His life style alone can explain why a crisis situation arose. The life style will tell us what avenues have to be opened for a resolution of his problems, for the improvement of his emotional and mental condition, and for the rehabilitation of his social functioning.

The concept of the life style, and the technique of soliciting it, characterizes the Adlerian approach. Adler provided a definite and rather simple technique for a clear understanding of a person's basic personality pattern, which he called the life style. This very pattern, which distinguishes each individual, is developed in early childhood. It is impossible to understand any adult without information about his formative years, for that is when he developed his concept about himself and about life, concepts which are maintained throughout life, although he may remain completely unaware of the premises upon which he acts.

A clarification of the patient's life style requires an investigation of his family constellation. This investigation reveals the interaction within his first group. It shows the circumstances under which he developed his personal perspective and biases, his concepts and convictions about himself, his fundamental attitudes and approaches to life, all of which are the basis for his character, his personality.

An essential factor of the family constellation is the order of birth. It provides an immediate impression of the grouping within the family and of the characteristic place which the patient occupied in it. His impressions of his environment will be different if he is the first, second, middle, or youngest child, an only boy amongst girls, or vice versa. However, the birth order by itself does not explain the development and movements of the patient within the family setting. This development depends on his interaction with the other members of the family, primarily with the one sibling who is his main competitor. This one is most different from the patient in character, temperament, and interest. Their difference, indicating competition, results from the fact that where one succeeds, the other will give up his efforts; and where one fails, the other moves in. As a consequence, each becomes different. Conversely, the siblings who are most alike are the allies. Competition may coincide with rivalry, but is not identical to it. The personality and character traits of each child can be used, therefore, for an understanding of the lines of alliances and competition. They express the movements which each child made toward finding a place in the family group, the interactions which took place among all, and the way in which they influenced each other.

The powers behind the scene are the parents. They facilitate, by their approval or disapproval, success and failure of each sibling. But it is not so much their direct relationship to the patient, their emotional interaction, their favoritism which affects the patient's development (unless he is an only child). More important than the parental attitude toward him is the success and failure of other siblings. Even a favored child will feel defeated if his neglected competitor should be more successful.

The patient's description of his parents rounds out the picture of his family constellation. His parents establish the family atmosphere, and set the pattern for all interpersonal relationships within the family. They provide guiding lines for conduct and are the prototypes of the roles of men and women. Other people living with the family have to be included for the complete picture.

After the setting is established, we can determine from the patient's early recollections the conclusions which he drew under circumstances. From the multitude of experiences to which he has been exposed in his early childhood, he remembers only those which coincide with his outlook on life. All early recollections show, therefore, the same pattern; where they differ, they supplement but never contradict each other.

(3) Interpretation

A certain amount of interpretation coincides with investigation and analysis. As a rule, whatever material comes up is interpreted to the patient. In this sense, psychotherapy constitutes a learning procedure. The patient learns about himself, about his motivations, intentions, and goals.

The most characteristic aspect of our interpretations is the constant emphasis on goals. We are less concerned about how the patient feels, and do not explain to him why he does so but rather for what purpose. We confront him constantly with his movements, with his intentions. We explain his private logic, which he cannot see for himself. The most difficult area of gaining insight is provided by emotional experiences. Emotions by their very nature are not inducive to insight. As soon as they are recognized in their purpose, they diminish or evaporate.

All experiences of the patient, be they in the office, in his interaction with the therapist, or outside as revealed by his report, are utilized to explain his goals and movements. Constant reference is made to his basic premises, to his life style. An improvement presupposes a change in the life style, at least a partial correction of some of the fundamental basic mistakes. The patient is never told what to do, but is always informed about the purpose of his behavior. It is then left to him to draw his own conclusions.

Not only actual experiences, but fantasies and dreams indicate the patient's movements. Their interpretation provides insight. Dreams permit an evaluation of the patient's attitudes, progress, or relapse. They are the "factory of emotions." They reveal the private logic, not restricted by demands of reality, and, therefore, indicate the patient's real intentions.

(4) Re-orientation

This is the most important phase of psychotherapy. Its extent, intensity and duration spells success or failure of therapy. Certain psychological dynamics take place in this process of reorientation which have not been discussed in the previous phases. Reorientation can be accomplished without uncovering or interpreting procedures, as witnessed by the success of non-analytic forms of therapy, such as hypnosis, wake-suggestion, and others. This indicates that reorientation must have its own dynamic elements. It is uncertain whether it can be permanent and satisfactory without deeper understanding and analysis of the problems involved. However, since each school of thought is inclined to doubt that the other provides real insight, it actually becomes questionable how far insight is necessary for reorientation. As an example, one school may consider any therapy as superficial which does not explore the unconscious, and another may have a similar reservation if the life style is not recognized and dealt with. We are inclined to regard as inadequate any therapy which neglects to explore, to understand and to correct the social and psychological mechanisms behind the patient's difficulties.

To motivate reorientation, I employ a mirror technique, confronting the patient with his goals and intentions. Moreno also employs a "mirror technique" for similar purposes in psychodrama. Interpretation of goals is singularly effective in stimulating change. When the patient begins to recognize his goals, his own conscience becomes a motivating factor. Adler called this process "spitting in the patient's soup." However, insight into goals and intentions is not merely restrictive; it makes the patient aware also of his power, of his ability to make decisions, of his freedom to choose his own direction.

But insight is not the only therapeutic agent. Our understanding of the dynamics of deficiency and failure makes encouragement appear as the essential factor in stimulating rehabilitation, adjustment and cure. It is essential in all corrective endeavors, the basis of all "supportive" therapy. Feeling inferior means having no place in society; that is worse than death. Our competitive culture increases this danger of not measuring up.

This fundamental discouragement requires counteraction in every therapy. This may be done deliberately and consciously or it may be a by-product. Success of a therapist depends entirely on his ability to provide encouragement; conversely, corrective failure is generally due to an inability of the therapist to encourage.

The trite use of the term "encouragement" prevents a full recognition of its significance and the complexity of its application. As a basis of reorientation, it is a means to restore the patient's faith in himself, the realization of his strength and ability and the belief in his own dignity and worth. Without encouragement neither insight nor change is possible.

Imparting to the patient a sense of worth and value contradicts many social influences to which he is exposed. Society puts a premium on prestige; therapy minimizes its significance. It attempts to eliminate vanity and anxiety about status, which society stimulates. We try to free the patient from the vertical movement by which he constantly measures himself against others. In this way, psychotherapy attempts to replace wrong social values. In this sense, again, therapy is primarily an educational process.

The Goal of Therapy

Unfortunately removal of symptoms does not guarantee success of therapy. The patient may get well to avoid therapy, to escape facing himself and changing basic mistakes. Evaluation of progress is only partly based on the improvement of the patient's overt behavior, of his subjective feeling and better functioning. The final proof of the patient's satisfactory reorientation is the change in his basic mistakes, indicated by a change in his early recollections. If a significant improvement has taken place, new incidents are recollected, reported recollections show significant changes or are in some cases completely forgotten. An examination of the patient's function in life indicates whether he still continues to operate on his old concepts and premises, or whether he has changed them.

We cannot expect a complete change in the patient's outlook on life. But some significant changes of the most detrimental premises are necessary to presume a more permanent adjustment. However, the therapeutic process does not end with the termination of therapy. Changes during therapy are probably less significant than the changes which are made after termination. The final result of the therapeutic experience is the extent and the nature of a new training. Therapy puts the patient on a different track, so to speak. In this sense, it may prove to be successful even if, at the moment of termination, which may be accidental or forced, no beneficial result was apparent.

THE TECHNIQUE OF PSYCHOTHERAPY*

Ever since the first systematic attempts to influence man's psychic life therapeutically, various theories have been held with a view to furnishing a scientific foundation for the different therapeutic methods. Let us cite those of Charcot, Bernheim, Dubois, Coue, and Freud, besides that whole army of practicing psychotherapists who have developed numerous theories to support their own more or less individually-colored methods of treatment. Alfred Adler's Individual Psychology has given us a definite approach to psychotherapy, and has provided us with insight into those factors which are significant in every psychological treatment. This method uses rationalization to influence emotions. It attacks the problems directly, and thereby avoids many time-consuming detours. It appeals to the common sense of the patient. Some of its techniques are restricted to the practice of psychiatrists who can spend much time in the treatment of one patient, but some procedures can be applied by any physician who tries to influence his patients.

It has often been held that the therapeutic efficacy of psychiatric work—and likewise, in a great measure, probably of any medical therapy— depends on the individual physician's personality. The notion persists that the method one uses is of less importance than the person who uses it. There is much to be said for this, when we consider the significant roles which suggestions, confidence, and power of persuasion can play in the course of any treatment, especially of a psychiatric treatment. This influence of a strong personality seems quite logical, since the neurotic person is, above all, one who is discouraged. A self-confident physician, sure of his ability, will

* *Chicago Medical School Quarterly*, 1944, 5, 4-7, 35.

therefore have a much more encouraging effect than one who is not so confident. His power will probably even be overestimated by the patient, to whom the contrast with his own weakness is especially obvious; thus the physician will enjoy a measure of trust which will cause all of his prescriptions to be regarded as salutary. Moreover, everybody unconsciously works towards bringing about that which he expects—be it pleasure or pain; therefore the expectations evoked by the physician have a great stimulating effect.

A therapist with a so-called "strong personality" may much more easily establish close contact between himself and the patient. A great ability to make human contacts is probably one of the reasons for the success of many practitioners. It does not matter so much what else goes on. As long as the patient is in contact with the therapist he feels strong, and hence, is well. How important it is for the therapist to arouse in his patient a feeling of community is also to be seen in the fact that every experienced psychotherapist can observe fluctuations in the success of his work. The reason for this is primarily that he is not equally ready at all times to adjust himself to his patients.

To a certain degree this also applies to the psychiatrist's attitude toward the individual patient. Yet the relationship is quite complex. A strong emotional interest in the patient does not necessarily imply great probability of success. Indeed, the opposite is true; the more interested a psychiatrist is in the cure of a particular patient, the worse is the prognosis. Adler has pointed out repeatedly that in psychotherapy, as in life generally, in order to do the right thing unself-consciously and with assurance, one must have no preconceptions in one's work. He who is too eager to accomplish a certain task, come what may, is actually afraid of failure and therefore cannot act objectively. Aside from this, a too strong interest on the part of the therapist in the cure of a particular case delivers the therapist over completely into the hands of the patient. The latter then easily dominates the therapist's behavior by rewarding with improvement whatever he regards as agreeable, and by responding to unpleasant information by getting worse. Thus an occasional improvement or relapse in the course of the therapy may signify merely the personal relationships, while the really important point, after all, should be the patient's change in his attitude toward life, the change of his life style, so that he can fulfill the demands of human society.

The outstanding factor in treatment is the elucidation of the situation, the illumination of the field of operation in which the patient lives and within which all his behavior patterns have a definite meaning. This orbit within which the patient's life runs its course is established in earliest childhood. What matters, therefore, is that the patient would come to recognize his own life style, the plan according to which he has arranged his life. Reading and studying Individual Psychology can play a great role in everyone's self-education and no doubt contributes toward the gradual changing of one's behavior. This process, however, takes place very slowly and has its limitations. In cases of severe disturbances reading alone cannot accomplish a cure. Otherwise we should merely have to hand our books to our patients instead of submitting them to long drawnout and expensive treatments. Books, of course, may furnish the patient with correct knowledge which he will probably apply in his judging others. He may even learn to recognize and understand more about himself. But not often will he, by himself, be able to see through himself. He will not distinguish between important and unimportant matters, he will claim characteristics for himself which he does not have and will deny that he has others which he possesses to a high degree. All human beings are unwilling to give up their life plans, to which they are accustomed and which seems to offer techniques in dealing with dreaded difficulties. It is an arduous task, which must be undertaken by the therapist and patient together, to provide the patient with the necessary degree of self-knowledge which will enable him to see the misconceptions behind his life style.

It happens often, during a somewhat superficial procedure, that the range of the patient's life pattern as an entity is ignored, and that the therapist may be satisfied with explaining —perhaps correctly, but a bit too generally—the patient's present behavior and symptoms. The pointing out of inferiority feelings, of lack of social interest, of striving for prestige, of discouragement, of "arrangements," of lack of security, etc.; may be correct; but such general formulations will hardly make any great impression on the patient. Though these devices are used differently in every individual case and show innumerable nuances, there still exists the danger that through the poverty of language we may make use of similar formulas for the most varied individuals. The result will then be that at the end of the treatment the patient will not have seen clearly his own life style, but will have retained only general phrases which he will repeat on all possible occasions, fitting or not. It is necessary to show the patient his own personal behavior in such a way so that he can actually see himself in his own peculiarities.

In order to make this easier for the patient, and above all in order to simplify for him the mnemonic reproduction of this knowledge, we might search in the life of individual patients for situations which in the lives of other persons would hardly be possible, revelation which, acting like a lightning flash, will illuminate the entire life style. An individual's every slightest action, every behavior symptom, is characteristic of the whole individual, and like a stone from a mosaic, it indicates the style of the whole. From the way a person talks, moves, reacts to certain events, the traits, characteristic of his life style, can be more or less easily recognized. Thus in the course of treatment we show our patient how to a very great degree his past experiences as well as the entire sum total of his life to date are dependent—and always have been dependent—on himself, on his own life plan. However, in the life of almost every person situations can be found which not only illustrate how his personality created his experiences, but which also indicate his personal characteristics. The following may clarify this point.

A man suffering from compulsion neurosis tells the following experience from his eleventh year. At that time he was attending a school, far from his home. He was fairly good in his studies. One day he was called to the principal and shown a letter full of the vilest language, directed to the principal, with his, the patient's name signed at the bottom. He was not asked whether he actually wrote the letter. The principal whipped him and threw him out, although he had been completely innocent and had not had any previous knowledge of the letter. At first glance, it seems as if he must have been quite innocent in regard to this affair. Could the poor boy have helped it if mischievous lads used his name and unjust teachers punished him without reason? We perceive, however, that there is more to this than accident, when we find out that the same boy, at the age of six to seven, in an entirely different environment, often was unjustly punished by his mother, because his playmates accused him of deeds which he had not done at all. These identical experiences somehow have been conditioned by his personal behavior. How is that possible?

Even as a little child, he always felt himself to be at a disadvantage and suppressed, at first probably not without justification. He was taken from his home at an early age, while his sister was allowed to stay with her parents. He was ill treated by strangers. At the age of four he felt badly because his aunt, with whom he lived, always gave preference to her own son. He had the feeling of being without rights, and with all the means at the disposal of a recalcitrant child he attempted to make himself disagreeable to others—as, for instance, by soiling himself. His entire environment was against him. With this attitude he returned home, alien to his mother, alien to his brothers and sisters, treated by everyone like a "bad" child, and full of spite towards the whole world. He remembers that his mother once said to him: "You will grow up to be a bum—you're going to land in jail!" These words, which would not be likely to give a child courage and lead him to the path toward better things, caused quite a peculiar change in him. He thought to himself: "I won't give you the satisfaction!" From then on he endeavored, almost compulsively, to be good, to fulfill all the demands of his environment, to do nothing that was forbidden; but every time he was engaged in fulfilling a demand he had a curse on his lips. He was filled with revolt against everybody. His outwardly good behavior was nothing but a protest against the opinion which prevailed everywhere about him.

It is obvious what kind of results such behavior would give rise to in school. Everyone discerned the revolt within him. It must have been quite evident from his expression. At the same time he was apparently good and obedient. In class he was not one of the good boys; he was regarded as obstinate and recalcitrant. However, he was not one of the bad boys either; he never was involved in any pranks. One can imagine how the solidarity of the "bad" boys, which can be observed in every classroom, was directed against him. When they played a prank, he was blamed for it, especially so, because, conscious of his innocence, he never ran away. And the boys soon found pleasure in revenging themselves on him because of his goodness. The result was unjust accusations, and so, finally, the letter to the principal came about. If the boy who wrote the letter had signed it with the name of a really good pupil, he would have run the risk of having the teacher not believe the signature; the matter would have been investigated and the actual letter writer perhaps might have been found out. Hence the letter signed with the name of the patient, while it was directed against the teacher, was at the same time directed against our seemingly well-behaved patient.

This experience is particularly characteristic of the life style of this patient. Today, as much as then, this man conceals behind an outstanding decency and conscientiousness a boundless obstinacy and opposition against everyone, particularly against all duties within the human community. Outwardly, he is employed by the police department and is thus a representative of public order, of the law. Inwardly, he has a severe compulsion neurosis, which forces him laboriously to wrest out of himself every one of his good actions, the fulfillment of each order. Also, he constantly has obscene thoughts in his head. The opposition to the entire world and at the same time the ambition to appear especially good and fine, dominates his life plan. These are the identical factors which, as we have seen, were the basis for the childhood experience at the age of eleven into which we have looked.

The exact opposite of this can be demonstrated in a second case. A woman patient tells of an occurrence during her high school years. She had put a nettle in the teacher's hair and had thrown stink bombs. Though it became known that she was the guilty one, the whole class was punished—with the exception of her alone. She was generally looked on as the victim, led astray by the others. How did she come to have this experience characteristic for her?

She had an older sister, and even as a little girl she was much prettier than this sister. She was quite pampered by her parents, but always felt her slightness of stature to be something very undesirable. She remembers several occasions when she was not able to do things because she was too little. She now learned, with the help of her attractive appearance, to press parents and relatives into her service and make use of them in the battle against her sister. She annoyed her sister a great deal and always escaped punishment for it. In school she was a good student and was always regarded as well behaved. (She says she regrets this even now.) She had always made an effort to be disagreeable, but at the same time had understood how to gain sympathy of others, so that she achieved an apparent superiority over other people in a peculiar manner—by doing things which were not right and then avoiding the consequences. She takes a keen delight in every sort of prank. This offers her, she believes, the only possibility of apparent success. For she feels incapable of any actual accomplishment which might satisfy her ambition. Within her set she is regarded as unapproachable and refined. One would not dare speak of sex in her hearing. At the same time, she likes to read the most vulgar books, is homosexual, and, with an inordinate impudence openly discusses the most daring of adventures. Whenever she becomes surfeited with the timidity which her colleagues—she is a bank employee—show toward her on account of her "refinement," she gives vent to some vulgar remark. Then they all think that in her complete innocence she doesn't realize what she is saying. Here too the childhood experience clearly shows the life style typical of this patient.

Another woman patient had grown up in the country with two older brothers. Parents and brothers adored her. She was pampered by her brothers and regarded with special solicitude because she was a girl. Later she had two younger sisters whom she herself tenderly cherished. No matter how often her parents made the effort to get her to accept the company of playmates her own age she always rejected it. She did not go to public school. She tells of an experience which clearly shows her life style, her attitude toward the human community. When the patient was nine years old her mother brought home a girl from the neighborhood, of about her own age, to play with her. The first thing the patient did was to try to find out who was the stronger. In doing this, she wrenched the girl's arm so violently that the arm became dislocated and the girl ran away crying. It could not be any better demonstrated that this patient never felt herself to be an equal among equals, that she acknowledged her fellow human beings only when she was pampered by them or was able to pamper them herself. When her own children had grown up and her life style became incompatible with the conditions of her life, she broke down because she had not learned to understand any other form of human communion and, hence, had always rejected any other type of accomplishment within this community.

Another patient relates the following experience: She went to the theatre with a boy, and was told to be home by ten o'clock. The performance was not scheduled to end until eleven-thirty. In order that she might not be too late, she went half an hour before the end of the play with the violent disapproval of her boy friend. In spite of this, she was severely scolded by her mother because she had not come home by ten o'clock. Thereupon she had a fit of rage. She felt that she was being treated unjustly because, after all, she had left half an hour early. This, at first glance, seems like a harmless situation; yet it is very characteristic of this person's life style. Had she really wanted to comply with the wish of her mother she would have been home at ten o'clock. But if she had wanted to ignore this wish and please her boy friend, she could have stayed until the end. All her life this patient felt that she was an innocent victim of the injustices of others. Here, too, she had endeavored to act as if she intended to obey, without, however, really conforming to the desires of her parents. Thus she was punished, and yet she had not done what she had wanted to do.

This patient has an older sister, who, on account of her special competence, makes the patient, who is prettier than she, seem inept and inefficient. Her discouragement regarding her own work was intensified by the constant nagging of her mother. Our patient has always attempted to prove her good intentions apparently, never, however, fulfilling the tasks expected of her. At the present time she "apparently" is a good wife to her husband, and does not do anything that is objectionable. Yet she is dissatisfied with everything, and, of course, frigid, too. Just as she herself is always dissatisfied, she never satisfies anyone else.

These brief examples obviously cannot do justice to the entire significance of each individual case. But they are not intended to be case histories; they merely serve to show how we can illustrate the uniqueness of each individual by reference to particular experiences. We can thus make clear to the patient what we mean when we speak of life style. We can compare other experiences with those. We can show the patient how he acts everywhere in life according to this attitude. Therefore characteristic experiences, such as these, prove to be effective means of throwing light upon the range within which each individual patient's life takes place.

In the treatment it is important to impart to the patient in a vivid manner the necessary self-knowledge. One really absorbs only that which made a deep impression. The success of therapy depends upon the extent to which the patient recognizes his mistakes in his accustomed attitude toward the human society, in his accustomed goal. It is quite possible to distinguish a merely apparent recognition, an acting "as if" one recognized all this, from the actual experienced understanding which is automatically translated into action and can therefore be proved objectively by a change in behavior. For all our actions spring from our interpretations and goals, i.e., the sum total of what we have "recognized" in our lives. This is true even when we do not admit to ourselves the psychic background of our actions, when it seems as if we do not know this background.

We must not overlook the point that the mere disclosing of psychic connections is in itself an experience for most people. For this reason psychological writings and talks are so popular, though their effectiveness in reshaping the neurotic life style is sometimes comparatively negligible. Similarly, we find in most patients, at the beginning of the treatment, a striking improvement and a sensation of relief. This is absent only in those cases in which the patient submits to treatment involuntarily, either under the pressure of relatives or so as to make it appear as if he intended to do something about removing the neurotic symptoms which have disturbed his environment. For in all those cases in which the patient is driven to the therapist by the suffering from his ailment, in those cases in which he seeks treatment because the war costs of his customary battle with human society have become too great for him, the patient experiences a feeling of relief at the beginning of his treatment, as the result of the opportunity for discussion, the understanding which he suddenly finds in another person, and the dawning of fresh possibilities for self-knowledge. There are patients who are so shaken by the mere disclosure of their "arrangements," by the recognition of their accustomed goals, by the discovery of their control of their further deviation and mistakes, that this experience alone furnishes the momentum for successful conclusion of the cure. These are often very ambitious persons who above all would not want to appear stupid and for whom the accusation of not correctly understanding something contains a severe challenge. These individuals derive from their ambition the strongest impulses for a completely rational comprehension of the problem—an understanding which, as said before, in the cases may be synonymous with the change in attitude. For them, rational understanding is at the same time a very intense emotional experience. In the case of most patients, however, sooner or later we arrive at a situation where the theoretical discussion of psychological problems fails to bring any further visible progress, irrespective of whether the situation of the patient has been elucidated or not. Even for the patient who at first follows with enthusiasm and great readiness there will often come a period of stagnation. He will then be just as one who was in opposition from the beginning.

In all these, cases, rational explanations will not suffice. Other techniques must be used to convince them and to train them in a different orientation to life.

The goal of psychotherapy as that of any medical treatment is to cure the patient of his ailment. In psychoneuroses that cannot be accomplished without a change in the patient's attitude to his present life problems which he evades by being sick. The present attitude of the patient results from the impact of his personal life style and the acute life situation for which he is not prepared. As it is generally impossible to alter the objective life situation, therefore it is necessary to change the patient's whole life plan so that he can meet more successfully the tasks of life which confront him.

Uncovering what is taking place in the patient, revealing the purpose which dominates his present behavior, is part of an organized effort to challenge the patient to a new orientation.

However, words have their limitations. Explanation is only one method of education. No education can be effective if it remains totally on the verbal level. Presentation of ideas and rationalization must be supplemented by vital experiences, by psychological action. Every psychotherapy reaches a point where the patient, for the time being, is not amenable to logic. The treatment must become dramatic to jolt the patient out of the complacent security which he provided for himself by using his illness as a protection from life.

Every therapist develops his own technique to overcome such a deadlock and psychological blockage and to create experience which make the patient receptive to further rational discussion. A change in the thought process of the patient is still the fundamental factor in psychotherapy; for upon understanding alone rests the change of the life plan, and hence, the success of the therapy. For this reason we must warn against, not only any over-estimation of psychological tactics, but also, above all, against a careless and too liberal application of them. They may easily endanger the whole treatment. Indeed, they put the heaviest demand upon the therapist's sense of tact. For it may happen only too easily that the patient will feel duped. If this is the case, further cooperation between therapist and patient is definitely disturbed. Moreover, the use of maneuvers may cloud the atmosphere of complete confidence which is so necessary. Finally, the position of the therapist is jeopardized by the use of cunning because he then appears to the patient in a position of especial superiority, a thing which from the viewpoint of psychotherapy leads to a state where the patient finds it easy to make the therapist responsible for his own failure. The failure, then, is not due to lack of readiness on the part of the patient, but rather to the inability or the errors of the therapist, who is more likely to be exposed to this criticism once he has entered the field of influencing through management. Nevertheless, sometimes artifice cannot be avoided when other ways of appealing to the patient's intelligence seem impossible for the time being.

Naturally I cannot enumerate all the devices which we have acquired. I shall merely attempt to point out some of them. How the individual therapist applies these principles is, of course, entirely dependent upon his creative faculties and his ability to put himself in his patient's place.

First we might mention the tactic of surprise, of staring. We must remember that when the therapeutic work comes to a standstill, this stagnation is caused by the fact that the patient has secured himself completely in the maintenance of his accustomed life style, even against the psychiatrist—and these safeguards cannot be broken through by words or simple information. Astonishment, first of all, makes the patient listen; he does not want to know what he is up against. Thus he will already have given up his set attitude and become receptive to any remarks which may help him in seeing his recent situation more clearly. Naturally this surprise must not have in it anything that might hurt the patient's feelings or set him against us. We must merely do the thing that he would least expect. Often it is enough if we abandon an opinion which we have held previously or express the opposite of what, with justification, he might expect of us. He is then forced to get new bearings, to work out new devices for obtaining his old stability.

Often through discussion of these problems the contact is reestablished. The element of surprise is actually in a measure fundamental to all therapeutic stratagems.

It is the same when we suddenly appreciate the patient's point of view and, contrary to our usual practice, attempt to defend this standpoint of his own arguments. In the moment of surprise the patient often suddenly takes over the attitude of his opponent, in our case that of the therapist. He proves in this way that he had not really believed the play-rules of human society, and, also contrary to all logic, that which hitherto seemed incontrovertible to him contradicts itself when no one else contradicts it. Let anyone else seriously attempt to defend his obviously illogical attitude and the error becomes immediately apparent to the patient. To carry on such a discussion with changed roles, a high degree of diplomacy is necessary, of course, so that the patient will not feel ridiculed from the start and reject the procedure. However, when it is possible to set such a discussion in motion, even occasional exaggeration will do no harm.

A young girl of nineteen who suffered from states of fear suddenly felt very ill in the course of treatment. She was obsessed by the idea that she had a stomach cancer. She felt that she had to stay in bed, and plagued her parents, who were obliged to quiet her continually. I tried to demonstrate to her that by this behavior she was endeavoring to evade the approaching first problems of her love-life and that, being a very pampered child, she wanted to do what she always had done in difficult situations—force her parents to give her special attention and sympathy. It was impossible to draw this otherwise very intelligent girl into a reasonable discussion. At the same time she refused to eat and actually lost weight at an alarming rate. Then all at once I remarked to her that perhaps she really did have a cancer. In a flash the situation changed. First she was surprised, then she objected that no physician, though her parents had already consulted many, had found any signs of cancer. Besides, she was much too young for cancer, etc. All that those around her had unsuccessfully sought to prove to her before, she now used against me. I insisted, however, that it might be cancer. Then she began to weep and was —as I found out later—justifiably angry with me, especially since I had recommended that no one should contradict her. But the thought of cancer had definitely been abandoned, and the path had again become open for further treatment.

Thus we come to one of the most dangerous weapons at the command of the psychotherapist and one which all of them occasionally use: this is irony. An ill-advised dose of it can result in the patient's staying away forever. But, discreetly used, nothing can illuminate a situation in which the patient tries to evade the logic of our arguments so well as an ironical remark. The patient must first consider how such a remark is intended, must, as it were, work out for himself the therapist's trend of thought. And, what is even more important, something is made clear to him without his really being able to contradict. Moreover, the point of the argument, the solution which had not been possible to present before, through discussion, is suddenly stripped of its seriousness and turned into the comic. The therapist must not forget, however, the fact that nothing has quite so wounding an effect as irony. If wounds are not to be inflicted, irony must be set forth in an atmosphere of benevolent consideration and every reaction of the patient carefully sounded. If this is done, one sentence may often explain more than might be possible in a long debate.

Irony is also an ingredient somehow of all finesses, a reason why the latter are so dangerous. Now this irony may be concealed in various ways. One may be sarcastic and still remain serious. When the patient cannot easily decide whether certain remarks are meant seriously or not, they become so much more effective. Sometimes it is advantageous if the therapist can succeed in assuming a stupid role. When the patient is faced with the necessity of explaining in detail his reason for his attitude, often he readily comes to realize the senselessness of his own behavior or the purpose which he had wished to attain by means of his behavior, and which previously he had not admitted to himself.

A rather unique technique which not only yields results with amazing promptness but also affords theoretical insight into the mechanism of the "nervous" symptoms was described repeatedly by Alfred Adler and has been called by Erwin Wexberg "anti-suggestion." It consists in this: the patient is advised, under some pretext and with no implication that he is being insulted, to practice just that very thing which up to now he has apparently been fighting against; i.e., to aggravate his symptoms. If one persuades a patient who cannot sleep that it might be good for him to try to stay awake once in a while, if one tells a patient who cries all day long to cry to his heart's content—then suddenly sleeplessness and weeping cease to function so well. One can observe again and again in functional disturbances, in states of fear, compulsion-impulses, etc., that the symptom diminishes in intensity when the patient consciously tries to intensify it. It might even disappear entirely if these attempts were continued for a longer period of time. However, it never comes to this, because the excessive use of any measures which are employed longer than merely for the overcoming of a temporary standstill in the therapy guarantees the failure of the therapy, and usually is answered by the patient's discontinuing the treatment.

Through anti-suggestion it can be most impressively demonstrated to the patient that his apparent battle against the symptom is not a priori useless, but actually calls forth the symptom. It is the tension which he creates through this apparent battle, be it in the organic, mental, or sensory sphere, which makes possible the symptom. When he ceases to struggle and the tension abates, the symptom, too, disappears. This happens when he attempts to intensify the symptom instead of fighting against it. When he stops fighting he attacks the foundation upon which he has constructed his symptom. In this revelation alone lies the value of anti-suggestion. It cannot help him in actually getting rid of his symptom, for the premise for this would be that he would not need the symptom any more, that his inner development had already progressed to such a degree that he could avoid any effort on the useless side of life —for such is the nature of every symptom. No trick, but merely his own growing insight and regained courage can help him to change his attitude and behavior.

How does the patient get into a situation in which logical discussion will, for the moment, no longer be effective and thus compel the therapist to resort to artifices? Freud is of the opinion that this "resistance" is always directed against the uncovering of "unconscious" sexual thoughts and experiences. He believes that this shows itself most in the "transference." The latter, according to Freud, is the patient's love for the analyst, who is for him the symbol ("Imago") of all the persons he loved before, especially those he loved in his earliest childhood. Freud makes the distinction between a "positive transference" of affection and a hostile "negative transference," the latter originating in the revolt against this love, in hatred for the analyst. The "resistance" which jeopardizes the success of the treatment is, according to Freud, the result either of the negative or of the positive transference when the latter represents repressed erotic instinct. The "component factor capable of being made conscious and not objectionable" is to Freud the nucleus of success in psychoanalytic treatment. In this assumption which regards a hypothetical instinctive life as the core of every treatment really necessary? Do we not everywhere see in daily life that people resist when one demands something of them which they do not like? Do we need the hypothesis of an erotic attraction or rejection between physician and patient? At the same moment when the patient resists us we know for a certainty that we are expecting something from him which he does not like. When he rejects an insight, he does so, not because of some embarrassing sexual revelation or because he hates us, but rather because he expects from this revelation a burden on his life which he does not feel strong enough to bear. He is not yet courageous enough to dare to go out into life without the protection of his devices for security, which his symptoms provided, and he is afraid of being deprived by us of these weapons. Is it not understandable that he should resist?

It cannot be doubted, however, that his attitude toward the therapist may intensify or mitigate this opposition. For between therapist and patient there exists, after all, a human community, the purpose of which is to cure the patient. If the therapist is so awkward as to insult the patient, then, as in every human community, the insulted one will revolt, possibly strike back. And the only weapon with which a patient believes he can strike the therapist is a relapse, a devaluation of the therapist's work by proving it a failure.

It is not always easy to separate a flight from health from revolt against the therapist. The patient will have some criticism of the therapist's personality to express when he revolts against the result of the treatment to date. The moment when the patient suddenly notices that his physician is, after all, not the right one is very typical. This can be observed with special clarity in the case of patients who have knowledge of other psychotherapeutic theories. For quite a while they have no doubt as to whether the method is applied right or not. Suddenly they will put the question as to whether in this or that instance another psychological school of thought might not perhaps be more correct. We can be sure that this is the moment when the patient wants to escape from the pertinence of our arguments. His search for excuses with which to destroy the foundation of the discussions proves this. I have found this supposition to be correct in every case. We find similar motivations existing when the patient suddenly brings forward political or religious objections to the therapist.

The fact that personal objections to the therapist are often mere rationalizations does not justify us, of course, in excluding the possibility of a mistake on our part. On the contrary, since we are all only imperfect human beings, all of us quite frequently make mistakes and commit errors. In most cases this does not do much harm. For everywhere in life mistakes can be remedied when the right understanding is present. And certainly our mistakes do not justify the patient in withdrawing from his obligations in life, or to put it concretely, in refusing to continue the course of treatment. Through the revelation of these very interconnections and an open confession of one's imperfection, much may be accomplished toward the establishment of a really human contact between therapist and patient. If a patient nevertheless finds us objectionable because of our imperfections, he would probably do so even if we spoke with the tongues of angels or had other supernatural powers at our command. For in this case he is not yet ready to add anything himself to the improvement of his life situation, that is, to change himself.

This combination of revolt against the therapist and flight from health often takes place because—as Adler emphasizes—rebellion plays a great role in any patient's life. This rebellion has not been provoked necessarily by the personal attitude of the therapist. The mere fact that the therapist appears as the representative of the human community, as the herald of the needs of human fellowship, will call forth that spite which the patient feels against human society. Up to now he has known how to withdraw successfully from life's demands and he will attempt to continue this way if these demands are presented through the mouth of the therapist. This rebellion and the intention to escape from our interpretations probably make up the main roots of the resistance which occasionally occurs in every treatment.

Though we have to reject the theory of a libidinous attitude on the part of the patient when we consider the difficulties of treatment, the question presents itself as to what role is played by impulses of love in the attainment of success in treatment. It probably infrequently happens that female patients are in love with their male therapist or that male patients fall in love with women therapists. This, however, seems not to be due to the character of the treatment as such. We must remember that all neurotic persons have special safeguards for one's self; and happiness in love demands the capacity for unconditional devotion. Discouraged, neurotic patients are not capable of this. Here, in relation to the therapist, they are in an unusually favorable situation. Nothing is demanded of them; on the contrary, the therapist attempts to get close to them, to understand them. Is it any wonder that the therapist may be idealized by the patient? Yet this is not so common as one might think and as psychoanalysts are eager to maintain. Of course, some sort of tie between therapist and patient must exist. It could not be otherwise, considering the close personal cooperation and the measure of confidence which this work demands. The frequent discussions of most intimate problems, too, may perhaps occasionally call forth amorous impulses. However, the latter occur so frequently and easily in the life of every individual, unless he guards himself against them, that they cannot be considered as evidence of special love for the therapist. The desire not so uncommon among patients for entering into personal contact with the therapist also usually originates in their resentment at being nothing more than a case to him. They suffer from not being pampered enough, as they had always desired throughout life. They do not care to realize that before and after them there are other patients whom the therapist will meet with the same friendliness and courtesy. They want to be exceptions. Their interest in the therapist as a person originates in their striving for prestige. Perhaps occasionally some women patients will offer the only treasure which alone in their feeling of inferiority they believe they still possess: the fact that they are females. But even this does not justify us in supposing that any real attachment for the therapist exists.

Since the hypothesis of love for the therapist is a dubious one, this applies even more in estimating the effect of this factor in relation to the success of the treatment. Occasionally a special affection for the therapist will increase the readiness to accept his point of view. It is, however, more than doubtful whether such an acceptance of insight really signifies a lasting success. For when this insight is built upon a feeling of love for the therapist, the logic of reality sooner or later will bring disappointment and newly-won courage are followed then by an even deeper depression. It may also happen that a woman patient, feeling that the psychiatrist may—to use the characteristic phrase—become "dangerous" to her, will be tempted to abandon the treatment. In other cases, too, affection for the therapist may tend to impede the treatment, even when this feeling is "brought to consciousness and is not found objectionable." How often is the treatment nullified under these circumstances! The therapist as a man is placed on a pedestal so that whatever he says in his professional capacity may be discounted. The content of his arguments is dismissed as negligible, while the patient regards only his personality as important. This apparently positive attitude is very often aimed directly against the treatment.

Even without "love" a certain degree of mutual experience in the treatment is possible, yes, even very important for its progress. The patient in the doctor's office shows himself in his true colors. He behaves no differently than he does in his outside life. And his attitude toward the psychiatrist reveals the sum total of his personality as does the review of his past life, his characteristic experience, his dreams, etc. When the patient learns to understand this, he will know himself. And if he behaves well in the treatment, in this definite task, then he will also behave well in life.

The characteristics and the life style of a patient are revealed with emphatic clarity in the course of collective therapy. In the joint discussions with several patients, the latter learn to know themselves with much more ease because they are able to make observations about one another. Once the first resistance against taking part in an association for the purpose of therapeutic treatment has been overcome, much ground has been gained on the way to a quicker and more thorough recognition by the patient of his own personality. Above all, this method eliminates any last remnant of a personal battle with the therapist. For as long as psychiatrist and patient face one another, in any sense of competition, the latter will feel himself threatened in his prestige. He may regard his possible cure as a personal defeat and may consider the treatment's failure as a defeat for the therapist. Conduction of the treatment in the spirit of a duel is the greatest handicap to its successful outcome.

It is therefore important that any authority, yes, even any comparison of respective personal values, should be avoided during the treatment. The patient, who shows his life style in his behavior during his treatment, attempts to measure his strength against the therapist's and to construct an "above" and "below," instead of a cooperation of equals. Either he directly repudiates the therapist from the fear that otherwise he might feel his own inferiority too strongly, or he places the therapist in a special position to him. In this case he believes in the therapist's "power of suggestion" or he expects that this be brought into play, sometimes demanding it directly and explicitly. It may be that the role which the therapist is supposed to play is, as Freud believes, often patterned after the image of the father. If so, it is only because the patient had learned as a child to misuse the dreaded authority of his father as an excuse for his own weakness. It is much more comforting for the patient to acknowledge the therapist's authority. Thus he is relieved of any obligation to work toward his cure himself. And, above all, procedure burdens the psychiatrist with full responsibility for success and failure of the therapy.

Hence it is imperative to reject consistently the attempt of the patient which is made in the course of every treatment—to represent himself as small and dependent, the therapist, on the other hand, as the omnipotent leader. For many a patient it is no doubt a heavy burden to have to realize that it is not the therapist and not any mystic "treatment" that is to make him well, but that he himself alone is able to do this. For then he is oppressed by his pondering over the question of why he did not take this path long before, if he alone is the one upon whom it devolves. Some miracle performed by the therapist ought, he feels, to free him of the mistakes of his past. Nevertheless, the recognition of the patient's own strength is the foundation for a cure and for the permanence of its success.

For this reason prescriptions which are given for the treatment of psychoneuroses—often with the best intentions—can be harmful. Medications as well as prescribed rules of behavior do not strengthen the patient's self-confidence, which alone can help him in solving the problem of himself and his own life, of his relationship to others. Prescriptions rather infringe upon it. What is most important in every treatment is encouragement. The most effective therapeutic factor is shown to be the uncovering of unjustified feelings of inferiority. On the other hand the revelation of the striving for prestige often calls forth obstinancy, for the neurotic striving for prestige disappears only when the feeling of inferiority, which is its basis, is overcome.

Revelation and challenge of the accustomed life plan, and encouragement: these are decisive factors with which our treatment is concerned. Only in that way can the social interest of the patient be increased, his social adjustment, which is synonymous with his cure, be accomplished.

PSYCHOTHERAPY AS CORRECTION OF FAULTY SOCIAL VALUES*

The value system on which the patient operates has always been a focal point for Adlerian psychotherapy. This has often been criticized because the introduction of "moralistic" elements into psychotherapy was considered improper. Not until the advent of group psychotherapy did it become obvious to many that psychotherapy involved the study and change of mistaken values. The group, utilized for the therapy of individual patients, became recognized as a value-forming agent, affecting the social orientation of each patient and his guiding lines in dealing with others. Every group requires norms to be respected by its members; and the therapeutic group apparently established norms different from those to which the patient had been exposed and accustomed, through its "unique social climate" of equality (6).

Regardless of the criteria which may be used to assess therapeutic results—be they the disappearance of symptoms, the solution of problems, or the change in personality structure—successful psychotherapy always results in the patient becoming a better human being. Even psychoanalysis, originally most reluctant to consider moral or evaluative judgments, aimed to bring about emotional maturity, which certainly implies a form of moral judgment.

The consideration of values during the psychotherapeutic process poses new and difficult problems. Are we in any position to determine which values are good for the patient and

* *Journal of Individual Psychology*, 1957, 13, 150-158.

which not? Do we simply accept the standards of the surrounding community, of society, and help the patient to become adjusted by learning to conform better? Or is there a yardstick by which we can measure the adequacy of value systems in various societies and come to a normative description of positive and negative, beneficial and detrimental, values and standards?

The present confusion in psychiatry and psychology is largely due to the fact that no scientifically valid basis for evaluating human behavior has been evolved by the social sciences. In the absence of scientifically established norms for social relationships individuals and groups looking for a more reliable and moral orientation, sought this in religion or assumed a transcendental origin of ethical systems (3). The individual, torn between the inclination to conform, in order to have social status, and to rebel against outdated autocratic social prescriptions, is likely to succumb to a state of anomie (Durkheim), of social disorganization. MacIver considers anomie "a state of mind in which the individual's sense of social cohesion—the mainspring of his morale—is broken or fatally weakened" (10). And Ansbacher is quoted by Merton (11) as stating that anomie is the equivalent to lack of social interest which latter, according to Adler, is the basis for cooperation, for harmonious social functioning.

Adler's concept of the "logic of social living" (2) suggests the existence of basic laws for cooperation; it presents a normative formulation of social relationships. In this light, existing societies are not the final authority for the establishment of proper social values and standards. There is a yardstick by which they and their institutions can be measured, one which permits a scientific evaluation of social values from the standpoint of mental health, which means harmonious social functioning. Adjustment, then, means not mere conformity to existing standards, but the movement toward an improved social organization which will better fulfill the requirement of the "ironclad logic of social living."

We may find normal reactions of normal people to abnormal conditions (12), or pathological reactions of people to either normal or abnormal conditions. We are concerned, therefore, with evaluating both the individual reactions and the conditions under which we live. In psychotherapy we try to improve the abnormal reactions to reality, which includes partly normal and partly abnormal living conditions.

Despite the fact that the individual is not the product of circumstances, the environment does furnish probabilities for the individual's reactions. Thus, from the standpoint of the logic of social living, certain present-day social values are undesirable, because they are inimicable to cooperation, the requirement for coping with the problems of life, which are all social problems.

Psychotherapy is concerned with establishing a psychological basis for cooperation. We find four attitudes essential for cooperation, with their counterparts disrupting it (5). These are: 1) social interest—hostility; 2) confidence in others—distrust and suspicion; 3) self-confidence—inferiority feelings; 4) courage—fear. Social interest is an expression of a sense of belonging; lack of social interest limits or impedes cooperation and makes an opponent appear as an enemy. Fear seems to be the chief obstacle to adequate social functioning in a democratic atmosphere; it can be regarded as the sin of free man (7).

The fundamental underlying premise of social equality for everyone—which implies that each individual is entitled to respect and dignity, to full and equal status, regardless of any personal quality or deficiency—finds little realization in our competitive society. The climate of our communities is not too inducive for the development of courage and self-confidence. A variety of contemporary standards, norms and social prescriptions merit close scrutiny in their highly detrimental effects on cooperation, harmony, and mental health. They are the mistaken guiding principles, the faulty social values, from which we try to extricate our patients in psychotherapy. They all constitute a violation of the basic principle of human equality and of respect for each individual, as he is.

Desire for Self-Elevation

A desire for self-elevation seems to be stimulated in every member of our society, from early childhood on. Nobody is ever told or given to understand that he is good enough as he is. On the contrary, such an assumption is considered as most unfortunate and detrimental; it would lead—so we are told—to contentment and apathy, blocking any progress, growth, or accomplishment. But such convictions are fallacious and reflect a misconception of human nature, revealing little faith in man.

Actually, the desire for self-elevation is not a basic human desire, but culturally and artificially induced. It is a compensatory striving, resulting from a sense of social inferiority. This has been instilled in each member of our civilized society, because since its beginning, seven to eight thousand years ago, it has been based on the assumption of the superiority of a few and the inferiority of the masses. The democratic evolution with its emphasis on human equality makes a more adequate evaluation of human nature mandatory.

The desire for self-elevation is by no means a prerequisite for growth and accomplishment. Another motivation, so far less recognized, is much more reliable and less costly. It is the desire to be useful, without regard for personal compensation, be it material or social. Such desire is natural, the result of social interest, of a feeling of belonging, of a genuine interest in the welfare of others. The "drive" behind such movement is enthusiasm, love, interest and the enjoyment of living, in contrast to the other motivation which is lust for glory, power and self-aggrandizement.

Desire for self-elevation versus desire for usefulness may be understood to lead to movement on the "vertical plane" versus movement on the "horizontal plane," to use the terms which were introduced by Sicher (13). Although many beneficial contributions to mankind have resulted from vertical movement which also affords growth and accomplishment, its effect on the individual is fundamentally different from the effect of horizontal movement . The vertical movement of self-elevation, regardless of the height it leads to, both in status and accomplishments, can never bring lasting satisfaction and inner peace. There is a constant danger of falling and failing; the gnawing feeling of real or possible inferiority is never eradicated, regardless of success. There is no sense of security possible on the vertical plane; one remains highly vulnerable. The competitive individual can stand competition only when he wins.

Quite different is the function of horizontal movement. The desire to be useful can never be frustrated. Whatever life may have in store, something can be done about it. There may be no perfect solution to a predicament, but there is always a way to improve the situation. It becomes less important what one receives in return, because the satisfaction in doing is deeper than any reward can provide. Self-fulfillment no longer depends on what others think or do, but on what one can contribute. Concern with status is unnecessary, since one can be sure of one's place in the group as an equal.

This basic distinction between self-elevation and usefulness has far-reaching consequences for the evaluation of other social values. Once the assumption that everybody is good enough as he is can be accepted without the fear of disastrous results, both for the individual and society, a new orientation in social living is possible—and mandatory.

Perfectionism

The idea of perfectionism, which seems to be more pronounced today than at previous times, is another faulty social value. Women, in particular, seem to succumb to the mirage of perfectionism. And who can quarrel with them? Is it not highly desirable to try to be as good and right as possible? Most people would be inclined to answer this question positively. However, such determination to be good and right may merely serve as a means for personal superiority or self-elevation. The desire to be good is in most cases a desire to be better than others. Goodness and righteousness as well as accomplishments do not always express a sincere interest in the welfare of others.

A related mistaken value, fostered in our society and requiring therapeutic consideration, is the idea of masculinity and feminity. Many men suffer from the assumption that they are not very much of a man, and many women are striving desperately to live up to a feminine ideal, established in their childhood, often emulating a superior mother figure. While actually the functions of men and women have changed greatly with the increasing social equality of women, the traditional ideals of a man and a woman are still widely maintained. But we can no longer permit ourselves to stress characteristics which provide superiority, and bemoan deficiencies which deprive us of it. It is more important that we stress the humaneness, rather than the sex. Instead of trying to be a strong man and a good woman, we need to become better human beings. In therapy, the freedom from sex-oriented behavior patterns is part of the necessary reorientation.

Fear of Mistakes

Behind perfectionism there usually lies a fear of mistakes. Our whole culture is mistake-centered. This is reflected in our educational systems, dedicated as they are to the prevention and correction of mistakes as a means of developing knowledge and skills. This concern with possible future or past mistakes, universal as it is, is based on two fallacious suppositions.

Firstly, making a mistake is considered dangerous. But actually, dangerous mistakes are rare, the exception rather than the rule. For example, even in driving an automobile only very few mistakes lead to accidents; and only very few accidents result in injury or death. The fatal mistakes form a minute fraction of the vast number which the average driver makes, almost daily.

The second erroneous assumption is that one must consider all possible mistakes in order to avoid them; otherwise one would become careless and make more mistakes. The opposite is true; the more concerned one is with the possibility of making a mistake, the more one is prone to make one. One can be cautious without fear of making a mistake. Many people devote much time and effort to preventing mistakes, thereby creating a side show which diminishes their efficiency in dealing with the real problems at hand.

Actually, making mistakes is unavoidable, and the mistake is less important in most cases than what the individual does after he has made the mistake. If he is discouraged, demoralized and beset with guilt feelings, he cannot face the situation as it is. But if he is a courageous person, the predicament may often lead to benefits which would never have been possible without the original mistake. What is needed is not concern with what we have done wrong, but the determination to meet the demands of the moment.

In view of these obvious consequences of a mistake-centered orientation, why is it then maintained? Two possible reasons seem evident. One is a vestige from an outgrown autocratic society. In such a society, doing wrong means not doing what one is supposed to do, and this is intolerable, as a defiance of authority. The person in power cannot make mistakes, because whatever he does is right; there is no one to tell him differently. Only subordinates can make mistakes. A second cause for our preoccupation with mistakes lies in the competitive strife on the vertical plane. Making a mistake implies humiliation; it lowers one's social status, as being right increases it.

This is at the root of our concern with goodness and righteousness: We are interested in it primarily because we are interested in our own prestige and status. Once we free ourselves from our fear of being inferior and recognize our worth and dignity, we no longer fear making mistakes—and therefore make fewer. This is learned in psychotherapy. Our educational institutions are not yet prepared to teach this new social value of the courage to be imperfect (9). The ability to make mistakes graciously and to accept the ensuing predicament in the same spirit as if it had occurred without our fault, is essential for functioning as a free man, as an equal amongst equals.

Personal Success

Similar to the desire to be right and correct is our concern with being a success. Personal success is highly valued in our society, as failure is condemned. In this way the vertical movement is strongly encouraged. The ambition to succeed is perhaps the most outstanding social stimulation of our times. Few realize the tremendous costs which we have to pay for this mistaken social value. We instill in each child the conviction that he has to become better, be more, achieve more—otherwise he will be no good, a failure. But for every one child who can satisfy his over-ambition in a useful way—socially, academically, athletically—there are literally thousands who have no chance to feel important and be significant. They either give up altogether, or switch to the useless side. Most failures are the result of the inevitable discouragement which results if the confidence in one's ability does not keep in line with the self-ideal, with what one thinks one ought to be or do. Most criminals and juvenile delinquents are the victims of a perverted ambition instilled in them in a prestige-hungry society. They can only feel important by breaking the law and waging a "heroic" battle against society and its representatives.

Moving on the horizontal line does neither provide the sensation of personal success nor the torture of failure. Doing one's best does not require comparing oneself with others, nor depending on the opinions of others, their approval and disapproval. Everybody likes approval; but the free man, sure of his own value, does not depend on it. Our patients need to learn this inner freedom, of which Adler constantly spoke when he advised his students not to have a personal stake in whatever they may be doing. If it turns out well, so much the better; but if it does not, we must go on. If we feel defeated, our ability to go on becomes greatly impaired; but nobody can make us feel defeated except we ourselves. The failure to accomplish what we wanted can be an important experience and part of a learning process. But this requires that we do not take it as an expression of our lack of personal worth or ability. We need to distinguish between the deed and the doer. What we do may be wrong, stupid or mistaken; but this does not mean that we are stupid or a failure. Society does not teach us this lesson yet; psychotherapy cannot proceed without teaching it.

Reason and Objectivity

Therapeutic theories and practices have generally supported the cultural tradition of establishing yardsticks to measure superior and inferior, good or bad. In addition to moral concepts which served such purposes came psychological value judgments. Reason appeared as good, emotion as bad, objectivity as desirable, subjectivity as deplorable. According to Adlerian psychology, however, reason and emotion are not in conflict with each other. A holistic picture of man does not permit the fallacious separation of various functions into pairs of contrasting forces. Behind the individual's emotion there lies his "private logic" (1). Consequently, emotions, which are presently held in considerable disdain, are not irrational; they do not dominate man, but are his tools. He uses them for his purposes, just as he uses his ability to reason. And objectivity is by no means always preferable to subjectivity; we need to be subjective, to have preferences and dislikes, in order to participate actively in the social evolution (8). Besides, a "biased apperception" (1) is an intrinsic human feature. Subjectivity and objectivity are a continuum, are complementary modes of functioning; together they permit apperception and movement on the social plane.

The same continuum exists between conscious and unconscious processes. There is a varying degree of awareness, but no such entity of an "unconscious"—as Freud postulated it. The unconscious was the source of all evil which only the conscious could overcome. But it is questionable whether conscious or unconscious processes are more responsible for detrimental behavior. Since the individual is unaware of the vast majority of mental and physical processes within him, only a few unconscious motivations have detrimental consequences; but his conscious thoughts may more frequently interfere with his well-being and functioning.

Contrary to the assumption to which the patient is exposed in his environment, he learns in psychotherapy to trust his emotions, his unconscious processes, to accept his inevitable subjectivity, and to enjoy both the freedom and the obligation to choose and to prefer. He stops trying to "control himself," as he has been advised to do since early childhood, by realizing that he is going to do what he decides anyhow regardless of how much he may pretend to object to his actions.

Conclusion

It is obvious now that all the mistaken social values which prevail today, and are responsible for the neurotic inclination of most contemporaries, particularly those in metropolitan areas, are characterized by an over-emphasis of good and bad, right and wrong, up and down. This is what Adler has called the "antithetical mode of apperception" which he found characteristic of the neurotically disposed individual.

Conversely, the therapeutic effect on the patient emphasizes the horizontal move toward usefulness. In this direction, good and bad, up and down, are part of a normal pattern, like light and dark, harmony and discord. They belong together as alternating phases of a meaningful process. The absolute values disappear with the vanishing authority, on the judgment of which they depend. Instead of such value judgments, the relative significance of each act of behavior in the total situation must be seen and understood.

A new concept of man emerges, fortified by our psychological observations in therapy. New types of motivations result from different social orientations. Group psychotherapy, particularly, has opened the way to an exploration of human relationships where deficiencies no longer imply inferiority, and people can respect each other fully, despite their intimate awareness of each others' faults. We can, therefore, conclude that changing the value system on which patients operate constitutes an essential part of psychotherapy.

REFERENCES

1. Adler, Alfred. *Understanding human nature.* Greenwich, Conn: Fawcett Publications, 1954.

2. Adler, Alfred. *Social interest; a challenge to mankind.* New York: Putnam, 1939.

3. Adler, Felix. *An ethical philosophy of life.* New York: Appleton, 1918.

4. Ansbacher, H. L., and Rowena R. Ansbacher (eds.) *The Individual Psychology of Alfred Adler.* New York: Basic Books, 1956.

5. Dreikurs, R. *The challenge of marriage.* New York: Hawthorn Books, 1946.

6. Dreikurs, R. The religion of democracy. *Humanist,* 1955, 15, 210-215; 266-273.

7. Dreikurs, R. The unique social climate experienced in group psychotherapy. *Group Psychotherapy,* 1951, 3, 292-299.

8. Dreikurs, R. Adlerian psychotherapy. In Frieda Fromm—Reichmann, and J. L. Moreno (eds), *Progress in psychotherapy.* New York: Grune and Stratton, 1956.

9. Lazarsfeld, Sofie. Dare to be less than perfect. *International Journal of Individual Psychology,* 1936, 2, No. 2, 76-82.

10. MacIver, R. M. *The ramparts we guard.* New York: Macmillan, 1950.

11. Merton, R. K. *Social theory and social structure.* (Revised and enlarged edition). Glencoe, Ill.: Free Press, 1957.

12. Plant, J. S. *Personality and the culture pattern.* New York: Commonwealth Fund, 1937.

13. Sicher, Lydia. Education for freedom. *American Journal of Individual Psychology,* 1955, 11, 97-103.

MINOR PSYCHOTHERAPY

A Practical Psychology for Physicians*

The importance of psychological factors in almost every medical case is well recognized. Whether they are at the root of a complaint or symptom, or generated by an organic ailment, these psychological factors should never be overlooked and need consideration and attention. For this reason one can understand the current interest of the general practitioner as well as of every medical specialist in developing diagnostic and therapeutic skills in dealing with the psychological problems of his patients. The first assignment in preparing physicians for this task is to provide them with a reliable approach to a psychological diagnosis. By this we do not mean the ability to label the patient, but rather to recognize the nature of his psychological problems.

Even more important than the sensitivity to the psychological needs of the patient is the physician's role in responding to these needs. To what extent can and should the general practitioner be able to help the patient resolve his problems So far, no uniform answer has been given to this question which is of crucial importance to the medical profession. Can he, in the rush of his medical service, take the time with any one patient to help him psychologically? In other words, should he provide psychotherapy, or rather leave this form of treament to the specialist, the psychiatrist? At the present time, each medical practitioner relies on his own inclination. One is more ready to refer his emotionally disturbed patients to a psychiatrist, while another one hesitates to do so, and not always because he feels

* *Transactions,* Fifth Annual Meeting, Academy of Psychosomatic Medicine, 1958.

capable of dealing with his patient. To be sure, if every medical practitioner would send all his patients who are emotionally disturbed, and may profit from such referrals, to a psychiatrist, he would lose a good part of his practice. Consequently, general practitioners are obliged to attend to the psychological needs of their patients as well as they can, and make use of referrals only in the most severe cases.

This, then, is the second assignment in training and guiding physicians: to increase their ability to provide adequate psychological help to their patients within a busy medical practice. They can do it, to be sure. There are many practitioners whose treatment consists of more than writing prescriptions and only giving medical attention. It is less the lack of time which prevents a physician from providing psychological help; it is his skill alone which permits him to do so.

At the present time, both an understanding of the patient's psychological problems and the ability to resolve them depends less on the formal training of the physician than on his common sense, his empathy with the patient, his feeling about what the patient needs and wants. He acts more as a friend and guide than as a therapist, relying more on his inclinations than on his knowledge as to what to do and why. It seems necessary to prepare physicians, both on the undergraduate level at the medical schools and on the post-graduate level, through workshops and similar educational facilities, with skills and knowledge which would enable them to attend to the psychological needs of their patients in a more systematic fashion and on safer grounds. We may call this medical service minor psychotherapy.

This implies a similar distinction within the field of psychiatry to that which is universally accepted in regard to surgery. Major surgery is performed in the hospital by a specialist; minor surgery is surgical intervention which the general practitioner can perform in his office. In both instances, similar tools are used under similar basic requirements of asepsis, etc. Only the scope of the surgical intervention is different. The same holds true for the distinction between minor and major psychotherapy. The latter, reserved for the skills of the further trained specialist, is indicated when a more profound change in the personality of a patient is needed. But many emotional problems which lead to the development of symptoms or accompany somatic disturbances, do not require such basic reconstruction. It is often the impact of a given situation with which the patient feels unable to cope, which creates the emotional upheavals leading to his ailment and leads to his request for medical attention.

At the present time the physician seeking a psychological orientation and technique which he can apply in his medical practice, is confronted with a variety of theories and procedures. Psychiatry, at the present time, does not provide any generally accepted body of knowledge, but is in a state of development where various schools of thought propose different approaches, based on often conflicting theoretical assumptions. The physician is at a loss as to which school to follow, and may even distrust all of them because they cannot come to terms with each other. This makes it difficult to propose any one technique as more applicable than another. However, we suggest a technique which may meet the practical needs of the physician. It has proven its value in training physicians. This method shall be presented here.

When we try to understand a patient's motivation, we can look to his background, into his unconscious; we can see emotions, out of control at times and almost irrational; we can distinguish cerebral, endocrine or metabolic stimulations; assess hereditary and environmental influences. We may then try to gather and integrate them all, with the hope of gaining thereby a total picture of his personality and present condition, psychologically speaking. Widely used as it is, such a procedure does not provide a true picture of the patient. In contrast to the impressions gained through a summation of all mechanisms and influences which have supposedly contributed to the total personality is the holistic picture of the individual, which may be —and very often is—quite different.

The holistic theory, first developed by Smuts (1), maintains that the whole is more than the sum total of all its parts, and therefore, cannot be explained by its parts, its partial processes and genetic influences. When we are confronted with a person, we cannot know all the factors which were involved in building his personality, or which prompt him today; but we can perceive and understand him, nevertheless. We can see him as a whole when we sense or know his intentions, his movements. The whole personality can only be understood by the goals which the individual pursues at the moment; and these goals are not determined by any given set of antecedents. They are the result of choice and decision. Another person under exactly the same physical or mental conditions may decide to move in a different direction.

The holistic concept of man presupposes that behavior is purposive, that the individual himself determines his own direction. He is neither victim of hereditary nor of environmental influences; he is neither slave to his mind, emotions, or body, but has control over himself and all the forces within him to a much larger extent than is generally assumed. It is not a relationship of mind over body, since both are mere abstractions and under the direction of the individual who uses all his qualities and resources for his own end, be they physiological, mental, intellectual, or emotional. Understanding a person, then, means understanding his goals. This teleoanalytic* approach to human behavior is characteristic of the psychology of Alfred Adler, who emphasized the social nature of man and his desire to find his place in society, deviating emotionally and mentally if he feels frustrated in his efforts to find a place for himself and to belong. (2)

This general orientation led to specific techniques of analysis and treatment of emotional and psychological problems.

Like any technique, its mastery requires training and experience. Only broad outlines can be presented here. However, they may be sufficient to indicate to the medical practitioner certain new avenues in dealing with the emotional problems of his patients, and support perhaps some of his practices

* Teleological means goal-directed (from Greek, telos or teleos.)

which he developed by himself, more on the strength of common sense than on the basis of a well-founded orientation. Even those who worked effectively will find a well-defined frame of reference beneficial; it provides a guide by which one can clearly distinguish between effective and fruitless procedures. It adds a sense of security, because actions become more deliberate when one knows their significance, instead of having to rely on a vague feeling of what should be done.

All forms of psychotherapy which are analytical, uncovering and interpretive, consist of four basic steps which often overlap and yet have their own dynamics. (3) These four steps are: 1) The establishment of a therapeutic relationship; 2) The exploration of the psychological dynamics (analysis); 3) Helping the patient to understand himself (insight); 4) Helping the patient to replace mistaken attitudes with more correct ones (reorientation). The various theoretical presuppositions lead to different therapeutic procedures; some forms of psychotherapy, like hypnosis and suggestion, client-centered therapy and what is commonly called supportive therapy, neglect or disregard the need for steps 2 and 3, and move directly toward reorientation, once a satisfactory therapeutic relationship has been established.

Our concept of man as a social being, who pursues self-determined goals in line with the concepts and beliefs which he holds about himself and life, gives each of the four steps a distinct meaning and practical significance. The fundamental principles on which we operate, are as valid for major psychotherapy, in the treatment of severe neurosis and maladjustments, as in the minor adjustments necessary in dealing with specific problems, like the therapeutic efforts of the general practitioner (Minor Psychotherapy).

Step 1, the establishment of a proper *therapeutic relationship,* should not pose any difficulty to the physician. After all, a great many of his regular medical procedures are based on psychological principles. Without having a proper therapeutic relationship, he could not treat any patient; failing to establish it, he would either lose his patients or encounter constant resistance, even to strictly medical management. It is self-evident that every physician must win the patient's confidence and his cooperation in carrying out therapeutic prescriptions.

However, certain aspects of the therapeutic relationship, as they become evident in the study of psychotherapeutic dynamics, may help the medical practitioner in difficult cases. Every form of treatment requires a high degree of cooperativeness. This mutual cooperation may either be impaired at crucial moments, if the physician does not know how to maintain it, or it may continue only if the doctor succumbs to the undue demands of the patient, because refusal to submit may mean losing the patient. In all these instances, an understanding of a sound basis for cooperation may be helpful.

Harmonious working together is only possible when both doctor and patient have the same goals or objectives. When the patient comes for help, he naturally wants to get well, and this desire is in line with the doctor's intention. Most difficulties arise when the doctor's ideas about what should be done do not meet with those of the patient. Such opposition poses relatively little difficulty if it is openly expressed. The trained physician will find many ways to overcome the patient's resistance. However, it requires more psychological sensitivity and skill to sense the patient's opposition if it is not openly displayed. Disregarding it may prove highly detrimental, both for the present therapeutic effort and for the future relationship. In order to maintain the therapeutic relationship, one has constantly to be aware of the patient's attitude and intentions. Bringing them into the open for frank and friendly discussion may go a long way toward overcoming an otherwise highly damaging, although sometimes only minimal, opposition.

More complex is the question of the common goals when the patient actually does not come in order to get well, but for a variety of other reasons. He may want to prove that he just cannot get well, or he may seek someone who will take responsibility for him in a tough life situation; he may consider the physician an excellent accomplice in maintaining a sideshow in his life, being more concerned with himself than with his obligations. In all these cases, the physician who is not prepared to deal with the psychological problems of the patient, will either antagonize and eventually lose him, or become a victim of the patient's unconscious scheme. If he accepts the role of manager, either by his desire to be helpful or by his pride in the extreme confidence of his patients, then he becomes an almost eternal slave, while acting as guide and manager. To resolve this predicament, the physician will have to take step 2 and attempt to understand the patient's psychological problems, through a short analysis. It is a mistake to assume that such a psychological venture has to be time-consuming. If the physician knows what to ask for and can go directly to the important points of investigation, he can get all necessary information he needs within a very short period of time.

Step 2, *analysis,* is the crucial point in psychotherapy, be it major or minor. To be sure, one can help a patient, even psychologically, without understanding him and his problems. However, such help will not bring lasting results, if the problems of the patient have not been recognized and resolved.

What the medical practitioner needs to understand in almost every case, not only in those where psychological or emotional disturbances seem to color the picture, is the total situation in which the patient operates, his current field of action. This kind of investigation has been commonly called taking a social history. We consider an exploration of the social and environmental forces to which the patient is "exposed" is inadequate. It is less important to know what the patient encounters at the present moment of his life, than what attitude he takes to it, how he responds, or—even more important—what goals he has set for himself in dealing with a given situation. He is not merely a victim of circumstances, but a most active participant. For this reason, it is a mistake to assume that the conflicts in his life are the cause of his anxiety, tension, guilt feelings and similar psychological mechanisms, which supposedly produce symptoms and ailments. The patient may develop anxiety and symptoms as his means to escape responsibilities, to avoid facing and resolving his problems. But his psychological condition and emotional upheaval is *his* creation, and not the consequence of detrimental forces around or within him, in his "unconscious." In other words, it is less important to know what the patient is confronted with, than how he intends to deal with his predicament. Similarly, his physical ailment becomes an important factor in his total life situation, even if he is not neurotic, maladjusted, "emotionally unstable," or immature. All depends on the function his ailment plays in his situation, or—more accurately—what use he makes of it. In other words, we cannot consider the situation of the patient merely as an array of forces to which he is exposed. Such contemplation eliminates the *patient* as the most important agent in the situation, at least as far as his physical and mental functioning is concerned.

Understanding the patient's *intention* is a prerequisite for assessing the psychological and emotional involvement in any disease, be it physical or strictly psychogenic. At the last meeting of this Society, the writer had proposed an examination which permits a reliable differential diagnosis between organic and psychogenic symptoms (4). Such differential diagnosis cannot be made merely by default, through absence of organic pathology, or because of the general nervous and emotional condition of the patient. The neurotic nature of a symptom is evident only if its function within the total situation has been established. By asking the patient what would be different if he were well, one can ascertain against whom or what his symptoms are directed. This kind of investigation has proven highly reliable, although no diagnostic tool is infallible. In cases where the symptom did not serve any purpose the patient was, time and again, returned to the referring physician who had been convinced of the psychogenic nature of the complaint. Upon insistence on our part, an organic pathology was eventually discovered.

Since even organic ailments can be used by the patient in his struggle with the exigencies of life, the distinction between organic and psychogenic ailments becomes less important. It does not matter on what basis the person is sick. Once he is suffering and seeks medical attention, the physician has to deal in his therapeutic efforts with the total situation, with organic pathology as well as with social and psychological realities. In the last analysis, it is not the disease nor the social stress with which the doctor is confronted, but a human being who is suffering and seeks help. It is less important, then, to assess the situation objectively, both in regard to the medical as well as the social condition of the case. Naturally, the medical aspect will determine the therapeutic effort, and the realization of social conflicts and tensions will make the physician aware that a strictly medical procedure may be insufficient. However, if he would entirely rely on his own "objective" evaluation of the situation, he may not be able to get the patient's full cooperation, without which no therapeutic procedure can succeed. For this reason, it is important to know what the patient thinks and feels, how he regards and evaluates his own position, both in regard to his ailment and to his environmental stress. He cannot always openly express his intentions, because he may not be aware of them. The physician needs skill and experience to recognize the patient's "private logic" on which he operates, his real convictions and beliefs, which may differ from his overt and conscious thoughts. One does not need to rely on intuition and vague impressions to "sense" the patient's inner logic, if one is trained to observe human actions as movements toward others and toward life, if the ability to recognize and analyze purposive behavior has been fostered and systematically developed.

While the medical practitioner is concerned with a patient, and his therapeutic efforts are limited to the solution of his immediate predicament, it may help greatly to understand its significance if he knew the patient's basic personality structure. The same social conflicts may have different effects on different people. One may get sick when he loses his job and cannot find another, while another patient may get sick because he has to take on a job. It would be disastrous if the physician considers the patient's predicament only in the light of how *he* would feel if he were confronted with it. He may find it difficult to perceive the patient's reaction and attitude unless he knows the latter's basic concepts of himself and life, his "style of life," as Adler called it. It may sound presumptuous to suggest that a busy medical practitioner should be expected to ascertain such facts, when current psychiatric practices require a long series of interviews for a reliable evaluation of a patient's personality pattern. The writer has described in his paper, "The Psychological Interview in Medicine," (5) a technique which every physician could use to understand the life style of a patient.

A clear formulation of the patient's life style can be obtained through an investigation of his *family constellation,* his position and interaction with other members of his family during his formative years. This investigation reveals his field of early experiences, the circumstances under which he developed his personal perspectives and biases, his concepts and convictions about himself and others, his fundamental attitudes and his own approaches to life, which are the basis for his character, his personality. After we know the setting, we determine from his *early recollections* the conclusions which he drew under those circumstances. From all the millions of experiences to which we are exposed in our early childhood, we remember only those which coincide with our outlook on life. All early recollections show, therefore, the same pattern; where they may differ, they supplement but never contradict each other. Only if one changes one's life style in therapy—it cannot be done without outside help—only then do recollections change, in accordance with the new outlook on life.

The examination of the family constellation and of the early recollections is a simple procedure, but nevertheless requires some skill and training. The order of birth shows the patient in his characteristic position of a first, second, middle, youngest, or only child. The one sibling who was most different from him is the most important figure in his life, since difference in character, temperament and interest always indicates competition. In most cases the next younger brother or sister is the main competitor. In asking the patient to describe the personalities of his brothers and sisters, he provides insight into each one's movements in their competitive effort to find a place in the group. Character traits are an expression of social movement. Where one sibling succeeds, his competitor gives up every effort; where the other fails, he may move in. This results in the development of different personalities amongst competitors. Through a set of questions about the patient himself as a child and about his brothers and sisters in regard to their individual successes and failures in various activities, the patient's function within his family group becomes visible. His final assets and deficiencies can thus be related to his movements within his family circle. Parents are the powers behind the scene; their relationship sets the pattern of all interpersonal relationships within the family. Some other people living within the family may have contributed to the role which the patient played as a child.

In soliciting the early recollections one must distinguish between a recollection and a report. Descriptions of actual incidents may be inaccurate, but they reflect the patient's impression of life. The incidents which are remembered are not important because they happened, but only because they are remembered. Every person has experienced falling down and hurting his knees; but only those will remember such an incident who still think they cannot take care of themselves and are in constant danger of falling down and hurting themselves.

Interpreting the information about the family constellation and about early recollections requires skill and experience. The ability to recognize all aspects and implications of the information obtained distinguishes the expert from the student. However, everyone who uses this technique will know more about a person than is possible without such information or without knowing its significance. The beginner can grow by investigations of this kind, and familiarize himself with a method which can provide, in a short period of time, reliable information about the patient's concepts, about his goals in life, his ideas of success and security. On the strength of this knowledge, the physician may see the present situation with which the patient is confronted in a quite different light than he would were he not aware of the patient's basic attitudes and biases. It may explain why the present juncture in his life became a crisis situation to which he responded with sickness, either developing psychoneurotic symptoms or intensifying incidental organic ailments.

Step 3 consists of providing *insight* through interpretation. Nobody knows himself, and we all hide our intentions from ourselves, if they interfere with our consciences. It is at this point that the physician is obliged to accept the role of a psychotherapist as part of his medical practice. The patient does not know why he is sick or for what purpose; the trained medical practitioner should know it and help him to see it. This cannot be done by criticizing the patient and pointing a finger at him in an accusing way. Nor will it help to minimize his predicament, to admonish him in either a moral or preaching way, telling him to control himself, to forget his fears, to pull himself together, and the like. It is obviously wrong to tell him that there is nothing wrong with him, because he actually does suffer, and his suffering can be well understood, because it is meaningful, at least to the patient in his predicament.

The art of interpretation requires certain skill; it presupposes a genuine understanding without condemnation or pity. It is usually advisable to make interpretations not in a dogmatic way. Instead of "stating facts" by telling the patient what he is doing, what his intentions and purposes are, how he uses his symptoms and illness, it is preferable to speak in tentative terms. Could it be that he tries to avoid a task, seeks excuses for not functioning, puts the blame on his condition rather than face his problems and solve them?—or whatever the case may be. In such an approach the patient is more willing to listen and to consider the possibility. It is of utmost importance that interpretations are always made in regard to *goals* and purposes, not about psychological *conditions*. It is of little help to the patient to be told that he feels insecure, suffers from fears and anxieties, that his tension or his guilt feelings make him sick. Such interpretations, even if they are correct, have no value. On the contrary, they confirm the patient in his assumption that there is something wrong with him, and he cannot do anything about it. He can change his goals and intentions, but he cannot change his anxiety, fear, tension, guilt feelings, or what other technical terms a well-meaning but ill-advised physician may throw at him.

Step 4, the *reorientation,* is the main goal of all therapeutic efforts. All other steps are a preparation for this, and have to be considered as means to this end. Therefore, it is essential to know the psychological dynamics which can induce a patient to change his attitudes, intentions, and goals. Let us first state clearly what kind of advice actually *prevents* the patient from changing and improving. Everything that induces him to fight with himself will inevitably lead to a worsening of the condition. Neurotic symptoms develop and are maintained by the patient fighting against them. Consequently, any advice to control himself and the like is bound to intensify the patient's condition. We are dealing here with a cultural misconception of psychological dynamics. Most people think that in order to change they have to fight with themselves. They do not know that we can change only if we realize that what we are, and what we are doing, rests upon our own decisions, which we usually make without being aware of them.

This is the starting point for a therapeutic reorientation. We use the mirror technique to show the patient which of his decisions led to his sickness and keep him sick. (6) This interpretation can motivate the patient to reconsider what he is doing. We use past history, his life style, only to explain to him his present plans and intentions. If he was an oldest child who always had to be first, and is now confronted with a situation which prevents him from being on top, or if he was the youngest or a sickly or an only child, who always depended on the support of others, and now has lost such support, then this knowledge of his general pattern can help him to understand what he is doing now. He is not bound by the past, although it explains why he feels as he does. His conscience is one of the motivating factors to reconsider his intentions once he becomes aware of them. Another therapeutic factor is his growing realization that he has the power to make decisions and, therefore, can decide whether he will remain sick or get well.

In many cases such insight may be sufficient to bring about a reorientation; in the majority, it is not. Here we need other psychological incentives. They are not specific for the individual patient and his problems, but are needed and effective in all cases of emotional or social maladjustment.

General therapeutic approaches are usually called supportive therapy. However, their characteristic elements apply to all forms of therapy, since reorientation is hardly ever accomplished without these dynamic approaches.

It seems that *encouragement* is one of the most essential factors in all corrective endeavors, since every deficiency is based on discouragement. Only if the patient is discouraged, has lost faith in himself and in his strength and ability to cope with his predicament, does he switch to the "useless side." (Adler) Without encouragement, without having faith in himself restored, he cannot see the possibility of doing or functioning better. Regaining his self-respect, he can recognize his strength, instead of seeking constant new proof of his assumed weakness. It is the doubt in himself which makes him build the defenses against whatever may threaten his place in life, which makes him sick.

The process of encouragement is much more complex than most assume. It consists of more than a kind word or a pat on the shoulder or telling him that he is strong and capable. These are often empty words, and not accepted by the patient, even if they are sincere. Encouragement presupposes self-confidence on the part of the physician that he will be able to help. One of the greatest obstacles in encouraging others is our doubt in our own ability. Encouragement presupposes that the physician recognizes his own therapeutic potential and is convinced of the patient's strength and power of decision. At the present time, the general practitioner is inclined to regard the neurotic patient as a liability, as an almost insurmountable obstacle to his best therapeutic efforts. This is so, to a large extent, because the physician is not yet trained to utilize effective methods in dealing with such cases.

One of the most frequent sources of emotional strain and distress is the concern with personal prestige. The patient considers himself a failure because he cannot live up to the high standards which he has set up for himself and which he then blames on society. His sickness is often his alibi for not doing better. We are here confronted with a social value system which is responsible for the widespread neurotic tendencies in our population. The physician has to assume the responsibility of an educator. As he teaches his clientele to respect the requirements of general hygiene, so he is in a position to teach also some of the basic requirements for mental health. It is mostly endangered by everyone trying desperately to elevate himself, with the inevitable consequence of constant fear of slipping, of failing. The physician could well counteract such tendencies in his patients, both as a preventive and therapeutic measure, provided he could free himself of such faulty social orientation.

Part of the necessary training of medical students for the psychological aspects of their medical practice is indoctrination in proper mental health aspects. Therapeutically, the physician has to provide his patients with new social values, counteracting those to which they are exposed in our neurotic society. Communication of a new outlook on life is, therefore, an essential part of the process of reorientation. Healthy living requires acceptance of hygienic prerequisites, be they physical, social, or psychological.

Without accepting the responsibility of influencing his patients psychologically, no physician can be effective as a medical practitioner. It is interesting to note that the medical specialists who responded the strongest when psychodynamic principles were first discovered and utilized for the development of psychotherapy, were the surgeons. While their therapeutic efforts are strictly physical, they realized the tremendous significance of psychological factors. These, and not the surgeon's skill, determine often the outcome of an operation. What is true for the surgeon is true for all medical practitioners. In order to deal with the psychological aspects of all their patients, physicians need training in psychological methods which are practical and applicable in every office. We have attempted to present an outline of a method which may fill this need.

BIBLIOGRAPHY

1. J. C. Smuts, *Holism and Evolution,* New York: MacMillan, 1926.
2. Alfred Adler, *Social Interest, A Challenge to Mankind,* New York: Putnam, 1964.
3. Rudolf Dreikurs, *Adlerian Psychotherapy,* in *Progress in Psychotherapy,* New York: Grune and Stratton, 1956.
4. Rudolf Dreikurs, A Reliable Differential Diagnosis of Psychological or Somatic Disturbances, *Int. Rec. of Med.,* 1958, 171, 4.
5. Rudolf Dreikurs, The Psychological Interview in Medicine, No. 3, 4, *American Journal of Individual Psychology,* 1954, 10.
6. Rudolph Dreikurs, The Goals of Therapy, *American Journal of Psychoanalysis,* 1956, VIX, 1.

GOALS IN THERAPY*

The function of the psychiatrist differs in many ways from that of any other medical specialist. With the exception of the psychiatrist in mental institutions, he does not see the most serious cases and those most in need of psychiatric help. As a rule, it is not the severity of the condition which prompts therapy, but the patient's decision to do something about it.

Furthermore, in many instances those who do come for treatment do so for reasons other than to get well. Psychiatrically speaking, even the term "getting well" is ambiguous and full of complexities since the disappearance of symptoms does not necessarily imply cure.

We cannot assume either that the goal of psychiatric therapy is to satisfy the purpose for which the patient came. Almost every patient believes that he is seeking help, that he wants to get well. This may not be true. The patient may not believe that he ever will get well. Seeking psychiatric treatment is merely a demonstration of his willingness to do everything possible; but while outwardly cooperative, he is bent on proving that even the best doctor cannot help him. Or he may look for sympathy or may wish to put somebody in his service, to solve his problems and make decisions for him. Some may seek support in their fight against others and hope that the psychiatrist will be their ally. It is obvious that the satisfaction of such demands cannot be the goal of therapy.

---

* *American Journal of Psychoanalysis,* 1956, 16, 18-23.

Differences of opinion about the nature of the therapeutic process itself confuse the issue further. The goal of psychotherapy will vary according to the postulations of a particular school of thought. All dynamic schools consider a change in the personality structure as essential. However, no agreement has been reached, as yet, about the nature of the pathological mechanisms and, consequently, of the kind of changes which are necessary to produce mental health and cure. It is the purpose of this paper to present the Adlerian point of view, the dynamic processes interpreted in the light of Alfred Adler's Individual Psychology.

Psychotherapy, as we see it, is a learning process. The object to be studied is the individual. Nobody knows himself. As long as he is functioning adequately, he does not need such knowledge. But if he does not function well, if he becomes deficient or maladjusted, then he cannot change unless he first knows what to change. Everybody knows when he does something wrong, but he does not know why he is doing it. Psychotherapy permits uncovering the motivation of the individual and the nature of his difficulties. It remedies the mistakes made in the natural learning process by which the child developed his personality.

This formulation indicates clearly the nature of maladjustment and emotional disturbances as seen from our point of view. It is a wrong social approach which the individual developed as a child and which eventually led to his difficulties in coping with the problems of life. Emotional and mental illness is an expression of withdrawal, a declaration of partial or total bankruptcy. Consequently, the goal of psychotherapy is more than emotional adjustment; it is actually social adjustment. This requires the recognition and alteration of the basic assumptions and premises on which the individual functions.

The question then arises, what kind of reorientation is attempted which, if accomplished, indicates success of therapy? It is obvious that a temporary change of attitudes cannot be regarded as satisfactory, although it may bring about a disappearance of symptoms and an improvement in the immediate conflict situations. The second question then is whether a permanent change of personality is possible. This leads to still a third question: If a change of personality can be achieved, and can remain permanent, do we attempt a total change of personality or is a partial change satisfactory?

We can distinguish four phases in psychotherapy: (1) The establishment and maintenance of a proper therapeutic relationship. (2) Analysis in its wider sense, understanding the patient. (3) Interpretation, providing insight. (4) Reorientation and re-education. Only in an interpretative and uncovering therapy do we find all four phases. They are not separated entirely but overlap. At certain points, therapy is more concerned with one or the other.

The establishment and maintenance of a proper relationship is more than a means of therapy. It is a prerequisite for the cooperation necessary in therapy, but in many instances it implies also a therapeutic goal. For many a patient the relationship with the therapist is the first good and close relationship he has experienced. This type of relationship with its give and take, its resilience in conflict and its endurance under the impact of hostility can well form a pattern for future and more satisfactory relationships. This phase, then, implies a retraining for better interactions almost an action experience. The conflicts between patient and therapist are not considered as an expression of "resistance" but rather as a clash of goals and interests. Through the interpretation of his attitudes and conduct toward the therapist, the patient learns about his own personality, his goals and intentions. The action pattern of their relationship supplements significantly the verbal level of the treatment. The training of a better form of relationship is one of the goals and objectives of psychotherapy.

Phase 2 does not in itself have any bearing on the goal of therapy, except as an indispensable prerequisite to Phase 3. It involves the exploration of the patient's life style of the basic premises on which he operates, his basic mistakes about himself and life, the goals which he has set himself.

Phase 3, providing interpretation, is one of the most important steps toward promoting reorientation. Since Adlerian psychology is characterized by its socio-teleological interpretation of behavior, our exploration of motivation is concerned with goals and not with causes. We try to make the patient aware of the purpose both of his deficiencies and his symptoms. This is the kind of insight which seems to be singularly helpful in promoting reorientation. Introspection as such, recognition of past influences and present "feelings," and concern with heretofore unknown mechanisms do not promote motivations to change as strong as the recognition of self-determined goals and purposes. The neurotic, particularly, is in a conflict between his conscience and his true intentions. The symptoms have the purpose of covering up his real intentions, his private logic. Bringing them to his attention is an important step in motivating him to change them. As Adler pointed out, one of the most effective therapeutic means is "spitting in the patient's soup." He can continue what he is doing, but it doesn't taste so good.

Naturally the most important phase of psychotherapy is the process of reorientation. Its extent and intensity alone indicate the success or failure of therapy. This reorientation occurs, at least to some extent, if the goal of the three other phases has been accomplished.

However, certain psychological dynamics take place in this process of reorientation which are necessarily part of the three other aspects. If reorientation did not have its own dynamic premises, it could not be accomplished without the preceding uncovering or interpreting procedures. As we know, therapeutic successes can be accomplished without them. It is questionable whether they are as permanent and satisfactory, but this is not certain, either. Since the analysis and the insight provided to the patient differs so widely in content and scope among the various psychological schools of thought, each school is understandably inclined to doubt that the other provides real "insight." As an example, psychoanalysts tend to consider Adlerian therapy superficial and merely supportive because it does not explore the unconscious and, therefore, cannot come to the root of problems.

Adlerians, in turn, maintain that no approach provides real insight which neglects the recognition of the life style, the basic premise on which the patient operates. If the insight provided by one form of therapy is questioned in its validity by the practitioners of the others, then one can well understand why certain therapists refute the need for any exploratory phase in therapy. Once they have established a good working relationship with the patient, they immediately move toward reorientation, as in Roger's Client-Centered Therapy, Slavson's Activity Group Therapy, Low's Self-Help Group Therapy, and many others, like hypnosis, waking suggestions and other forms of noninterpretative psychotherapy.

From our point of view a psychotherapeutic endeavor which neglects an exploration of the social and psychological mechanisms behind the patient's difficulties would be considered inadequate. However, we appreciate other elements of psychotherapy in their psychological effectiveness. Certain generally valid therapeutic endeavors may lead to reorientation without any detailed analysis and interpretation. We use such general procedures, which are often called supportive, if the patient is too confused or too upset to face himself in his motivations, purposes, and intentions. Even with patients with a low tolerance for psychological insight we never fail to attempt a communication of their basic goals. A permanent rehabilitation probably requires some change in the basic mistakes in self-evaluation which the patient made during childhood.

The dynamic processes which lead to reorientation indicate both the methods which need to be used to bring it about and the goals to be achieved. The important question with which we are confronted at this point is: can a person change, and, if so, what would motivate him to do so?

Let us state firmly that everybody can change. Man is not driven nor determined, but a self-directed and self-determined being. True, he follows fundamental goals which he has set for himself long ago and of which he is not aware. Therefore, his professed willingness to change may be stymied by his inability to know where to start. Consequently, many people try to change by doing exactly what prevents a change—they fight with themselves. Similar subjective experiences impress people with the conviction that they cannot change even if they want to. Actually, they are the victims of a fallacious assumption. We can change only if we realize that what we are, and what we are doing, rests upon our own decisions which we usually make without knowing it.

This is the starting point for a therapeutic reorientation. We use a mirror technique to show the patient which of his decisions lead to his actions and movements, including those from which he suffers. This interpretation can motivate the patient to reconsider what he is doing. We use past history only to explain to him his present plans and intentions. He is not bound by the past, although it explains why he feels shackled. His conscience, his desire to conform to social standards, is one of the motivating factors, the other being his growing realization of his own power to make decisions and to change his behavior accordingly.

In some cases such insight may be sufficient to bring about a reorientation; in most instances it is not. Here we need other psychological incentives. They are not specific for the individual and his problems, but are similarly needed and effective in all cases of emotional, mental or social maladjustment.

From our point of view the strict distinction between analytic and supportive therapy is unwarranted. What is called "supportive" is essential in any successful therapy. The term "supportive" seems somewhat superficial and misleading. However, reorientation in any form of therapy would be impossible without these elements which constitute a so-called supportive therapy.

Our model of man makes us emphasize certain dynamic approaches. Accordingly, widely known and used mechanisms take on a different meaning. From our point of view, encouragement is one of the most essential factors in all corrective endeavors. It is the basis for any "support" we can give a patient. In the last analysis, strengthening the ego is nothing but encouragement. But, on the other hand, encouragement implies more than is usually assumed when one talks about it. It is by no means "superficial" if it is recognized in its true significance and used properly.

As we see it, every deficiency is based on discouragement. It is so much easier to function well that nobody would be willing to take on all the tortures, suffering and sacrifices which disfunction entails—unless he had lost faith in himself, the belief that he can do what he ought to do, and do it well. Only if he is discouraged does he switch to the "useless side" (Adler). This discouragement may occur in a crisis situation, or it may be permanent, dating from early childhood. All mistakes in the life style can be understood through the humiliations and frustrations which an individual experienced in his childhood. Without encouragement, without restoring faith in himself, he cannot see the possibility of doing better. Deliberate and persistent encouragement can stimulate the patient to develop a better and more accurate picture of himself. It counteracts his prejudice against himself, which is found in every neurotic; the psychotic, the sociopath, generally cover it up, but they, too, do not believe in the possibility of finding their place in society through useful means.

We are dealing here with an essential point in Adlerian psychology: its emphasis on inferiority feelings as a genetic factor of maladjustment. This emphasis has often been considered as far-fetched and onesided. How can one single dynamic factor explain all the varieties of deficiencies and maladjustment? To understand its significance, one must realize the social constitution of man. The fundamental desire of every human being is to belong, to have status in the group of which he is a part. He can fulfill himself only within a group. Without belonging, he is lost and meaningless. For this reason, the concern with status is understandable in its pivotal significance. In our democratic society a feeling of belonging requires a realization of being equal to others. Being less than the others, inferior to them, deprives us of status, and with it, of being part of the group. This fear of being inferior and, thereby, of being deprived of a place is accentuated in our competitive society. The child is impressed with the fact that he counts less if he is inferior to others and that only superiority guarantees him a place in the group. This assumption of being a failure if one does not live up to high standards and cannot maintain superiority over others, at least within certain areas, is often responsible for the declaration of bankruptcy which emotional and social maladjustment implies.

It is obvious that any procedure which conveys to the patient his sense of worth and value promotes a reconsideration of his self-concept. He just is no longer the same person when he loses his prejudice against himself and discovers that he is good enough as he is. The similarity of this process with that in psychoanalytic therapy of helping the patient overcome his guilt feelings is obvious. It seems to be one of the primary goals of every psychotherapy to help the patient restore faith in himself, to regain his self-respect, to recognize his inner strength instead of seeking constant new proof for his assumed weakness. Rehabilitation implies the discovery of one's own dignity. These goals of therapy are essential in every case and implied in all forms of therapy, from faith healing to psychoanalysis.

Overcoming one's own inferiority feeling has far-reaching consequences on behavior. It removes all defense mechanisms which are understood by us as defenses against the social threat of humiliation and ostracism. The individual, sure of his place in the group, no longer has to defend himself against its social demands. Social interest which is based on a feeling of belonging and leads to full participation can only develop in the absence of inferiority feeling. Social interest and the feeling of inferiority are in converse proportion to each other. The removal of inferiority feelings opens the way for an increase in social interest. Such increase is the indispensable proof of social and emotional improvement. It alone permits the individual to function well in a social setting and to take the ups and downs of life in his stride without becoming frustrated, discouraged, demoralized, or sick.

The other by-product of encouragement is the realization of one's own inner freedom. Free from the fears of inadequacy, of loss of status, the individual can utilize all his heretofore unrecognized inner potentialities. He can devote his energies to whatever is important and useful, instead of being tied down by fears, apprehensions and wasteful defenses. Inner freedom and social interest are not contradictory, but supplementary. Only a free person can truly be a social person, not the victim of social and other pressures, but a free agent as a social being.

This process of learning implied in psychotherapy does not concern itself with personal qualities nor with feelings, assets and deficiencies, but with social values. The influence which we try to exert on the patient contradicts many social influences to which he is exposed. His inferiority "feelings" which are a wrong judgment of self, express the contemporary social contention that everybody who is not superior is necessarily inferior. Psychotherapy tries to instill in the patient a sense of equality to all others, in a society which speaks about equality and grants it to none. Society stimulates vanity and apprehension about status which psychotherapy attempts to eliminate. Society puts a premium on prestige—we try to minimize its significance. We try to remove the patient from his vertical movement by which he constantly measures himself with others. He establishes a fictitious superiority in one moment and an equally unrealistic inferiority in the next. We try to bring him to the horizontal movement which alone can bring fulfillment and self-realization through cooperation, in contrast to the false triumphs over his fellow men in a successful competition. Psychotherapy cannot avoid discussion of the value systems which have formed guiding lines for the patient. It attempts to replace wrong social values with those more beneficial.

This concern with social values, with the "ironclad logic of social living" (Adler) characterizes the Adlerian approach to therapy. It is not surprising, therefore, that the Adlerians were among the first to use group psychotherapy (since 1921). The individual therapist may overlook or deny that he is stimulating new social values in his patients regardless of the type of therapy he practices; the group therapist cannot escape this realization. The group is a value-forming agent. In the therapy group the patient becomes an equal, irrespective of individual assets and deficiencies. This forces him to reconsider his self-concept and his social attitudes and movements.

We are now in a position to answer the questions which we raised before:

(1) It is now clear what kind of reorientation we consider necessary in a successful therapy. This change implies alteration in personal concepts and in social orientation. Therapy puts the patient on a different track so to say. He may regress into his old patterns, but the new trend counteracts such tendencies.

(2) Can we speak of a permanent change of personality as the result of a successful therapy? I think we can. The patient certainly is not the same individual before and after therapy. And this change is permanent, regardless of temporary relapses or even reccurrence of symptoms. We have seen in cases of recidivism that some significant changes had occurred during the previous treatment but apparently were not sufficient to fortify the patient against new demoralizing influences.

(3) This seems to answer the third question, whether we attempt a total change of personality or whether a partial change is satisfactory. From our point of view, any partial change is actually a total change, since the individual no longer is what he was. However, if total change implies a change of all fundamental concepts and aspects of the personality, then it is obvious that such a kind of change is neither necessary nor possible. The correction of one mistaken concept is progress. Whether the extent of change is sufficient for future adequate living, only time can tell. In many instances, relatively minor changes in concept and approach proved to be sufficient. The patient, encouraged by his "success," grows, intensifying the changes made in therapy. By and large, whatever changes have been accomplished during the therapy are probably less significant than those which occur after termination. The patient finds himself moving in a different direction. The final result of the therapeutic experience is the extent and nature of his new training. Therapy may have been terminated successfully, and still a relapse may occur. Or conversely, a relatively insignificant change in a prematurely terminated therapy may lead to a sufficient and permanent adjustment of the individual.

THE PSYCHOLOGICAL INTERVIEW IN MEDICINE*

The development of psychosomatic medicine and the general acceptance of its basic tenets, namely, the interdependency of psychological and somatic processes, has stimulated medical practitioners to an increased awareness of, and interest in psychodynamics. There is hardly a physician who does not know that psychological conditions of his patients have to be taken into consideration; they can be either entirely responsible for the patient's complaints, or they may adversely affect somatic ailments. But while progress in medicine has firmly established the importance of psychological factors, it has left the medical practitioner without much assistance in his efforts to understand the psychodynamics of his patients and to evaluate properly the psychological factors in any given case. One is justified in questioning the extent to which physicians in general "understand" their patients. The same problem arises in regard to teachers, who are supposed to understand their pupils in order to help them in their progress and adjustment. But do teachers by and large really understand children? And if they do, on what premise is their understanding based?

We find ourselves in the peculiar position wherein the need for psychological understanding has been well impressed upon the practitioners of various professions, yet at the same time little training has been available to them for a scientifically sound evaluation of psychodynamics. Consequently, physicians,

---

* *American Journal of Individual Psychology*, 1954, 10, 99-122.

teachers, and others dealing professionally with people, have to rely on a pre-scientific, almost intuitive approach, based on ability to "sense" psychological factors, mostly through empathy.

We cannot blame any individual teacher or physician for his or her deficiency in this regard. It is in the scientific evolution of psychology that we find the reason for the inadequate knowledge of psychodynamics among professional workers.

Real progress in this field depended on the breakup of autocratic social organizations. In an autocracy it is neither necessary nor even advisable to "understand" the individual. Psychological considerations were only given to the masses which had to be subdued. It is characteristic for autocratic concepts to consider human behavior as being based on heredity (1), divine guidance, or predestination; this being so, there is nothing to understand, nor much to change; force alone can stimulate or suppress. All progress in psychological understanding has been made by investigators who were rebels and opposed certain cultural pressures of their time.

When psychology was recognized as a coming science, attempts were made to apply to the human being those approaches which had been found effective in natural and physical science. Experimental and statistical research provided valuable and new information about psychological mechanisms. But none of them could do justice to any one individual, explaining him in his uniqueness. Various theories were advanced in psychology, each one revealing other facets of the human mind and personality; but none provided an approach permitting insight into one specific person. One of the first theories, especially on the American scene, which attempted to analyze and to understand one individual, was Watson's "Behaviorism." It explained the individual in a mechanistic-physiological way, considering him as the result of innumerable stimulus-response patterns. While this theory offered some direction for corrective procedures, through exposing the individual to new stimuli in order to offset the past detrimental ones, it actually did not provide the professional worker with any tool to really understand the person, since no one had information about all the innumerable stimuli to which the individual had been previously exposed.

A revolutionary change in scientific methods of understanding individuals came from medicine, or more specifically, from its psychiatric branch. The physician has to apply whatever information science supplies. The psychiatrist uses "applied psychology." He cannot wait for statistical evidence, nor can he be satisfied with theoretical considerations of isolated mechanisms. He has to treat a patient and to find scientifically supported methods to do so. Consequently, it was a psychiatrist, Sigmund Freud, who revolutionized the science of psychology. He devised methods applicable to an individual case not only for therapeutic purposes, but to gain insight into psychological dynamics. But Freud was the product of a mechanistic-deterministic era dominant in science throughout the last few centuries. He could only see biologic-instinctual processes which seem to dominate man, making him a pawn of hereditary and environmental influences. The rather involved and often farfetched interpretations of the psychoanalytic school do not provide the medical practitioner with tools to understand individual patients. A psychiatric specialist is required to spend many hours to determine the psychodynamics of a person. The psychoanalytically oriented physician can only assume certain mechanisms which may operate in his patient. Actually, all he does is use an analytic label instead of the previous moralistic one. The old-fashioned physician may call a patient hysterical, selfish, irresponsible, stupid, or whatever quality he may need to explain the patient's inability to function. The modern physician may speak about repressed hostility, anal or oral personality, guilt feelings, self-punishment, etc. It is questionable how much real understanding is accomplished by either giving such a verdict or treating the patient on the basis of it.

II.

An accurate and rather quick understanding of an individual is available by what may be called the socio-teleological approach. It implies the recognition of the human being as a fundamentally social being, a zoon politicon (Aristotle.) All his actions have social significance, all his functions have meaning within a social setting. The realization of the social nature of man is generally associated with another concept, namely, man's self-directiveness, his striving for goals which he sets for himself. In this perspective all actions are purposive, and their goals are of a social nature. In his goals all the past experiences and stimulations of a person come into play. Therefore, the teleological approach is holistic, and no holistic approach seems likely without the recognition of the social purposiveness of man's behavior. In his goals, which bring about his actions, feelings and thoughts, the individual reveals his total personality.

The socio-teleological approach is the most recent one in psychology, although Adler developed it about forty years ago. It leads away from the causalistic-mechanistic concepts of the past. It presupposes man's ability to decide for himself, to be a self-regulating agent. Such concepts are in line with the democratic atmosphere which surrounds modern man. The power of any one force upon man becomes dubious and is even questioned in physical science. The causal principle assumes that a force can affect a passive object; however, it is established that no such passive objects exist, and that any organism "responds" to any force to which it is exposed. It is this response which determines the effect of the original force. This is true within the inanimate world, more so in the biological sphere, and most obvious in man. Man not merely reacts, he acts according to his own self-determination. This spells the end of an exclusively causalistic orientation.

The socio-teleological approach was perhaps first defined and clearly established by Alfred Adler in his Individual Psychology. His perspectives were later adopted by other analysts who broke away from the orthodox school of Freud, beginning with Otto Rank, Karen Horney, the Washington School of Harry Stack Sullivan, Erich Fromm, Frieda Fromm-Reichmann, Clara Thompson and the Chicago group of Franz Alexander and Thomas French. Each of them is in a different stage of breaking with the biological-instinctual past and discovering the socio-teleological future. Some, like French, still are blocked by their assumption that goals are mainly biological and concern the conflicts within the individual but are all moving in the same direction.

This development is universal wherever the new aspects of man and life are perceived. In contrast to the early vitalists who left the door open for mystical concepts, the modern teleologically oriented scientists have no such inclinations and regard teleological mechanisms as part of natural forces. "The concept of teleological mechanisms, however it may be expressed in different terms, may be viewed as an attempt to escape from these older mechanistic formulations that now appear inadequate, and to provide new and more fruitful conceptions and more effective methodologies for studying self-regulating processes, self-orienting systems and organisms, and self-directing personalities. But these new concepts carry no psychic or vitalistic assumptions, nor do they imply that any mysterious supernatural powers or psychic forces or final causes are operating the system or guiding the organism-personality. The idea of purposive behavior is not a regressive movement to an earlier stage in the history of ideas, but forward movement toward a more effective conception of the problems we face today." (L. K. Frank—2). The terms feedback, servomechanisms, circular systems and circular processes express the same basic mechanisms and substantiate in mathematical and scientific terms what Adler visualized half a century ago. At the same time he was considered "unscientific" when he rejected a mechanistic explanation of human behavior and recognized man's ability to set his own goals and to maintain them against outside pressure by establishing his own life style. Similar trends toward a new scientific orientation are reflected in the formulations of the "elan vital" by Bergson, the "cellular consciousness," by Pierre Jean, the "aristogenesis" by Osborn, the "nomogenesis" by Berg, Smuts' "holism," Rosa's "hologenesis," Driesch's "entelechy," du Nouy's "telefinalism."

This rather theoretical discussion is necessary as a preparation and justification for the technique which Adler provided in examining the personality structure of a patient, a technique which permits a rather quick and reliable psychological analysis.

Every physician should be familiar with such a technique which permits him a more objective psychological analysis of each patient, since psychological factors cannot only cause symptoms and disturbances, but aggravate pathological conditions. In many cases a differential diagnosis between psychogenic and somatic illness is hardly possible without a proper evaluation of the psychological condition of the patient.

Our technique of eliciting pertinent psychological information follows the well established pattern of Adler. Its slightly more systematic presentation became advisable for the teaching of medical students and the training of young psychiatrists. A questionnaire was evolved which facilitates the collection of all pertinent material within a short period of time. When Adler once declared that he, within an hour interview, could understand a patient, his problems and his whole personality, we, his students, stood in awe of his genius. Today we know that everybody can learn to do so, if not as efficiently. Every physician can learn, by using this technique, to understand the patient and his problems within a relatively short time.

In interviewing a patient for the first time, we let him talk about his condition, his symptoms, his discomfort and disfunctions. He gives us then—as we call it—the "Subjective Condition." We know then how he feels, what he experiences within himself, what he came for.

Then we examine the "Objective Situation" of the patient. We want to know the field in which he moves, the condition under which he lives, how he actually functions. Adler gave us the framework for such examination by pointing to the three life tasks which include all human actions and endeavors, work, social relationships, and relationships to the opposite sex.

Both areas of inquiry require some skill. No experienced physician should find it difficult to obtain a correct picture of the subjective condition of the patient. All it takes is the ability to prod the patient to express himself. The clarification of the objective situation requires more specific skill. Some medical practitioners may not yet have acquired it, although a good physician generally can, so to say, read between the lines or "listen with a third ear." That is necessary in many cases. Particularly if the patient sees no reason why the doctor should ask personal and intimate questions, he may be inclined to pass over the pertinent data and answer the question about the three areas of functioning with, "Everything is fine." He likes his job, his family, gets along wonderfully with his wife, sex activity is "normal," he has many friends. This may be so, although it is questionable whether any one of our contemporaries can lead such a well-adjusted life. Such answer of a patient is even more dubious if the subjective complaints indicate some nervous tension. Then we can be quite sure that conflicts and dissatisfactions exist within the three areas of living. The difficulty is to induce the patient to talk freely. This requires skill, an attitude of sincere interest and understanding, tact, but also acumen in not missing certain clues which would lead to the exploration of a conflict situation. We have seen inexperienced students give a patient a clean bill of health in his field of action, when a slight scratching of the surface brought forth deep disturbances in human relationships and functions. It is our opinion that a correct evaluation of the present field of action is mandatory in any case of serious illness, of whatever kind it may be. This information is at least as essential as a careful anamnesis of past illness.

In many cases it may be advisable to examine the field of action as it was at the time of the onset of the present illness, at least if neurotic symptoms are present or suspected. However, one should not be satisfied with the patient's report of any one upsetting incident. For example, a young man traced the beginning of his phobias to an auto accident; nobody was hurt, and he merely got frightened. But since then he could not walk alone on the street or even be at home by himself; somebody had to be with him all of the time. It was only after insistent probing for about half an hour that the patient mentioned the death of his grandmother which had occurred around the same time. How did her death affect his life? She had raised him and had acted as his mother. He felt completely lost and helpless since she had passed away. The "crisis situation" was not provided by the car accident, but by the new life without special service for which he was not prepared. One "trauma" by itself is never sufficient to produce symptoms; it is always the total life situation which has to be examined, first at the present time, then at the time of the onset of the disease.

After the subjective and the objective situations have been gleaned, the two sets of data have to be integrated. This is done through "The Question." This is the most important part of our dynamic approach. The patient is asked what would be different in his life if he were well. This question is generally received with some surprise: the patient does not know. He begins to think. In many instances he may not be able to give an answer at all. We may have to prod: "Let us imagine I gave you a pill and you would be completely well as soon as you left this office. What would be different in your life, what would you do differently than before?" Eventually, some statement is made. It is of the utmost significance. It indicates whether the symptoms have psychological significance or not; and if so, what their significance is. Naturally, if a patient with a broken leg is asked The Question, he may point out what he would do without the handicap. It generally is easy to judge whether a present lack of function is in accord with the actual physical disability or exceeds it. In the latter case the disfunction has both physical and psychological implications.

The answer to The Question indicates against whom or against what condition the symptom is directed. If he were well the patient might look for another job, do better on his present job, get along better with his wife, or perhaps he would get married; or she, the wife, might be able to divorce her husband or take on a job. All such answers are self-explanatory. They indicate why the patient is sick, if the illness is entirely neurotic, or what use the patient may make of an actual physical ailment. They reveal a psychological superstructure which has to be investigated regardless of any actual organic pathology.

The teleological premise of our technique becomes obvious now. Every neurosis has a purpose. Purposiveness is not a new concept in medicine. Around the turn of the century the neo-vitalists recognized the purposive nature of pathological conditions. The cell is fighting for its existence, engaged in a struggle for life, does not merely react to outside stimulations, but opposes them. Life has direction. Neo-vitalism opposes "the great mechanistic school around the middle of the past century" (Moriz Benedict—3). Fever became recognized not merely as a pathological process caused by certain noxes, but represented a healing process in the affected organism, and eventually became a method of treatment, being artificially induced.

One of the reasons for the difficulties in recognizing the purposive nature of neurotic symptoms is the still prevalent mechanistic-deterministic trend in psychiatry, originating in its organistic tradition and fortified by Freud's psychoanalysis. Freud was not always so adverse to teleological thinking. In his book *The Psychopathology of Everyday Life* (4) written while Adler was still closely associated with him, Freud comes very close to the recognition of the social significance of disfunctions which he called "Fehlleistungen" (slips). In one of his case histories (5) we find the following statement: "And he resolved his conflict which was in fact one between his love and the persisting influence of his father's wishes, by falling ill; or, to put it more correctly, by falling ill he avoided the task of resolving it in real life." Later on, Freud states, "The chief result of his illness was an obstinate incapacity for work which allowed him to postpone the completion of his education for years. But the results of such an illness are never intentional. What appears to be the consequence of the illness is in reality the cause or motive of falling ill." Here we have in Freud's own words a clear formulation of the socio-teleological principle. However, his preoccupation with biological-instinctual mechanisms prevented Freud from maintaining this direction, later taken up by his straying followers who called themselves Neo-Freudians; Freud himself could only discern a "secondary gain" of neurotic disturbances, since the underlying conflicts appeared to him primarily as intra-personal frustrations and not as interpersonal friction as they appear to Adlerians.

It is the existence of a social benefit from symptoms or its absence which provides the most reliable if not the only basis for a differential diagnosis between organic and neurotic illness. This dynamic consideration is essential that its neglect greatly impedes a physician's ability to determine the nature of his patient's illness. Without awareness of the possible social implication of a disease or a symptom, no reliable differential diagnosis can be made. The increasing frequency of psychogenic disturbances, superimposed on an organic pathology, or without any, confronts the physician constantly with the need to make a differential diagnosis between functional and organic symptomatology. This is generally attempted on the basis of positive or negative organic findings. If a symptom or complaint of a patient cannot be explained by physical examination and laboratory tests, if these negative findings occur in the case of a patient who shows signs of nervous tension or other social and emotional maladjustment and instability, then the diagnosis of functional disturbances seems justified—to many medical practitioners. Such a far-reaching diagnosis, which generally implies abandoning further clinical investigation, cannot be made by default, merely by the absence of positive clinical findings. As long as the practitioner has no means to base his diagnosis on positive proof of psychogenic involvement, he will try to rely on the proof of general emotional unbalance concomitant with a lack of clinical evidence. The only way to attain a more reliable proof for or against the psychogenic nature of a symptom is through an analysis of the social implication of the disease complex. As long as physicians are not familiar with such a technique and are not even aware as yet of the significance of the social involvement, we as psychiatrists are time and again put in the unpleasant position of sending a patient back to the practitioner who referred him to us for psychotherapy, because we find no evidence that the patient's emotional condition is responsible for his complaints; further study revealed in each case the existence of organic pathology, not recognized before. Such cases prove convincingly that emotional upset and absence of organic findings are no justification for making a diagnosis of psychogenic, functional, or neurotic disturbances.

In this light, The Question gains utmost significance. A short discussion of a case may demonstrate the point. A patient with gastric disturbances consented finally to consult a psychiatrist, having rejected this suggestion for years, since he considered himself physically sick and felt insulted by the implication that he needed a psychiatrist. His condition cleared up completely when he began to realize its function. He was overambitious, tried to please and to make a good impression, and could not say "no" to anybody; his stomach "spoke up" instead of him. If he could not "stomach" a situation, he got sick. At that period of his life he had become increasingly doubtful about his ability to maintain his moral superiority, and consequently was sick most of the time. He not only understood in a short while what he was doing, but was able to change his basic assumptions, and develop a new perspective of life. He was an out-patient at a medical school clinic, and returned year after year as a token of gratitude to be demonstrated to the students. One time, after several years of well-being, he came and complained of a "relapse." He was sure that his pains which had reoccurred were again psychogenic, since they first appeared on the train which brought him back to the city from a vacation. Consequently, he came directly to the psychiatric clinic. Upon closer scrutiny it became obvious that the pains were not "used" by him in any way; he functioned fully at home and on his job, and did not excuse himself from any participation or contribution. Therefore, the pains could not be psychogenic this time, although the patient felt the painful sensations as similar to those of years ago, except that the location was somewhat lower in the abdomen. He was sent back to medicine and to surgery; a small tumor in the testicles was found, and upon its removal the pains subsided. The patient was in no position to distinguish between the psychogenic and organic pains—they both were identical. Only the exploration of the patient's functioning and the use of the symptoms permitted a differential diagnosis.

In most cases the medical practitioner will be satisfied if he can understand the patient in his present situation; such understanding will enable him to evaluate properly the function of the patient's disease. However, the incidence of psychogenic implications is so frequent that it is utterly impossible to refer every patient with functional disturbances to a psychiatrist. It seems necessary, therefore, that all medical practitioners, not only those in general practice, but also all specialists, have some knowledge of psychotherapeutic procedures for both diagnosis and therapy.

A considerable amount of psychotherapy takes place in every medical effort by doctors who are not psychiatrists and often may not be aware of the actual role they play in the treatment of their patients. Closer analysis would reveal the extent of psychological factors in supposedly medical treatment; without psychological effectiveness no physician could maintain a practice. In most cases, the medical practitioner relies in his psychotherapeutic endeavors on general principles of conduct, good bedside manner, authoritative role of a father figure, and similar empirically developed approaches. This will remain so until all medical practitioners are trained in the rudiments of physchotherapy. Then we will be able to distinguish major psychotherapy limited to trained specialists, from minor psychotherapy as used by the general practitioner and any other non-psychiatric medical specialist.

At this point we are concerned with an approach toward an understanding of the patient, as it can be used by any physician. So far we have described an approach to understand the patient in his present setting, in his field of action. In many cases it becomes advisable, then, to know more about the patient's personality structure which got him into his present predicament. After all, any crisis situation is created by the impact of a given life situation on a certain personality. What upsets one may not upset another. One patient gets sick when he loses his job and feels unable to get another one, another patient gets sick when he is suddenly confronted with the need to take on a job. Without some insight into the personality makeup of a patient it is difficult to comprehend the nature of his predicaments and difficulties.

Adler provided a definite and rather simple technique for a clear understanding of a person's basic personality pattern, which he called his "life style." This very pattern which characterizes each individual and all his movements through life is developed in early childhood. It is impossible to understand any adult without information about his first four to six years of life, which are the formative years. In this period, every person develops concepts about himself and about life which are maintained throughout life, although the person remains completely unaware of the premises he has developed for himself and upon which he acts.

A clear formulation of a person's life style can be obtained through investigation of his family constellation, which is a sociogram of the group at home during his formative years. This investigation reveals his field of early experiences, the circumstances under which he developed his personal perspectives and biases, his concepts and convictions about himself and others, his fundamental attitudes, and his own approaches to life, which are the basis for his character, his personality. After we know the setting, we can determine from his early recollections the conclusion he drew under those circumstances. From all the millions of experiences to which we are exposed in our early childhood, we remember only those which coincide with our outlook on life. All early recollections show, therefore, the same pattern; and where they differ, they supplement but never contradict each other.

It is unfortunate that such a simple and—as experience has shown—most reliable approach to an understanding of the basic personality of a person should be so little known today, exactly forty years since Adler described this procedure (1913) (6). This can be explained by the overshadowing influence of Freud, who considered early recollections as cover-up recollections for the really significant but repressed, and therefore unconscious experiences (7). Only now that Freud's premises are critically re-examined do psychiatrists and psychologists take notice of early recollections.

III.

The examination of the family constellation and of the early recollections is a simple procedure, but nevertheless requires some skill and training. For the benefit of students and trainees, we have developed a questionnaire which assists the examiner in obtaining all pertinent information. Questionnaires are somehow tradition in Adlerian literature; but most of them have dealt with children (8). Wexberg devised one for the treatment of functional neurosis (9). Ours is concerned with information given by adults about their own childhood. It is presented herewith.

GUIDE FOR INITIAL INTERVIEWS ESTABLISHING THE LIFE STYLE

I. Family Constellation

List all siblings in descending order, including the patient in his position. Give patient's age and add after each sibling the years of age difference with patient, with plus and minus sign. Include siblings now dead.

A. Description of Siblings

1. Who is most different from you? In what respect? (Ask patient to elaborate.)
2. Who is most like you? In what respect?
3. What kind of kid were you?
4. Describe the other siblings.

B. Ratings

List highest and lowest sibling for each attribute, and if patient is at neither extreme, give his position as to similarity to either.

1. Intelligence
2. Hardest worker
3. Best grades in school
4. Helping around the house
5. Conforming
6. Rebellious
7. Trying to please
8. Critical of others
9. Considerateness
10. Selfishness
11. Having own way

12. Sensitive—easy to hurt
13. Temper tantrum
14. Sense of humor
15. Idealistic
16. Materialistic
17. High standards (of achievement, behavior, morals, etc.)
18. Who was the most athletic? Strongest? Tallest? Prettiest? Most masculine, feminine?
19. Who was the most spoiled, by whom, how, and for what?
20. Who was punished most, by whom, how, and for what?
21. Who had the most friends? What kind of relationship—leader, exclusive, gregarious?

C. Sibling Interrelationships

1. Who took care of whom?
2. Who played with whom?
3. Who got along best with whom?
4. Which two fought and argued the most?
5. Who was father's favorite?
6. Who was mother's favorite?

D. Description of Parents

1. How old is father? Mother?
2. What kind of person is father?
3. What kind of person is mother?
4. Which of the children is most like father? In what way?
5. Which of the children is most like mother? In what way?
6. What kind of relationship existed between father and mother?
   a. Who was dominant, made decisions, etc.?
   b. Did they agree or disagree on methods of raising children?
   c. Did they quarrel openly? About what? How did these quarrels end?
   d. How did you feel about these quarrels? Whose side did you take?
7. Who was more ambitious for the children? In which way?
8. Did any other person (grandparent, uncle, aunt, roomer, etc.) influence you? Describe them and your relationship to them.

II. Early Recollections

How far back can you remember? (Obtain recollections of specific incidents, with as many details as possible, including the patient's reaction at the time. Make sure that this is a recollection and not a report. Childhood dreams are early recollections.)

III. Conclusions

The summary of the family constellation and of the early recollections permits the derivation of the basic mistaken assumptions on which the life style is based.

This questionnaire requires some discussion in order to clarify the meaning and significance of the questions asked.

Family Constellation

Writing down the names of the siblings in their age difference from the patient provides an immediate impression of the grouping within the family. First of all, it shows the patient in the characteristic position of a first, second, middle, or youngest child, as the only boy amongst girls, or the opposite. The closeness in age separates one group of children from the others, and thereby often establishes clear indication of the subgroups. Such subgroups with their own inner tensions and conflicts are not only provided by the age distance, but by other factors affecting the family; change in domicile (American or foreign-born), and changes in economic status distinguish one group of siblings from the others. Siblings who died very young may have had considerable influence on the patient's life; they may be responsible for parental anxiety about patient's health and survival, or they may represent an unbeatable rival, since nobody can compete successfully with a dead brother or sister. Sometimes a patient may have felt accused or responsible for a sibling's death, so that his whole childhood life was affected.

Description of Siblings

The first question as to who is most different from the patient is of utmost importance. Difference in character, temperament and interest always indicate competition. Competition may coincide with rivalry, but is not identical to it. Open rivalry may be absent in a strong competitive relationship which is revealed by the differences of personality (9). The most different sibling, therefore, can be recognized as the strongest competitor. In most cases it is the next older or next younger brother or sister. (The first and second child are usually most different, indicating strongest lines of competition.)

Most patients have no difficulty in naming the most different sibling accurately except a patient who is over-concerned with being right and afraid of giving the wrong answer, or one whose desire for moral superiority prevents him from saying anything "bad" about a sibling.

In asking the patient to elaborate spontaneously on his dissimilarities with his main competitor, he describes each one's movements in their competitive effort to find a place in the group. Character traits are expressions of movements. Where one sibling succeeds, his competitor will give up every effort; where the other fails, he will move in. As a result, each becomes different from the other.

Conversely, the siblings who are most alike are the allies. The answer to question 2 indicates these alliances. The description of the patient himself as he was a child provides for his descriptions of the other siblings(not as they are today, but as they were as children.)

Ratings

So far we have let the patient provide us spontaneously with information, the significance of which is naturally unknown to him. We have to rely on what he can tell us, since in most cases we have no other access. Now we are proceeding by presenting the patient with a set of qualities, asking him to tell us which one of his brothers and sisters rated the highest or lowest in each of these qualities. In this way we obtain the lines of movement for each child, and can draw the diagram about the lines of competition and alliance, for the purpose of discerning the patient's own movements in his interaction with all the others.

The various qualities have been chosen because of their significance as to success and failure, high and low status of each sibling. Most of these qualities are self-evident in this regard. The last three questions (19, 20 and 21) permit a description of interactions with peers and parents. Twenty-one is particularly significant. Some siblings are punished for mischief, others because their non-conformity is based on their righteousness which does not permit them to yield to the "unfairness" of the authority.

Sibling Interrelationships

Here lines of rivalry or responsibility of function within the family group become visible. Question two generally indicates the "natural" grouping of the siblings. It must be kept in mind that the question of competitiveness does not necessarily come into play in questions three and four, which deal with getting along or fighting. Sometimes the main competitors reach a working agreement by which they get along famously, the successful one protecting his defeated and, therefore, "weak" competitor. Favoritism by parents leads to the exploration of the powers behind the scenes, of father and mother.

Description of Parents

We need to know what kind of person each parent was. We correlate the information about each with questions four and five, pointing to the likeness with certain siblings, who followed parental "guiding lines." This in turn provides us with a verification of the information which we received previously about each sibling. Question six is of eminent significance. The relationship between the parents sets the pattern of all interpersonal relationships within the family, be it between parents and children or between individual siblings.

Other people living with the family have to be included in their role within the family setting. Some of them may play a more important role for patient's development than the parents. Excluding them may give a wrong picture of the interactions which explain the patient's movement on the scene.

Early Recollections

The beginner is likely to get incomplete or inaccurate information about early recollections. We must distinguish, first, between a recollection and a report. Reports may sometimes have significance in reflecting the patient's evaluation of himself as a child and of life as he sees it. But reports are not reliable—recollections are. They represent a description of actual incidents which the patient remembers. It is not important whether the incidents did occur in this way; but it is all important that the patient thinks it did happen. Members of the same family may remember the same incident; but what they remember of it generally differs greatly, in accordance with their basic outlook on life. The details which the patient remembers are of utmost importance. Without them the recollection may be utterly insignificant, or its significance may be completely distorted. For example: a patient remembers a big flood at the age of three; men were working to repair some damage. Without details this meant little. It took prodding to get the details of the recollection: patient, helped by mother, was looking out of a third floor window, watching the big men working below. This is revealing. The little child who needs protection, and, compensating for his being small in a dangerous world of strong men, looks down on the strong who do the "dirty" work. (This was his basic personality pattern.)

Childhood dreams are memories. It does not make much difference whether the recollection contains an actual event or a dream. It would not be remembered unless it fitted into the general outlook on life.

One must keep in mind that the incidents which are remembered are not important because they happened, but only because they are remembered. Every person has experienced falling down and hurting his knees. But only those will remember such incidents who still think they cannot take care of themselves and are in danger of falling down and hurting themselves.

Conclusions

The summary of the life style which can be gleaned from the information about the family constellation and about early recollections constitutes the most difficult part of the whole procedure. It requires skill and experience. The ability to recognize all aspects and implications of the information obtained distinguishes the expert from the beginner. However, it can be stated definitely that everybody using this technique will know more about a person than is possible without having this information or knowing the significance of it. The expert may be able to know more, but this should not discourage the beginner from growing by his own experience and observations. If he has a chance to study with a well-trained Adlerian, he can expect to progress faster. But we have seen people who were able to train themselves, once they became familiar with the method, and progressed through their study of the literature, and by experience.

IV.

Let us finally present a case to demonstrate this technique.

Harry W., thirty-five years old, complains of extreme nervousness ever since his father and uncle died of heart attacks a month apart, half a year ago. He became afraid of suffering a heart attack, becomes upset when he thinks of them, developed a nervous stomach, lost thirty pounds the last half year.

Previously he had suffered with what he called "tension headaches." Since the two deaths, the headaches had disappeared. He is irritable, has a temper which he tries to control, has "bad habits," cracking his knuckles and swinging his foot. He worries about business unless other troubles come up. He dislikes being left alone, and has short depressions without apparent reasons. Always he has been a hypochondriac, always afraid something may happen to him, afraid of dying, constantly running to the doctor.

This is the subjective situation for which he seeks help. His objective situation seems outwardly well under control. He has been married for nine years, has three children, gets along well with his wife. There is no boss, just a give and take. However, he gives in if she gets aggravated. Arguments? Not more than "normal." When? If he does not do what she wants. Sex is "normal." The frequency depends upon how she feels, generally two times a month. He would like to have it more often, but she refuses if she is tired. She responds fully. He considers himself "very happily married," but goes regularly to prostitutes.

He has "loads of friends," is very gregarious. He likes people around and likes to go out.

He is a partner in a family business which his grandfather established. He is his own boss, the head of a separate department. He and his younger brother run the whole business since the father's death. The brother knows more about it and Harry gives in to brother to avoid clashes.

Outwardly the situation seems to be without conflict; at least, this is what the patient thinks. It does not take too much psychological sensitivity to feel the underlying tension, how he gives in to his wife, to his brother, how he feels deprived of sexual gratification and seeks it otherwise, how much of an inner anger and rebellion he has, which he tries to "control," or better, to conceal. This is clearly expressed in his answers to The Question. If he were well, that is, if he were not irritable and nervous, did not suffer with headaches and live in fear of heart attacks, he would take more interest in his children, not be interested in prostitutes, make more effort in his business.

It is obvious that the patient feels unable to solve his actual life problems and hides them behind a smoke screen of various physical and emotional complaints. A physician trying to treat his symptoms with medication would obviously help him as little as another who would tell him that he is physically well and everything is simply imagination. What is wrong with Harry is neither his body nor his "mind." It is his total personality in his specific setting which is his problem. One can neither cope with this by curing his body nor by calming his mind. One must help him to understand the impact of his personality and the situation in which he finds himself. In other words, anyone trying to help him would first have to understand him; then he could help the patient to understand himself, and eventually to change his outlook, his attitudes, his movement toward life and others. At this stage we had no idea about his life style, although he gave the impression of being a pessimist, of expecting not to succeed and, therefore, giving in and rebelling at the same time, of feeling weak and sorry for himself, of fighting against the dangers of life, never sure of anything. The two deaths apparently justified and intensified his distrust of life. We can assume that the death of his father may have put him in the difficult position of coping with his brother on his own, without the "control" of father over both. But why has he no confidence in himself, or in life, for this matter? The answer can be found only in establishing his life style.

The Family Constellation

The sequence of children is as follows:

Louise, +11; Robert, +10; Patient, 35; James, −1½; Blanche, −6. The age distribution indicates immediately the grouping of the children; there are the two oldest, the two middle (patient and James), and the baby. We can readily expect the answer to the first question as to who is different. Naturally, it is James, the brother closest in age to him, who establishes himself by this difference as his most important competitor. Interestingly enough, when patient is asked to elaborate on the difference, he gives at first a very superficial description. He considers himself more flashy, having fewer inhibitions than James, while the latter is satisfied with what he has. We will see later that this is true, but in a different way than the patient realizes. Who is like him; the baby, Blanche. Both are gregarious, like to have money, like to go out and have a good time. One guesses already what they have in common; they want to "get" things. Maybe both are convinced of their lack of strength.

According to our outline we let the patient describe his siblings and himself. He has something good to say about everyone. How does he describe them?

Louise is vivacious, energetic, very capable. She raised the younger children and took on responsibility at an early age. She is down to earth and everyone likes her.

We can expect Robert, the second child, to be just the opposite. He did not apply himself to school. Father was down on him because he did not live up to expectations. Robert is very generous, has a lot of humor. He will "give you his shirt," provided he likes you. We can see here a boy who is defeated and discouraged, but makes the best of it.

Now comes Harry, the patient. By his own description one can see immediately how he fits himself into the family pattern. Is he successful like Louise or a "failure" like Robert? Here is the answer. He, too, is generous and gregarious; he too, "disappointed" father because he did not live up to his expectations. He has never considered himself much of a man. But in contrast to Robert, he does not take his defeat as philosophically as Robert, but rebels—and makes demands. He was sick as a child and nearly died, which probably induced some spoiling and overprotection.

Now comes James, his main competitor. We can already imagine what type of person he is: down to earth, very conscientious, hard worker, does not show his feelings outwardly; in other words, does not indulge himself, but keeps on doing things.

Blanche, the baby, is the only other girl in the family, and, as such, like her older sister Louise. However, she is not as capable nor as intelligent as the older sister. It was stated that she likes to have a good time, to get things, in the same way as does Harry, the patient.

Here we have a pretty good picture of the lines of competition and alliance, of success and failure. As we analyze the various qualities and attributes of each sibling, the lines become more pronounced. In regard to intelligence, James is highest, the patient lowest. The same holds true for grades in school. In temper, Harry is highest and James lowest. James is father's favorite, and Harry mother's. James is most like father, and Harry is most like mother, in actions and thinking. Harry considers himself lowest in many other regards where James is not necessarily the highest. He has the least number of friends, considers himself least handsome, but he and Robert try most to please others. Robert does not stick out anywhere. He is generally in the middle of the ratings, except that he was the one most punished. (Which contradicts the patient's statements of Robert's philosophically accepting his defeat; he did not rebel openly with a temper, but more passively by being stubborn and "ornery.")

The parents are naturally responsible for the efforts of each child to find his place in the family in his own way. They encourage and discourage each child in his efforts and set the pattern for the whole family. In this family father established a very well defined masculine pattern. He was down to earth, always tried to do the right thing, was very ambitious, very well liked. He wanted the boys to go to college, but only James did.

Mother, on the other hand, took the patient's part. She got along best with him and Blanche, the baby. Patient in turn felt warmer and closer to mother who was very generous to him, her favorite, and tended to spoil him. She, too, was hard working; her family came before herself. In a certain sense she was the boss in the family because father was very much in love with her. Actually, her authority existed only through the strength of the father who gave her the outward status of the master of the family. They got along very well under this arrangement.

We see here a very definite alliance of the "masculine" people, consisting of father, James, and—peculiarly—Louise. (By the way, this possibility of girls following the masculine pattern of father and boys the feminine pattern of mother is only found in a democracy where women have gained similar status to men. In this regard the situation in the United States is quite different from that in many countries, where a girl is supposed to play the woman's role—and generally does so.) On the other hand, the feminine pattern was established by the close relationship of mother, Blanche—and the patient. Between the two triangles Robert was completely left out and had to shift for himself. This is the picture of the family constellation.

Early Recollections

Harry remembers an incident from age six. Dad came home with a new car. He and James got dressed; he put on black sox. All were anxious to see the car.

Here we can see what is important to Harry. He is a flashy dresser and feels that clothes make a man. Or a car. Those are the only things that count, things which one can "get."

At the age of five he remembers falling down brick stairs and breaking his nose. This is actually not a recollection but a report. Still it shows what happens to him when he has to rely on his own resources.

This comes out more clearly in another recollection. He was very young, doesn't remember the exact age, when he visited an aunt's house in a poor neighborhood. Someone sent him for cigarettes. It was a very dark street; he was scared. On the way back some man followed him. He ran home and could not run fast enough. That is how he looks at life and at himself in it. A frightened little boy, in a world full of danger.

At the same age a boy told him that he had found a dime in the grass. Harry asked where, and the boy showed him. He got down on his hands and knees, and he, too, found a dime. He told it to the boy, who did not believe him and called him a liar. Here we can see how even "getting" something will not give him status in this world. Nobody believes that he is worth while and can do things. At least, that is what he thinks.

At the age of six Robert, his older brother, was making a ring out of beads. Harry begged for a ring, too, but Robert did not have enough beads. However, he was willing to make Harry one if he would get the beads. Harry went out to ask another boy for beads. He ran across the street and was almost hit by a car. The boy "bawled the hell out of him," and did not give him the beads. We have to keep in mind that this incident as such had no significance for Harry's development. The importance of this incident does not lie in the fact that it happened, but that Harry, now an adult, still remembers it. This is what he thinks of himself in life: trying so hard to get something, endangering himself while doing so—and not getting anything in the end.

Summary

Patient is the third of five, the middle of three boys, and actually the first of two. He is overrun by his younger brother, who overran both older brothers. His older brother is completely left out between the two alliances of father, James and Louise, and Mother, himself and Blanche. This brother, in addition, was pushed down by a wonderful and capable older sister and an ambitious father to whose expectations he could not live up. Patient, too, felt unable to live up to father's expectations which were only met by his younger brother; but he, the patient, overran his older brother through his charm and his ability to get things, encouraged by his being the favorite of his mother. Despite this favorable position he, like his older brother, considered himself as a failure because masculinity as represented by father and younger brother seemed to be of utmost importance. He could not find his place in a masculine world, only with women. Stimulated by mother's protectiveness, he was more interested in getting (approval, money, sympathy) than in doing.

The early recollections show the conclusions he drew from the situation as he perceived it. Life is dangerous, and I get hurt, and there is no recognition for me, particularly in a masculine world. (All recollections are about men, who threatened, rejected or thwarted him.) Only by getting and by chance can I get somewhere, and even that will not be recognized by others, especially by men.

These conclusions permit the formulation of the Basic Mistakes which patient made in his childhood and maintained throughout life. We can point out the mistakes in his assumptions, somewhat as follows:

1. Neither life, nor the world of men is as dangerous as he thinks;
2. He has a place in the masculine world, but does not know it;
3. He does not recognize his own strength; therefore,
4. He does not need to "get" or to rely on chance, he can depend on himself and his own strength;
5. He neither trusts life around him nor within him.

Now we can see that our first impression was accurate. At that time we did not know why he was pessimistic, why he did not trust life, messed things up, and felt sorry for himself, why he could not fully cooperate on any level of life, and why he was so impressed with death. It was his doubt in his own masculinity, in his own strength, in his determination to "get" without doing. After six interviews his ability to "understand" himself led to some reorientation. His symptoms disappeared completely, not only his fears and nervousness, but also his headaches. He became more courageous, stopped being afraid of walking at night, catches himself when something looks dangerous to him, and realizes it is not. He began to see how he always magnified or provoked dangers. He found that he even used better judgment in business. He realized his unwillingness to "give" at home, being more interested in going to a ball game than in playing with the children, and is considering a change in this attitude also. He is by no means "well" or "adjusted" yet, but very much on the way.

Conclusions

The socio-teleological approach as developed by Alfred Adler permits an immediate examination of a patient's movement in life, both on the present scene and throughout his lifetime, beginning in his formative years. All actions and reactions can be understood by the direction of the movements. The total personality has mind and body at its disposal to be used in accordance with the intentions and the resultant movements. Only in the light of these movements can the significance of symptoms be determined.

A technique as we described here, if acquired, would enable every physician to "understand" his patient, and perceive his goals. Such understanding should be part of every examination, but is particularly necessary for the "minor psychotherapy" which every physician should be able to carry out.

BIBLIOGRAPHY

1. Nicholas Pastore. *The Nature-Nurture Controversy.* New York: King's Crown Press, Columbia University, 1949.
2. Lawrence K. Frank. "Teleological Mechanisms." *Annals of the New York Academy of Sciences,* 1948, 59, 4, 187-278.
3. Moriz Benedikt. *Das biomechanische (neo-vitalistische) Denken in der Medizin und in der Biologie.* Jena: Gustav Fischer, 1903.
4. Sigmund Freud. *Psychopathology of Everyday Life,* London, 1914.
5. Sigmund Freud. *Collected Papers.* Volume III, p. 336.
6. Alfred Adler. "New Leading Principles for the Practice of Individual Psychology"; "Individual Psychological Treatment of Neurosis"; both in *The Practice and Theory of Individual Psychology.* Totowa, N.J: Littlefield, Adams & Co., 1969.
7. Sigmund Freud. "Screen Memories." *Collected Papers,* V, 47-69.
8. An Individual Psychological Questionnaire, drawn up by the "International Society of Individual Psychology. *Intern. Zeitschrift f. Individual-psych.,* 1923, Vol. II, No. 2. Republished by Alexandra Adler in *Guiding Human Misfits,* New York: McMillan Co., 1936. An Individual Psychological Questionnaire, in Alfred Adler, *The Education of Children,* Greenberg Publ., 1930. Republished by Erwin Wexberg, *Individual Psychology,* New York: Cosmopolitan Book Co., 1929.
9. Erwin Wexberg. *Individual Psychological Treatment,* Chicago: Alfred Adler Inst., 1970.
10. Rudolf Dreikurs. *The Challenge of Parenthood.* New York: Hawthorn Books, 1948.

PSYCHODYNAMIC DIAGNOSIS IN PSYCHIATRY*

The diagnosis of psychopathological conditions is usually of a descriptive nature, based mainly on symptomatology. Dynamic factors are generally considered in the diagnosis only if they refer to organic etiology, such as senile, toxic, climacteric, or traumatic conditions and pathological changes in the central nervous system, the metabolism, the endocrine system, etc. Although such a diagnosis is important for therapy and prognosis, it is incomplete because it disregards important psychological dynamics. Psychological factors are recognized in the differential diagnosis of psychoneuroses, such as anxiety states, conversion hysterias, etc., but even here the diagnosis is mainly based on symptomatology.

Even more inadequate are the prevalent methods for the diagnosis of the psychological dynamics in each patient. Sometimes adjectives are used to describe the patient, according to his overt behavior, as timid, aggressive, repressed, suspicious, restrained, apprehensive, etc. Sometimes mechanisms are taken for granted because they were observed on other patients before, and the present symptoms are interpreted as being based on insecurity, hostility, discouragement, guilt feelings, Oedipus complexes or castration fears.

There are several methods available for diagnosing dynamic factors more objectively and not merely on the basis of superficial observations or haphazard guessing. The technique which

* *The American Journal of Psychiatry*, 1963, 119, 1045-1048.

I have developed, and which I hereby submit, is based on Alfred Adler's concepts.

Psychodynamic Differential Diagnosis

Neurosis, psychosis, and psychopathy are differentiated not only by their symptoms but by fundamental differences in their respective mechanics.

All psychopathological conditions are expressions of conflicts between the individual and his social obligations, since all human problems are essentially social in nature. Psychopathology is characterized by mental, emotional, and characterological conditions which prevent the individual from functioning at an adequate social level and keep him from participating in harmony with others. The fundamental interpersonal conflicts are reflected in the intrapersonal conflict between the conscience, which recognizes the social obligations, and the personal desires, which may stand in the way of cooperation. The conflict between the individual's private logic (private sense) and his conscience (common sense) may be resolved in three ways:

1. The patient may maintain his common sense consciously, but may look for alibis and excuses should he act contrary to his common sense. Thus, he uses his symptoms as alibis and yet maintains his good conscience. This is the characteristic mechanism of neurosis.

2. The conflict may be resolved by bringing the conscience in line with the demands of the private logic. This is accomplished through delusions and hallucinations which serve the patient as a means of escape from the logic of social living, his private logic acting as a substitute. This is a characteristic mechanism of the psychosis and is usually associated with certain predisposing conditions. These are organic inferiority of the brain, exhaustion, excessive stress, disturbance of the CNS, of the metabolism, toxic or infectious conditions, etc. These can be considered as release mechanisms in crisis situations and are

more and more recognized as favoring conditions, but not as causes, of psychosis.

3. The conflict between common sense and private sense may be avoided through neglect of the conscience as a result of inadequate training (excessive indulgence, suppression or neglect). This is a characteristic mechanism of the psychopathic personality.

The recognition of these dynamics permits a clearer differential diagnosis in certain borderline cases, such as between reactive depression and depressive psychosis, obsessive neurosis and schizophrenia, neurotic usage of alcohol and psychotic or psychopathic conditions. The most important feature of this dynamic differentiation seems to lie in the differential diagnosis between organ neurosis and organic disease. In all cases of neurosis and psychosomatic disorders a proper psychological diagnosis is imperative for treatment, management and counseling. The diagnosis of neurosis can no longer be based on the mere lack of evidence of organic pathology. The deciding factor must be the proper recognition of the purpose for which the symptom is used. If it serves as an alibi, then the case must be classed as a neurosis regardless of the presence and extent of organic pathology.

The technique I use permits a rather quick diagnosis of the psychodynamic factors of each case. We must recognize the dynamics of the present life situation in the light of the deeper dynamics of the whole personality. Our investigation is, consequently, directed towards a systematic examination of both aspects.

The Acute Situation. The examination starts with an inventory of the subjective symptoms and complaints of the patient. They represent his *subjective condition.* The next step is an investigation of the *objective life situation.* This consists of a careful examination of his participation at work, in social contacts, and in his relationship to the opposite sex, uncovering existing conflicts and dissatisfactions. The connection between the subjective condition and the objective situation is established by the question, "What would you do if you were well?" The answer will reveal the dynamics of the existing psychopathology. It will indicate against what person or what situation the symptoms are directed. Caution must be used, however, to determine carefully whether the non-participation is justified objectively (by the conditions) or is justified only subjectively, and really out of proportion to the existing personal and social conditions.

The evaluation of the present situation is then substantiated by an examination of the patient's life situation at the time of the onset of the disturbance. Such examination reveals a "crisis situation" in which the personality clashed with the then existing conditions and the patient retreated, withdrawing or limiting his participation.

The crisis situation cannot be understood in its dynamics without recognition of the patient's whole personality, i.e., his life style. No real difficulty in itself causes retreat if the person is properly prepared for it. As long as an individual is confronted with living conditions which permit participation on the basis of established patterns and approaches, no conflicts will arise and no psychopathology will develop.

The Life Style. It is possible to determine the "life style" of a person objectively by analyzing his *family group,* the early group situation during the formative first years of his life and by interpreting the *early recollections.*

The family group may be recorded diagrammatically; the diagram shows the dynamic interrelationships of all members. The most important factor is the position of the patient in the sequence of children, whether he is the first born, second, middle, youngest, or only child. Although the parents are the most important force, directing the mutual relationships between patient and all other members of the family, of greatest significance is the relationship to brothers and sisters. The interview will determine which one of the siblings was most different in character, interests and temperament. In most cases it is the next older or younger one. These differences indicate competition; in this competition the patient developed his ideas and concepts, and his manner of conduct contrasting to those of his rival. Further inquiries will establish possible favorites of father and mother, the personality of the parents, the nature of their relationship, the method they used in training each child, the alliances of siblings which is always expressed objectively in the similarity of traits and interests. These are the dynamic factors which influence the patient to develop a characteristic attitude towards society and the world.

These personal concepts and attitudes are revealed in the early recollections. The fact that one remembers from all the childhood experiences only certain impressions, makes these recollections highly significant. As all early recollections substantiate and supplement each other, they reveal thereby the general outlook of a person, and indicate his subjective interpretation of life.

The proper evaluation of early recollections requires training and experience in soliciting the material and in considering each detail in its full dynamic implication. The psychiatrist trained in this method is capable of making an objective diagnosis of the patient's life style on the basis of family group and early recollections.

The psychological examination as outlined can be accomplished in one or two interviews. It provides an objective basis for the evaluation of the problems and the personality of the patient. During psychotherapy other pertinent material may appear, clarifying the first diagnostic impression. But this technique provides information about the most essential psychological aspects and may protect the psychiatrist from making unsound assumptions or neglecting relevant material.

I report one short case to demonstrate the technique:

Subjective condition: The outstanding symptoms are pains in the abdomen, constipation, diagnosed as spastic colitis. Patient was examined in several hospitals and by many physicians. State of depression has occurred several times. He is in a state of anxiety, worries a great deal, has experienced several incidents of a "nervous breakdown" where he could not sleep, could not eat, felt weak and had to stay in bed. All objective findings were negative, but once an appendectomy was performed without any improvement in his condition. He has felt sick for the last 20 years.

Objective situation: At work he cannot work effectively, is constantly on the defensive against being called upon or criticized, cannot accept more responsible positions offered to him, has to lay off several times when he gets pains or feels sick.

Socially: Has a few friends but hardly sees people; is distant to people, suspicious when he meets new people, wants to be sure first.

Sexual and marital relationship: His wife has been sick almost since they were married. Very tense situation. He feels the victim. She is a perfectionist, demanding and criticizing him. Complains constantly.

Question: What would be different? He would have proven at his company that he is the best professional worker. His nervous condition has shattered all his hopes. Before he got so nervous, seven years ago, he blamed his wife for his failure. The attention and care which she needed prevented bigger and better jobs. Afterwards his pain kept him from accepting more responsibility. He would be more tolerant to his wife if he were well.

Crisis situation: Twenty years ago he had a mean boss who cursed him and laid him off despite hard effort. It was the first time in his life that he had failed. He went home hiding his face. At that time the first symptoms started. An acute recurrence of severe pains in the abdomen, seven years ago, when he was scolded at work. Five years ago a severe nervous breakdown, was unable to work for several months when his mother died without his having visited her. He blamed his wife who by her sickness prevented him from going.

Family group: He is the third of nine children. Most different from him is the oldest brother, three years older. The brother was a bad student, flunked in school, slow thinker, dislikes work, does not take on responsibility, but takes life easy and is happy. Patient was a favorite of the mother who expected him to be the only one to extricate himself from poverty. He helped around the house and in the field where he was the leader of the two older children. One sister, two years older, was more like him but soon accepted his leadership, too. The father was away in the war when the patient was ten years old, and he took on his place and responsibility. After the father returned, he accepted the patient as an equal. Patient picked on the oldest brother and made fun of the next younger one. All in the family accepted his superiority.

Earliest recollection: At 11, he was not allowed to go to high school, but went for himself to register. All the other children were well dressed and with their parents. He was ashamed. When it came to making the application, he started to cry, but the principal spent some time trying to console him.

At nine, the teacher put him in charge of the class while she left the room. He helped correct papers. Once she hit him on the hand: he felt innocent, cried for hours. The teacher felt sorry for him, apologized, and tried to console him. Actually, he had been at fault by not following instructions.

At five, patient had bitten the older brother, who was much stronger than he. He ran away, cried, and complained to his parents, who scolded the brother.

Evaluation: Patient wants to be first but knows he cannot be. Tries to conceal his antagonism by feeling innocent and by suffering. Instead of admitting his rebellion he blames others and circumstances for his "defeat."

Outcome: During psychotherapy he first changed his concept that he must be first or otherwise he would be lost. Then he realized his rebellion and antagonism and changed his attitude. He discovered the function of his pain as a means to escape humiliating situations. His stomach "spoke up" for him and permitted him to withdraw and to refuse participation. His relationships at work and at home changed. He became easy going, learned "to take it" without resentment and without retreat. His pain subsided completely; he became happy, accepted a higher position which he had refused previously because he was afraid of failing there. The condition of his wife improved, too, since he no longer used it for excusing his own inadequacy, instead of pushing her down, and gaining his superiority on the grounds of her complete deficiency. Patient has been seen periodically for a check-up during the last three years, without relapse.

A RELIABLE DIFFERENTIAL DIAGNOSIS OF PSYCHOLOGICAL OR SOMATIC DISTURBANCES*

The importance of a proper diagnosis of symptoms is self-evident. It alone permits an understanding of the underlying pathological processes, indispensable for determining the course of treatment. The need for a sound basis for a differential diagnosis between various organic disorders is well recognized and usually met. This is not so in the case of a differential diagnosis between organic and psychogenic disorders. The usual diagnosis of so-called "psychosomatic" disturbances is based on the absence of organic findings. If the lack of organic pathology is accompanied by obvious neurotic symptoms, such as marked anxiety, tension, tremors, or other indications of emotional unbalance, then the diagnosis of psychogenic disorder seems fully justified. It is the purpose of this paper to suggest that it is misleading to make such a diagnosis by default, merely on the basis of no evidence of organic pathology. We can well understand the tendency to rely on negative findings. Hardly any psychological or diagnostic method is available so far that would provide a positive proof of the psychogenic nature of a symptom.

However, it is possible to determine the psychogenic disturbance on positive grounds. Even more important, the method proposed here does not require time-consuming or involved examinations or tests. Every physician can acquire the skill to distinguish with reasonable certainty whether the symptom of which the patient complains is really of organic nature or of functional nature, so often called "psychosomatic." A few

---

* *International Record of Medicine.* 1958, 171, 238-242.

theoretical premises are necessary to explain the method and the results obtainable through it. The theory is based on the psychological system of Alfred Adler. He provided a frame of reference by which neurotic behavior can be clearly understood, and in a way differently from contemporary practices. Without accepting Adler's theory of neurosis, the method of a differential diagnosis as proposed here remains both unintelligible and impractical. On the other hand, the considerable reliability of this tool substantiates its theoretical assumptions.

The concept of neurosis depends on and varies with theoretical assumptions about the nature of man. The organicist, who believes that all human functions are determined by hereditary endowment, may consider a neurosis as a weakness of the nervous system, an organic neuropathic predisposition. Conversely those who consider environmental forces as causes for personality development may assume that stress and strain produce neurotic disturbances. Quite different is the function of neurosis when we accept the socio-teleological concept of man.

The suggestion that man should be regarded primarily as a social being and not merely as the product of drives, of physiological reflexes or inherited constitutional predisposition, is not difficult to accept. One can perceive all human qualities as expressions of social interaction with others, as movements toward others. The deepest human desire is to belong. Without belonging to others, without a place in the group, man can neither function nor fulfill himself. Most of his problems are caused by his uncertainty about his place and status, his doubt of his adequacy. Concern with prestige and status are often paramount compared to all other interests.

Adler's other basic assumption, the teleological concept of man, postulates that all human actions are purposive. That man can determine his own goals and then direct all his actions accordingly is quite in conflict with prevalent mechanistic concepts. When Adler first proposed the teleological interpretation of human actions, he was about 40 years ahead of his times. Despite the facts that finalistic teleological analysis of life processes had already been explored philosophically, and that the neovitalists had proposed such a point of view in medicine, scientific thinking was strictly causal and mechanistic, recognizing only the causal principle and refuting any other possible correlation of events. It is only recently that the basic sciences like physics have demonstrated the limitation of a rigid causal principle and replaced it with the law of statistical probability. Teleological principles, which imply freedom of will and self-determination, are no longer regarded with contempt, but found to exist within the universe. They are basic to the new orientation in epistemology. This new orientation has not reached the level of the educated layman or of the average physician, who is still deeply entrenched in traditional deterministic-mechanistic thinking. For this reason, our concept of neurosis may challenge cherished convictions. A new concept of man as a self-directed, creative being is necessary for an understanding of one of the most troublesome expressions of his creativity, namely, neurosis.

Neurosis can be understood as a self-inflicted ailment, created in self-defense against specific social demands. It always has a purpose, and its purpose is social. In contrast to Freud's assumption of a "secondary gain," we find every neurotic symptom of primary and entire social significance. This is obvious when the total movement of the neurotic patient is observed. Freud assumed an intrapersonal dynamic process as the basis for neurotic phenomena, which then served as defenses against repressed instincts, guilt feelings, and other unconscious impulses. Neurosis is the result of a conflict between instinctual demands and defenses of the ego. In contrast to these primary functions of the neurosis, its social benefits appeared then as "secondary." We can agree that the neurotic symptom is a defense mechanism, but the defense is of social nature, against the demands of a situation that the individual feels unable to meet.

Neurotic symptoms develop in what may be called a "crisis situation." One person may become ill when he loses his job and cannot find another; the other person, when he no longer can loaf and feels pressed to look for a job. In other words, what constitutes a crisis situation differs for each individual.

It occurs when the life style, the basic pattern of movement of the individual, clashes with the needs of a given situation. The convictions about oneself and life, which are the basis for the personality structure, permit adequate functioning only under circumstances favorable to the individual pattern of movement. We do not develop a neurosis as long as we feel we can function adequately.

Nervous symptoms begin to appear only when the patient experiences difficulties. This is a moment of discouragement. Then the individual withdraws from some life task, either from work or from social relationships or from love and marriage, because he feels inadequate. Such feelings of personal inadequacy is always present in a crisis situation. It creates the inner tension, the apprehension, which is a prerequisite for any neurotic disorder. The difficulties of the situation are always based on a subjective interpretation, dependent on the patient's goal in life, on his life style.

In this sense, neurosis is a safeguard, an excuse for not functioning. It creates a side show that commands the patient's attention and effort. Instead of solving his social problems, which he feels unable to do, he concentrates on his symptoms, and tries to suppress them.

It may be difficult to accept that one can develop symptoms in accordance with one's need. Obviously, symptoms cannot be produced deliberately. But the effort to fight and suppress symptoms actually produces and maintains them. It is a desire to overcome a disturbance in the function that leads to its continuation. Symptoms can develop only against the conscious intentions of the patient. The efforts to overcome the symptom serve the purpose of demonstrating good intentions. But struggling with himself, the patient increases his tension, which in turn helps him to continue and aggravate a symptom, which he needs to avoid a situation, a task or duty, or the obligations of a relationship.

These theoretical considerations are necessary to justify the technique that is suggested for establishing the neurotic nature of a physical symptom. It consists of the "question." The patient is asked what would be different in his life if he were well. The answer indicates against whom or against what condition or situation the symptom is directed. Sometimes the patient will answer immediately. If he were well, he might look for another job, do better on his present one, would get along better with his wife, or perhaps he would get married. All such answers are self-explanatory. They indicate why the patient is sick, if the illness is entirely neurotic, or that he uses a physical ailment for such purpose. Such neurotic superstructure may be revealed in the case of an actual organic pathology.

Sometimes it is not easy to get an answer to this question. The patient does not know. Then he may have to be prodded. We may ask him to imagine what would happen if we could give him a pill that would remove all his symptoms and make him completely well as soon as he left the office. What would then change in his life, what would he do differently than before? Eventually, some statement is forthcoming. It is of utmost significance. It indicates whether the symptoms have psychological significance or not, and if they have, what their meaning is. Naturally, a patient with a broken leg would act differently if he were well. By and large, it is not difficult to evaluate in the case of a physical ailment whether a disturbed function is in accordance with it or exceeds it. In the latter case, the psychological implications are obvious.

A few cases may indicate the significance of the question.

Case 1: A 42-year-old man suffered from gastric disturbances. The only clinical finding was hyperacidity, and he was referred for psychiatric attention. It was a year before he consented, in the meantime going to physicians. He was convinced that he was physically ill and considered referral to psychiatry as an insult. However, once he came, he was cooperative. His condition cleared up completely as he began to understand its function and to change his attitude toward life. He was overambitious, tried to please everyone and always to make a good impression. He could not say "no" and his stomach "spoke up" for him. If he could not "stomach" a situation, he became ill —but only after the "crisis situation" had developed. Previously, he had been able to get along adequately on his concepts. He did not have to fight, to argue, to assert himself aggressively, because he was a good worker and always able to maintain his superiority over others. Then he came to a point where he realized that any further advance in his position and status was impossible. He did not have the necessary education to get a higher position. At that time his willingness to participate in the give and take of life became impaired. An incidental upset stomach was maintained as a defense mechanism against any threatening situation; he could feel superior only by emphasizing wrongdoings of others. By becoming ill, he escaped tasks that he did not like. He limited his activities and was ill most of the time.

His answer to the question was clear enough. If he were well, he would not get upset so easily, he could get along with his fellow workers, he would meet friends and not stay home all the time. It was obvious that he wished to withdraw from all situations that did not permit him to feel superior, as he had before. He restricted himself to the safety of his own home, where his status was still maintained and even perhaps enhanced through his sickness, which required special attention and evoked sympathy.

In three months of therapy he not only learned to understand what he was doing, but was able to change his basic assumptions, and he developed a new perspective of life. The symptoms disappeared completely.

After several years of well-being he returned to us. The pains had recurred. And he was sure that they were again psychogenic, not only because he felt the same sensation, although a little lower in the abdomen, but because they had first appeared on the train as he returned home from a vacation. Being somewhat familiar with the mechanism of a neurosis, he suspected that he did not want to return home and to go back to work. However, closer scrutiny revealed that he was not "using" the pains in any way. He functioned fully at home and on his job. He did not avoid any participation, nor did he draw attention to his symptoms. Therefore, it was doubtful that the pains were psychogenic since they had no function. He was sent back for a thorough physical examination. A small tumor in the testicles was found, and upon its removal, the pain subsided.

This case is interesting for several reasons. First it shows how the same symptomatology can be organic or functional and how the answer to the question permits a clear distinction. But it is also interesting to note that the patient was in no position to distinguish between the psychogenic and organic pains. Both were experienced in the same way.

Case 2: A 25-year-old woman suffered for several years from severe "neurotic" symptoms. She was afraid of spells, which consisted of palpitations and shortness of breath and lasted for about 20 seconds. She said she sometimes wanted to faint but could not. She was afraid of brain tumor and was sure she had a serious nervous disease. Physical examination was negative, as was the electroencephalogram.

Her social adjustment was very poor. She was in and out of college, tried to get a job and quit, changed jobs and boy friends, was engaged several times. She was her father's favorite, and he supported her in all her whims. She admitted that she did things only if she liked to do them and had her own way.

This is obviously the picture of a severely neurotic woman. Without the benefit of the question, her case would be clearly diagnosed as such. And, no doubt, she was neurotic and could benefit a great deal from psychotherapy. But this was not the reason for her referral to psychiatry. She was referred because of her acute fear of spells, which were considered neurotic. The completely negative clinical findings and the general condition of the patient would support such assumptions. However, the answers to the question were negative. Nothing would change in her life if these spells were eliminated. She still would do what she liked, work when she felt like it, and give up as she pleased. There was no function to be detected for the symptoms, no use she made of them. Therefore, our diagnosis was organic condition. She was sent back to the general practitioner, who hospitalized her and returned her for psychotherapy since nothing could be found clinically. We insisted on further probing and suggested thorough neurological study. This finally led to the diagnosis of multiple neuroma, von Recklinghausen's disease.

Case 3: A 43-year-old man suffered for three years from hepatitis. Finally, an ameba was found, and he was treated accordingly. He made a slow recovery, and he had recurrent episodes of nausea and diarrhea, chronic physical weakness, tiredness, agitation, and was generally tense and apprehensive. He was told that this condition was the consequence of his disease. But somehow he was suspicious of his attitude, because he was not "like himself." Previously, he had always known what he wanted in life—now he did not. Previously his wife had depended on him; now he depended on her. He could not stay alone in the evening, and the children annoyed him.

When the question was put to him, he immediately responded with all the tasks that he avoided "because of his condition." If relieved, he would see more friends, would be more ambitious, more interested in his work, and would do a good job.

The diagnosis of a neurotic superstructure on an existing organic condition was made and verified in the course of psychotherapy. His physical ailment occurred in a crisis situation. He was a man with a determination to elevate himself professionally and suddenly found himself at the top of his particular career. There was no way to go any further, and he used his condition to detach himself from his work and from his social contacts, since, for him, absence of further elevation was tantamount to failure.

These case histories indicate the merit of this method of investigation. Naturally, like any diagnostic tool, it is not infallible. It requires a certain skill and sensitivity, as well as a proper evaluation of the presented information. On the other hand the results of this form of investigation have proved to be sufficiently reliable. The diagnostic impressions gained in this way often enabled us to rule out psychogenic involvement and to return the patient to the referring physician, who was convinced of the psychogenic and functional nature of the disturbance. Time and again, we had to insist on further study, because no function of the symptoms could be found. In many cases, unexpected and sometimes even hardly known disease processes were discovered, such as kidney stones, brain tumor, porphyria, and a variety of organic pathologies which had been completely overlooked and probably would never have been considered were it not for the negative results of this form of psychiatric investigation. Its only danger is that sometimes we may actually find a neurotic process, as revealed by the question, and then may overlook a concomitant organic ailment. So far, this theoretical eventuality has not occurred.

BIBLIOGRAPHY

1. Adler, A. *Understanding Human Nature,* Greenwich, Conn: Fawcett Publications, 1954.
2. Bergson, H. L. *Creative Evolution,* New York: Henry Holt and Co., 1911.
3. Benedikt, M. *Das biomechanische (neo-vitalistische) Denken in der Medezin und in der Biologie,* Jena: Gustav Fischer, 1903.
4. Frank, L. K. *Teleological mechanisms,* Ann., New York Acad. Sc; 1948, 59, 4, 187-278.
5. Fenichel, O. *The Psychoanalytic Theory of Neurosis,* New York: Morton and Co., 1945.
6. Dreikurs, R. The psychological interview in medicine, *American Journal of Individual Psychology,* 1954, 10.

PSYCHOLOGICAL DIFFERENTIATION OF PSYCHOPATHOLOGICAL DISORDERS*

The differentiation of mental or psychopathological disorders has been made in the past mostly on the basis of symptoms. Psychiatry was first—and for a long time exclusively—concerned with the description of the various types of disorders and their symptoms. Attempts to define groups led to the establishment of three main types of disorders which are still recognized today in their fundamental differences. They are the neuroses, the psychoses and the psychopathic personalities or states. A dynamic and psychological understanding was first achieved in regard to neuroses. Despite the extensive research to gain insight into the mechanism of psychoses, no generally accepted understanding of their dynamics has yet been reached. The psychopathic personalities are still causing complete confusion, although psychiatrists try to classify and interpret them psychologically.

Individual Psychology has made its contribution towards an understanding of the various disorders. Alfred Adler pointed to the defects in Social Interest, to the faulty life style and the discouragement which can be found in any case of mental or emotional disorder. However, this common background of psychopathological disturbances leads frequently to a summarizing reference in regard to all of them. Neurotics and psychotics are often mentioned in the same breath with criminals, drunkards, and perverts, indicating their common deficiencies.

---

* *Individual Psychology Bulletin*, 1945, 4, 35-48.

A differentiation between them has so far rarely been attempted, because we are fundamentally more interested in the individual patient and his unique personality than in any more or less artificial grouping and classification. However, the step toward a sensible demarcation and an understanding of the fundamental difference seems to be necessary. The theory and technique of Individual Psychology provide us with a key to a dynamic understanding, which is sought today by psychiatry in general. If we can shed light on the fundamental structure of all psychiatric disorders, if we can come to understand psychoses and psychopathic personalities as well as we understand neuroses, much confusion can be avoided in our own thinking and in the field of psychiatry as a whole.

General Differentiation

Due to the lack of other criteria, the differentiation of the various disorders has often been based on the assumed diversity of degree. However, the distinction between neurosis and psychosis is not a quantitative one. It is not permissible to say that a neurosis is so severe that it is *"almost"* a psychosis. Psychotic cases may be so slight that they are very little disturbed in symptoms and functions, so that they can continue to work and keep in social circulation, while a neurosis may be so severe as to keep a patient bed-ridden and produce complete invalidism. The difference between psychosis and neurosis is structural. The conflicts in each case are solved, or at least answered, in a different way.

All conflicts of any human being are social conflicts, resulting from a disturbance or straining in the social relationship of the individual, impairing his integration into the community and obstructing his participation in the social functions. It seems that the nature of the social conflict and the attitude of the individual to his own social maladjustment distinguish the various types of psychiatric disorders. In any case we find the Social Interest restricted. However, this restriction is not uniform. Again, it is not a question of degree. A person suffering from a neurosis might have more, or less, Social Interest than a psychotic, and even than a criminal. The degree of discouragement, of inferiority feeling, and of social antagonism may well be expressed in the severity of the case, but not in the type of disturbance. The structure of the inner conflict is different in each type.

As our social adjustment remains incomplete, we all have conflicts in regard to our social participation. This conflict is regarded by some as an expression of man's fundamental inability to become a truly social being. There seems to be no reason to assume any intrinsic obstacle in human nature which would prevent man from adjusting himself to the social atmosphere in which he lives and which makes him what he is, namely human. We know, too, the factors which prevent in each case the harmonious development of social personality. We know the obstacles to the development of sufficient Social Interest, namely inferiority feelings and discouragement.

We can watch the social growth of individuals when we lead them out of their inferiority complex and help them to change their faulty life styles, which had been based on their wrong interpretation of the logic of living together. The old saying "The spirit is willing, but the flesh is weak," characterizes the general social maladjustment during an epoch of human history when man has not yet learned to live with his fellowman peacefully. This obvious conflict between the "spirit" and the "flesh" *is the crucial* point for our investigation.

Many attempts have been made to understand this inner conflict found in most contemporaries and caused by their inadequate social adjustment. Freud described the Super-ego as the instance of social values and ideals which come in conflict with the urges and drives of the Ego, forcing those tendencies, which are not socially acceptable into the unconscious, the Id. In more popular terms the conflict is recognized as existing between the conscience and the "weaknesses" *or* "faults" of an individual.

Adler clarified the issue considerably by formulating the terms Common Sense and Private Sense. Under Common Sense we understand our thinking in common, our participation in general ideas, in values and morals accepted by the whole group to which we belong. The normal individual knows what he should do, what is right and what is wrong, how one should behave and act. But very few act always according to their own understanding, to their Common Sense. While we do not deny, principally, the desirability of a certain behavior, we do not follow this pattern if our understanding of ourselves leads us to move in another direction. What we think of ourselves is not always conducive to following our Common Sense. One should work; but if one considers himself incapable of doing a good job he might refrain from working. The Private Sense, as Adler called it, conflicts with the general rules of common understanding.

It might be well expressed in the sentence, "I know how one should act; but that is only true for the others; I myself gain more if I act differently." The interest of the others, of the community, conflicts in these instances with what the individual considers his own interest. His private goals, his life style, his interpretation of his own needs, interfere with his willingness to bring himself in line with the social demands, with evolution. Instead of following his social interest, he is concerned with his own security, with his prestige.

These universal conflicts find different answers in the various psychiatric disorders. The neurotic person meets the conflict by hiding his Private Sense from his own consciousness, by not admitting his own tendencies when they conflict with his conscience, his Common Sense. He looks for alibis to excuse his social shortcomings. If this description is correct, and we have every reason to believe it is, then it leads to the conclusion that we are all neurotic, fundamentally and structurally. It is then only a question of degree whether our alibis and our lack of social participation are more, or less, conspicuous and impressive. The line between normal and pathologic is very indistinct. It might be drawn by the existence or non-existence of a subjective feeling of being sick. If sickness or symptoms of diseases are used as alibis, the diagnosis of a neurosis is justified.

The person who becomes psychotic suffers from similar conflicts. However, in his case, the answer to the conflict is different. Under certain conditions, either on the basis of an organ inferiority of the central nervous system, or of infection or exhaustion, of toxic agents or organic brain lesions, an individual may be able to resolve his inner conflict by changing, temporarily or indefinitely, his recognition of the Common Sense. Through delusions or hallucinations, he can impress himself with an assumed reality, which then conforms with his Private Sense. He lives in a world of his own, in which his personal goals find complete justification. He no longer adheres to the logic of life; he has his own logic shared by none.

The psychopathic personality, as I understand it, is a person who also deviates in his actions from the logic of living together, from the social obligations to which he is exposed. However, unlike the neurotic, he has no inner conflict. He has failed to develop sufficient Common Sense. He denies the logic of others, never accepts their values and morals, and considers his own interests as the only motivation which counts. Therefore, he needs no alibis and flaunts his own interests and tendencies.

There is some fluctuating and overlapping between these three groups of personality disorders, which will be discussed later in greater detail. However, for practical purposes, these distinctions which I have formulated hold true. They explain the different behavior of these types of disturbances. We find insight into the condition only among the neurotics, as the psychotic and the psychopath have no realization of the conflict. One avoids this realization by adjusting his Common Sense and the other by not having such a sense. Of course, the conflicts exist in either case, but they are not recognized as such. The psychotic suffers from what he believes is reality, and the psychopath suffers from society itself. Neither of them considers himself sick, at least not in regard to his conflicts. Therefore, neither asks for help or is willing to accept treatment.

Only the neurotic recognizes his disturbance, as he uses and benefits by it. There are exceptions to this rule in any group, as some psychopathic personalities, might, in certain phases of their lives, act as neurotics; and even psychotic patients; either before the fully developed psychosis or in the period of recovery, might act more as a neurotic. This distinction has also far-reaching implications for treatment and therapy.

A more detailed examination of the three groups of personality disorders and of some psychological mechanics is necessary to understanding certain types and syndromes.

Neurosis

The diagnosis of a neurosis must be made on the basis of its psychological structure. Before adequate knowledge of the dynamics was available, the diagnosis of neurosis was merely made by default. If a person complained of symptoms for which no organic reason could be found, and which could not be explained on the basis of clinical and laboratory findings, then the patient was classified as neurotic and his symptoms as "functional" disturbances. Today we recognize the possible neurotic nature of any disturbances, independent of the existence of any organic pathology. Even organic pathology can be used for neurotic purposes, as an alibi for non-participation in life and as excuse for failure. In order to establish a definite diagnosis, one must recognize for which psychological purpose the neurosis is used.

The nervous symptoms begin invariably at a moment of personal difficulties in life. This is a moment of discouragement, when the individual decides that the social problem which he has to face is too difficult. It is the moment when he withdraws from some life task, either from work or from social relations with friends or relatives, or from love and marriage. A feeling of personal inadequacy always creates the inner tension, the apprehension with which the neurotic disorders began. There is no objective measurement for the decision whether any particular situation, or any particular social obligation, is actually too much and too difficult. All depends on the subjective interpretation of the patient, on his goal in life, on his life style.

A person with a very highly developed ambition, one who believes that he must be the first or he will be lost, the perfectionist, will get discouraged where someone else sees no danger to his social status. The person with Social Interest, who is less interested in his own prestige than in the welfare of others, who enjoy being useful and know how to be, the individual with courage, who knows that he can stand anything and that he will be able to make the best of any situation, will stand greater hardships without withdrawing, without becoming afraid, nervous, and sick.

As any nervous symptom is directed against some particular situation, against some social task, against some duty or some person, one question is helpful to determine the meaning of any particular neurotic disturbance. If a patient is asked what he would do or how his life would change if he were well, he invariably will reveal the direction of his neurosis. "I would get married," or, "I would get a job," or, "I would be able to do a better job," or, "I would go out and meet friends," or, "I would get along better with my wife," are some of the characteristic answers. They indicate that the patient is sick because he wants to avoid marriage or work, or because he needs an excuse for his failure at work, at social contacts, or in his family life.

The patient is not aware that he uses his ailment as an excuse. If he would admit to himself that his symptoms are not, as he believes, the cause of his failure, but only a device for avoiding his responsibility—if the patient could see these relationships, the symptoms would become futile. The neurosis is, therefore, a human creation built after the image of a disease. However, as the patient believes himself to be sick, and actually experiences the symptoms which he creates, he really is sick, for all practical purposes.

The distinction between various types of neuroses has been generally based on symptoms. However, all these differentiations connected with a host of names are very incidental and rarely significant. The neurotic symptoms are as varied as the human functions. There is no limitation in the symptomatology of neuroses, as any human function can be disturbed by an individual, who then regards himself as the victim of the disturbance which he himself has created.

It seems difficult to comprehend how one can develop symptoms in accordance with one's needs. No doubt, nobody can produce symptoms deliberately. And yet there can be no doubt, either, that the neurotic patient himself has created his symptoms. How can this be done? We know today the mechanism of establishing nervous symptoms. Two factors seem to be required. One is the psychic tension, provided by the apprehension in regard to some life task. It is fundamentally the fear of obligations, the fear of failure and of inadequacy. With this psychological strain the whole body is placed under tension. No symptom can be developed without this tension. It affects the vegetative system and through it influences all bodily functions.

The second requirement seems to be paradoxical, but there can be little doubt of the correctness of the observation. It is a desire to overcome some disturbance which creates the symptoms. In other words, the symptoms can only develop against the conscious intentions of the patient. As long as the patient does not mind being sleepless during the night, either because he wants to think something through or because he wants to read or to do anything else, he does not suffer from insomnia. This disturbance starts when the patient decides he must sleep. He does not realize that, while trying so hard, he actually disturbs his slumber. He would fall asleep without any effort, if he were not, for some reason, interested in being sleepless. There are many purposes for which insomnia can be used; as an adequate excuse for a possible failure at an examination; as a logical reason for an otherwise unexplainable lack of efficiency; as a demonstration for being overburdened with responsibilities. The patient fails to realize for what reasons he uses sleeplessness. However, he could not develop this symptom—in this case insomnia—if he did not try so hard to fall asleep. The efforts to overcome the symptom serve the purpose of demonstrating the good intentions of the patient, while he, struggling with himself, merely increases his tension, which in turn helps to continue and aggravate the symptom.

It can be demonstrated beyond doubt that the patient has it in his power to produce or stop any symptom. If one succeeds in persuading a patient to produce the symptoms deliberately, they will disappear. This technique, called "*anti*-suggestion" (Wexberg) is not a method of treatment because it does not even touch the deeper reasons for the development of a neurosis. But the prompt effect of the antisuggestion proves that no symptom can be maintained when the patient stops trying to overcome it.

It is, therefore, obvious that it makes little difference what kind of symptoms a patient develops. The neurosis remains the same fundamental structure, though some symptoms disappear and others are substituted. For the sake of classification we can, however, divide all symptoms into three groups: Disturbances of feeling, of thinking, and of bodily functions.

In the first category fall all emotional disturbances per se. There is, first of all, fear, which is most pronounced in phobias and anxiety states, but which exists more or less in any neurosis, as fear is the basis of the neurotic attitude toward life. To this group belong the various types of phobias like agoraphobia, claustrophobia, erythrophobia, fear of height, of disease of any kind, of death. Other disturbances of feeling are depression, temper, worries, irritability.

In the category of disturbances of thinking belong first the obsessive compulsive neurosis, but also all obsessive ideas, overexactness, querulousness, jealousy, lack of memory, inability to concentrate.

The third group, disturbed bodily functions, includes the wide field of organ-neurotic symptoms; they are the object of special study, for which Psychosomatic Medicine was inaugurated. The first type of neurosis which was recognized and described as a special disease consisted of organ-neurotic symptoms. It was called "Hysteria," because it was assumed that in old maids the womb (Greek: hysteria) was floating in the body due to lack of sexual gratification. The symptoms of hysteria are rather primitive reactions of simple muscular and sensory functions, convulsions and pareses, anesthesias and other disturbances of feeling, deafness and blindness, connected with various pains and emotional excitement. Later in the development of medicine, when nervous reactions were recognized also to affect men, a new syndrome of organ-neurotic symptoms was described and called "neurasthenis."

This complex of symptoms is connected with symptoms of weakness and general "nervousness," and often regarded as an expression of an assumed weakness of the nervous system. It has been attributed to mental or physical exhaustion, due to inherited deficiency, over-exertion, sexual over-indulgence, excessive mental stress, abuse of stimulants and drugs, and other similar excesses. However, fatigue and irritability are typical neurotic mechanisms of a defensive attitude toward some life problem. The emphasis on the physical sensation is the typical evasion of the actual conflict, which is of a social nature.

Other syndromes of similar nature were described and were given names, like "psychasthenia." In this group belong all the small symptoms of our daily life, irritability, weariness, sleeplessness, lack of memory, difficulty in concentration, various pains and aches, impotence and frigidity. These symptoms are often superimposed upon some minor organic ailment, as in arthritic conditions, polyneuritis, sinus infections, and similar chronic disorders of organic nature. The neurotic disturbances might affect certain organ groups and create gastrointestinal, cardio-vascular, glandular, and vegetative disturbances, all through the channels of the vegetative system. They are originally without pathological foundation, but through constant abuse of certain organs pathological conditions may develop, like gastric ulcers, hyper-thyroidism, and many other organic disfunctions. Most neuroses begin with rather simple symptoms and may then develop into quite complicated and organized psychopathological disturbances. They are dynamically and structurally alike, and their differences are more incidental than the emphasis on various terms may indicate.

There are no definite rules why certain symptoms are produced and not others. In some cases the symptoms develop in an organ group which offers less resistance to the strain of life. Inherited organ inferiorities make some organs more irritable and more responsive to nervous tension. Organs which were used early in childhood in an attempt to gain attention, sympathy, or special favors from parents remain always a locus minoris resistentiae. Such early training may produce certain character traits conducive to certain symptoms. Timid children may always incline toward phobias; overprotected children trained to watch the smallest physical ailment may develop hypochondriacal tendencies and somatic preoccupations; children exposed to pressure and trained to use symptoms as counter-pressure may develop an obsessive compulsive character.

Symptoms are often continuations of an incidental disturbance; upset stomach may lead to a "nervous" stomach; an incidental acceleration of the pulse rate may be maintained and repeated, an actual frightening event be used to establish lasting violent fears. Such "causes" are merely occasions which are used by a person who is under stress. Some symptoms develop as imitations of neurotic or organic ailments observed in others. Parents by their example often invite children to develop similar symptoms which have proved their efficiency. As a rule, every symptom presents the best and most effective answer a person has found in regard to his psychological needs. But we must keep in mind that these symptoms are chosen without any realization on the part of the patient. He remains completely unaware of his actions. Otherwise, he could not satisfy his conscience; he would not suffer as acutely as he does. The suffering is the price which the patient pays to demand absolution. Only psychotherapy can clarify the issue and help the patient back on the way to participation in life.

Psychosis

The mechanism of psychotic disturbances is completely different from the structure of a neurosis. The defensiveness against life is complete. A psychosis starts when the bridges between the individual and his social atmosphere are either completely, or are on the verge of being, broken up. Psychosis is no longer directed against one or another situation, but against social living together. It takes certain predisposing factors to break completely with the logic of life.

However, it must be emphasized that psychotic mechanisms are not at all alien to the normal personality. The dreams of the normal person have the same pattern and structure as the delusions and hallucinations of a psychotic patient. During our sleep we are removed from the social atmosphere of our waking life, from the logic of social life and the grammar of conscious talking and thinking. Our inner life creates its expression in dreams as does the private sense of the psychotic, who is similarly not bound by any logic of life or thought, nor by grammar or any other superimposed rule. He obeys his inner order, his private sense, as does the dreamer. This principle is true for all psychoses, regardless of the nature of the psychosis; the various types of psychoses vary only in regard to the outlets which they provide for the expression of the inner self.

There are first the so-called functional psychoses—schizophrenia, manic-depressive psychosis, and paranoia. They are called functional, because no brain pathology has yet been found to substantiate the mental disorder. The psychological understanding of these psychoses is still limited, as research has so far been mainly directed toward the structure of the symptoms and their mechanism. Few reports are available on the personalities of the patients and their life styles, to clarify the role which the psychosis plays in the life of the patient. The family relationship seems to play an important part and deserves more illumination.

The onset of schizophrenia is very often connected with a shocking experience that throws the patient off balance. Predisposing factors are probably organ inferiority in regard to certain brain functions, tendencies to withdraw and to concentrate on inner life experiences, exhaustion or drastic changes in the body equilibrium, like puberty or pregnancy. These predispositions alone seem not to be sufficient as long as the individual is not exposed to tasks which he is not prepared to solve or situations which he, according to his life style, cannot meet successfully. The psychosis is the admission of complete inner defeat.

Experiences with war schizophrenia will probably shed more light on the structure of schizophrenic breakdowns. Some observations point to a type of schizophrenic disorders which seem to include more neurotic elements and to approach the picture of hysteria. They are similar to psychoses observed in prisoners and seem to offer a better prognosis. One significant factor may be that the logic of life for those people is confined to the social atmosphere of army or prison life against which the psychosis is directed—from which the patient withdraws completely. Brought back to civilian life, he may be capable and willing to participate again and to accept anew the logic of living together.

The disturbances in the manic-depressive psychosis are more on the emotional side. The logic of life is also defied, but in a different way than in schizophrenia. Delusions are less violent, hallucinations less extensive and frequent; nevertheless, the patient follows his Private Sense at the expense of the Common Sense without inner conflict. Even the remorse and self-accusation of the melancholic is not in line with Common Sense, but is used as a weapon of attack against social responsibilities.

The element of anger seems to play an important part in manic-depressive psychosis, although it is converted and not obvious, as the patients very often are persons who do not permit themselves to express anger without losing self-respect. Suppressed anger probably plays a more important part in the so-called reactive depressions, which are more the type of a neurosis, and directed to a limited object, such as a person or situation. Release of anger very often removes the depression.

In a melancholic psychosis, however, the antagonistic attitude involves the whole world. In the manic phase, the defiance and aggression of the patient are more obvious, while he conceals these tendencies behind inertia and immobility during the depressive phase. The manic phase is the overt over-compensation for the feeling of complete defeat, "a flight into reality" (W. A. White), whereby the reality is rearranged according to the inner demands of the patient.

The periodic appearance or disappearance of depressions is less indiscriminate than might appear at superficial observation. The provoking agent in the life situation at the start of a relapse can be discovered only by careful analysis of the patient's life style and the relative significance of the conditions under which he lives.

An extremely interesting type of psychosis is paranoia. Here we deal with a psychosis which has not affected the ability of logical thinking. Very few individuals seem to have the capacity to impose their own logic and their Private Sense upon the logic of life without excuse of neurotic symptoms or without alienating their own logic from the Common Sense of others. Most such attempts lead to schizophrenic processes, and the difference between the inner logic, the Private Sense of the patient with the logic of the rest of the world becomes apparent. The paranoic concept puts the individual in the center of the world; significance of a defensive and intimidated individual is over-compensated into an object of general attention. The logic —or perhaps better, the distortion of logic—of the paranoid resembles somewhat the type of thinking we find in psychopathic personalities. Both are refractory to persuasion and, unlike a neurotic person, reveal by their rigidity their denial of the Common Sense.

In organic or toxic psychosis the apparent inability to participate in our mutual social sphere seems to be adequately explained by the organic damage to the brain. It can be on the basis of brain pathology due to tumors or other diseases of the brain; due to cerebral arteriosclerosis, senile changes, or syphilitic process; or as a consequence of endogenous or exogenous intoxication as through alcohol, various drugs and poisons; through acute infections like influenza, rheumatic fever, scarlet fever, typhoid, and others; or through disfunction of the inner metabolism in connection with childbirth, glandular disfunctions, and pathology of the blood picture. However, we seem justified in assuming that the various disturbances do not actually cause the mental disorder, but only provide a tool which can be used, under favorable circumstances, for pathological mental reactions. Exactly the same pathological condition can be found in patients with a psychosis and in those who are not mentally ill. The location of the damage plays a role, but not conclusively. It influences the type of mental disturbance, inducing and facilitating certain mental reactions. Organic psychoses tend to affect judgment, memory, and emotional stability, while toxic psychoses generally show vivid hallucinations of a delirious type, deep confusion, and agitation. These two syndromes already indicate the reasons why the patients lose their ability to maintain their Common Sense sufficiently intact. As the perception of our common world vanishes or disintegrates, the inner world of the patient becomes dominant.

New types of treatment have been found to be effective with various types of psychoses. Although the reasons for the success of shock treatment are not yet clear, their efficiency cannot be doubted. It seems that the breaking up of rigid channels of thinking and feeling is the determining factor. It is significant that in certain cases the psychotic derangement disappeared under the treatment while the presumably "causal" brain pathology remained unchanged. Such cases seem to indicate the rather loose connection between cause and effect, which we should better understand as a relationship of stimulation and response.

Organic and toxic conditions offer possibilities to which the patient with his attitudes, intentions, and life pattern may or may not respond. The problems with which he is confronted, the personality he has developed, may very well determine whether he responds with a psychosis, and even with which symptoms. We know, for instance, that alcohol may produce a great variety of psychotic disturbances, some almost entirely in the nature of an organic psychosis, like the Korsakoff Psychosis; others typically acute toxic, like Delirium Tremens; and others again with schizophrenic or with manic-depressive symptoms in the foreground.

We will see later that the same agent, alcohol, may as well produce disturbances of a neurotic or psychopathic type. It seems, therefore, that organic and toxic agents on one side and social conflicts on the other confront the individual, and that it is the patient who determines the outcome of the impact. Shock therapy does not remove the causing disturbance, but offers a new possibility for a new and better reaction. The solution of the psychological conflict may be removed by managing the life situations of the patients after shock therapy in such a way that they become more favorable to the patients' needs. The limitations of shock therapy may well be provided by psychological factors. The treatment attacks only the tool, the mechanism, but not the attitude of the patient.

Psychopathic Personality

The term "psychopathic personality" has been widely used and much abused. This type of mental disorder still presents psychiatry and culture with many puzzling and confusing problems. Very little agreement or clarity exists about the nature of this disorder and its origin. Many terms are used, such as constitutional psychopathic states, constitutional psychopathic inferiority, sociopathy and similar terms. There was a trend—and it still exists—to consider a person who is not insane in the sense of a psychotic, but who does not act like a normal person, not feel sick like a neurotic, as constitutionally deficient. Inheritance is and has always been the outlet for an etiological understanding when no more specific and concrete etiological factors could be found. Most classifications of psychopathic personalities are based on a mere description of their various emotional and social maladjustments. A dynamic understanding of these disorders seems to be missing.

However, attention of psychiatry and the public in general will probably center more and more on the problems of psychopathy. Psychiatry first was mainly interested in and dealt exclusively with psychoses. At the end of the past century, the emphasis shifted to the neuroses which occupy the first place in psychiatric interest and practice. Physicians of all specialities, and medicine in general became interested in the problems of neurosis as it was recognized as an integral factor of a great number of diseases. Right now we seem to stand on the threshold of a new psychiatric phase: The concern, the understanding, and the effective dealing with psychopathic personalities. Many psychiatric, legal, and social problems could not be solved due to this lack of understanding of the nature of psychopathy. Our dealing with criminals, our efforts to prevent delinquency, our attempts to cure the anti-social, were completely frustrated because there was no basis to rely upon in these efforts.

Psychopathic personalities are characterized, as was said in the beginning of this paper, by a peculiar deficiency of the Common Sense. They are persons who have failed to develop the necessary Common Sense in order to get along with others and behave in a socially acceptable way. Their deficient Common Sense is the causal factor in their maladjustment. Their deficiency may originate in an inability to conceive of the moral standards and values of the group in which the person lives. For this reason, I am inclined to regard the mentally deficient as one group of these psychopathic personalities. Some psychologists take exception to regarding mental deficients as part of psychiatry. However, we realize more and more the connection between emotional and social maladjustment and mental deficiency of varying degrees.

In many cases of mentally deficient children, the general inability of parents and teachers to inculcate children with proper social attitudes contributes to the resulting moral and emotional defects. Retarded children, instead of receiving the necessary better care, receive less of it and are therefore prone to become psychopathic personalities. However, psychopathy can in all cases be traced back to deficiencies in upbringing, due either to a lack of supervision and educational facilities or, more frequently, to a lack of ability on the side of the responsible persons who failed in their educational obligation.

The configuration of the Common Sense of psychopathic personality is extremely interesting and revealing. As nobody is completely devoid of Social Interest—or he would not have been able to survive—so everybody has a certain amount of Common Sense. This Common Sense, however, is identical with the ideals and values of those to whom he feels he belongs. But it ends there also. As this feeling of belonging of a psychopath is reduced, and as he opposes the society in which he grew up, so his Common Sense is not in line with the generally accepted social ideals and values. However, the gang to which he belongs, the group with which he identified himself, shares his Common Sense. This peculiar configuration of the Common Sense explains the social fluctuation in regard to certain types of psychopathic personalities. The same social behavior may be regarded as acceptable or as anti-social, depending on the social conventions of a group. Killing may be criminal or heroic, according to the Common Sense of a group. A rebel is regarded as criminal when the rebellion of which he is a part fails, and a hero when he succeeds. The difference can be understood only from the point of view of a Common Sense, of a set of values which the individual either shares with the society around him or which distinguishes him from them. In these instances psychopathy is obviously a question of social order and social nature, and the deficiencies of an individual are expressions of social inadequacies which are not necessarily faults of the individual. These facts should make it clear that delinquency and crime have to be recognized not merely as individual, intrapersonal problems, but as problems of social interaction. Any criminal may be a completely acceptable and dignified member of a group which shares his values.

For this reason, criminals of any kind must be regarded as psychopathic personalities; because their Common Sense and their understanding of good and bad as part of their mental setup is at variance with the social order around them. They belong in one of the three groups in which psychopathic personalities may be divided: They are (1) the Indulgent Personalities: The alcohol and drug addicts, the gamblers, the liars, the perverts, the truants, the swindlers, the eccentric and the excitable, the hoboes and malingerers. Then there are (2) the Defiant Personalities: The criminals, the delinquents, the morally insane, the active sex perverts and prostitutes, the impulsive and quarrelsome; and (3) there are the Mentally Deficient of all degrees, from feeble-mindedness to idiocy. They all have in common their limited acceptance of what is right and wrong, their limited acknowledgment of good and bad. As they do not feel sick and as they feel justified in their own behavior, they seek no help and accept no therapy. Prevention is the best cure. Helping parents and teachers in understanding and guiding their wards will be recognized as the prime objective. Psychopathic trends must and can be recognized very early. They cannot be suppressed by force, nor mitigated by indulgence. These two methods, predominantly used today with misbehaving children, are mainly responsible for the great number of indulgent and defiant personalities. Psychopathics are the result of our social conditions which do not induce educators and parents to deal with children in a human, dignified, restrained and encouraging way.

Once such personalities have been developed, the only therapy that seems to affect them is group therapy. They resist personal treatment in most cases, but they respond to group spirit. It is easier to change the objectives and tendencies of the whole group than of any individual alone. New group values must be developed to increase and improve the social values of an individual. That is the reason why group psychotherapy is so efficient in reconditioning delinquent youth and alcoholics.

This efficiency of group therapy will be increasingly recognized when we are dealing with mental disorders which tend to develop psychopathic personalities. There are some fluctuations between the various groups of disorders. An alcoholic might use his drinking as a neurotic symptom, excusing his failure by his "weakness." He feels sick and asks for help, as is typical of a neurotic. However, the chronic alcoholic very often is a psychopathic individual who refuses assistance. In this case individual therapy is almost hopeless.

Chronic neurotic persons very often react like psychopathic personalities; they are well entrenched and rigid in their indulgent or defiant attitude toward life. Although they maintain their symptoms, and continue to feel sick, they generally establish an attitude of definite declination to recognize and accept social obligations. Especially in cases of compulsive neurosis, one is confronted with a person who often shows a deep sense of justification for not playing a part in the social tasks. Shock therapy fails, as there is no mechanism here which might be broken down; but group psychotherapy, with the possibility of setting up new moral values, proves to be efficient.

The problem of psychopathic personalities will probably confront us with great violence after this war, when readjustment has to be made by the community to the returning soldier and by the veteran to his community. Clash of social values and mutual refutation will create innumerable problems which will require psychological understanding and psychiatric help. Group discussions and group psychotherapy seem to be the methods which offer the most probable help.

THE PROBLEM OF NEURASTHENIA*

This article is not intended to be an exhaustive study of the problem of neurasthenia. But it seems necessary to throw a little critical light on some of the opinions on this subject so strongly maintained both in lay circles and among physicians. The viewpoint of Individual Psychology is especially well adapted to this task of clarifying the meaning of the neuroses—both those that show predominantly psychic symptoms and those that manifest functional, physical disturbances.

The concept "neurasthenia," initiated by Beard in the second half of the last century, is based upon the idea that the nerve-substance can be injured or weakened, purely organically, by an excessive strain upon it; and that this injury is hastened by a faulty predisposition, a natural weakness of the nervous system. (Neurasthenia—asthenia, or debility, of the nerves.) According to this view, the causes of the injury include everything that overloads the "nerve capacity": great exertion, extreme fatigue, excitement, sexual excess, sexual abstinence, onanism, frustrated sexual stimulation, coitus interruptus, etc.

The subjective symptoms of the complaint appear in the form of intermittent pains in all possible parts of the body—the so-called "rheumatic" pains and "stitches" in various members; headaches, sensations of pressure on the head; lumbago; heart-pains; pains in the stomach; lack of stamina; sensitivity; irritability; spells of depression; vertigo; aversion to work; disturbances of the rational powers, of the memory, of the sexual

* *International Journal of Individual Psychology*, 1936, 2, 14-34.

function, etc. People with any of these symptoms come to the physician, say that there is something wrong with "their nerves," and attribute their complaints to one or another of the causes listed above.

Neurasthenia was an especially popular ailment at the beginning of this century. It was looked upon as the visible sign of great exertion and overwork, and for this reason was thought to be distinctively "masculine," hysteria being considered its "feminine" counterpart. Today this nomenclature has been supplanted for the most part by the term "neurosis," popularized by Freud, which does away with the sex distinction in the names of these diseases. But since the notion of an organic basis for these "nervous complaints" is still so unhappily prevalent, among physicians as well as the general public, we will first put forward a few arguments against its validity.

Corresponding to the subjective complaints of neurasthenic patients there are a series of objective symptoms. These can be divided into two groups. The first consists of a considerable increase of the reflexes—tremors of the fingers, the tongue, the eyelids, the head, and sometimes also of the lower extremities and the whole body; such as the unsteadiness to be observed in a negative Rhomberg. The other group of objective, seemingly organic, symptoms concerns the vegetative processes, debility of the vascular system, irregularity of the pulse, dermographism, hyperacidity of the stomach, derangement of the intestinal functions, increased formation of urates, etc.

To the best of my knowledge, no attempt has yet been made to determine the origin of the first group of objective symptoms. Alfred Adler was the first to point out the intense strain under which all neurotics live. And the symptoms just mentioned seem to me to be only an expression of this strain. Kretschmer has taught us that the trembling incident to hysteria results mainly from the tenseness of the extremities affected; it ceases as soon as the patient can be made to relax his limbs. That the fluttering of the eyelids is also the result of extreme tension is shown by the following observation. If it is desired to determine whether a person whose eyes are closed is really asleep, or only pretending to be asleep, one of the surest criteria is the condition of his eyelids. In sleep these are completely relaxed and still, but voluntary closure of the eyelid always produced a certain agitation and a scarcely detectable quivering. In the case of a neurotic in a state of great psychic strain, the voluntary closure of the eyelids leads to a pronounced fluttering. It is, therefore, the excessive innervation of the muscles and their antagonists that produces all these symptoms of uncertainty including the functional Rhomberg.

The facts are a great deal more complicated in the second group of symptoms. They all indicate disturbances of the vegetative nervous system—a root factor in all organic neuroses. Adler himself (among others) has shown that nervous headaches are very frequently the result of a dilation of the blood vessels passing through the bones of the skull, and the resultant pressure on the accompanying nerves. There can be no doubt that the vegetative nervous system is subordinated to the will, the psychic aims, of man not directly, but through a series of lower brain centers which make possible a central regulation. Hence there can be no question here of a primary organic change. Yet the majority of physicians assume that a peculiar predisposition is necessary to make possible the utilization of this system of nerves by the psyche. Here a question arises that is vital to our viewpoint. Is it possible that all disturbances in the equilibrium of the vegetative nervous system—for this is the point at issue here, too—are post foetal—i.e., developed and "acquired" after birth, through the behavior of the individual in human society? Even though the concept of vagotonia, proposed by Eppinger and Hess, (i.e., the complete, one-sided shifting of the equilibrium in favor of the vagus) cannot be supported, it cannot be denied that under certain conditions the vegetative nervous system may temporarily be in a state similar to this (vagotonia in sleep, during digestion, in pregnancy). W. R. Hess has made the important postulation that vagotonia corresponds essentially to the condition of the body in which the vital powers are turned away from the external world and devoted chiefly to the work of regeneration, the functioning of the internal organs (histotropic regulation); whereas the opposite condition, a decided turning toward the external world correspond to sympathicotonia (ergotropic regulation). It still remains to be determined whether a pronounced turning away from the external world (evidenced in part by an extreme addiction to lengthy daydreams) can lead to a disturbance in the equilibrium of the vegetative nervous system, perhaps even in early childhood. This could subsequently effect a general hypersensitivity of the vegetative functions (something like Bergmann's "vegetative stigmatization") or a heightening of the tone of the vagus. These changes are, however, always the organic correlate of the objective symptoms described above. At all events—and this is important for our later contentions, no one can any longer deny the psychic origin of the organic neuroses that consist of disturbances of the vegetative nervous system. In his study of organic inferiorities, Adler assumes in many cases a somatic basis for the origin of the organic symptoms of neurosis. But an organ can never "speak its dialect" unless the individual permits it to "speak"—unless he has a use for this symptom in his lifeplan, in the pursuit of his fictive life-goal. The nerves—the central nervous system with its sensory and motor branches—are, however, in no case and in no manner deranged. It is not the "nerves" that are responsible for the symptoms, and hence we cannot consider neurasthenia as a "nervous disease" in the sense of being a disease of the nerves.

At this point we must say a few words more on the question of organic, neuropathic predisposition, which, as we have seen, is often considered the basis for such a complaint as neurasthenia. Now it must be taken for granted that human beings are subject to precisely the same laws of heredity as those which govern all of nature and the regularity of which was first demonstrated by Mendel. It is beyond dispute that children at birth are not alike. Not only in their physiques—facial structure, color of hair, bodily build, etc.—do they show marked signs of similarity to certain forebears, but it is probable that their psychic and mental capacities, which are physically conditioned, are therefore also different. Adler's great service consists in recognizing that this hereditary endowment, unequivocal as it may seem at first, it not so fatefully significant in man for him to adopt a personal attitude toward the world (including himself) and, with this attitude as his guide, to regulate his entire being and either develop or neglect to develop his native equipment as the case may be. The faulty use or faulty development of a native ability naturally prevents this ability from evincing itself, and may give the individual the impression that his native endowment is actually defective in this particular. All this is self-evident. Adler demonstrates, however, that the opposite is also possible—that an original inferiority in endowment can be "over-compensated" through intensive training and developed into a definite ability. Thus the endowment is not significant in itself. "It is not what a man has to begin with that matters, but what he does with what he has." (Adler)

It has already been suggested that the same may also be true of the so-called neuropathic predisposition. In any event, the presence of one and the same abnormality in parents and children and other relatives cannot be taken as absolute proof of an hereditary predisposition. Children frequently imitate the behavior of their parents, especially if this behavior seems in some way advantageous to them. In their desire to be like mother and father, or to adapt themselves, particularly to one or the other, they often take parental faults too as models worth striving to emulate and so imitate their parents' vices. Then, too, the parents often directly transfer their weaknesses to their children through defective rearing. They themselves commit the same faults that their parents had been guilty of in their own upbringing. (Here we see the operation of a law that is of the greatest moment in the improvement of mankind —the law of the inheritability of faulty education. This does not, however, depend upon an organic predisposition, but results simply from the fact that most people have no better understanding of the significance of education than that which their

The vegetative, or sympathetic, nervous system has two counteractive nerves which regulate and promote or retard all the animal functions. These are the vagus and the sympathicus. Subject to their influence are: the blood vessels, the heart, the digestive system, and also the ductless glands, the metabolic and excretory functions, the secretion of urine, sugar, sweat, and sleep, etc.

parents exemplified for them in their childhood.) Hence the question of predisposition presents an almost insoluble problem today, except in those cases in which the training and life-plan of the individual can be traced through from earliest childhood and infancy. And, for this reason, the conclusions reached by a study of the family—an attempt to deduce the laws of human heredity purely from the finished products, the end results—should be accepted with considerable caution.

But if a "predisposition" to nervous debility and sensitivity seems a questionable explanation for neurasthenia, the other theories on "overloading" the nervous system prove themselves also untenable. It is generally believed that great exertion, if continued too long without rest periods, can produce neurasthenic symptoms. But a closer observation of individual cases shows that this is impossible. It is probably true that physical exertion leads to a poisoning of the muscles, to a diffusion of toxic substances in the blood stream, and hence to exhaustion. But this exhaustion, if extreme, results only in dullness and finally in sleep. It has been observed that almost superhuman exertions on the battlefield produced no nervous symptoms in the soldiers; whenever a lull in action occurred they simply fell to the ground wherever they happened to be, and dozed off. The neurasthenic symptoms appeared under quite different circumstances—on the not infrequent occasions when effort was made to induce them to over-exert themselves anew. The supposed effects of overexertion serve rather as a pretext for justifying one's own inability to perform some particular task. One can often observe in individual cases that long and taxing activity will be endured without disturbances of any sort as long as its results are gratifying, but that a much easier and shorter piece of work may produce strong symptoms, when it is unpleasant in itself or when the individual does not feel equal to it and fears a failure. In this event the neurasthenic pose serves the end of averting, evading the task.

Much the same is true of the supposed effect of frequent and long continued excitement. Not even psychic strains on the nerves can lead directly to the symptoms that characterize the neurasthenic patient. The behavior of the excitable individual is not—as he and his environment believe—the inevitable result of his previous experiences; for in this case, too, we see behavior serving personal aims, as a safeguard and a means of evasion. His state of excitement serves as a defense against his environment. This fact is clearly shown in the conduct of hot-tempered persons.

Superficially considered, the actions of hot-tempered individuals seem to result from the irritability of their nerves, and they themselves do not seem responsible for what they do. They often show signs of the most bitter remorse for the actions committed in fits of anger, and sometimes shed tears and beg forgiveness on bended knee. It actually looks as though the condition of their nerves could not permit any other reaction to certain stimuli. But closer observation proves that the seeming inevitability of their conduct is a device to evade responsibility for certain actions conducive to certain definite ends. The hot-tempered person is always an individual who wants to lord it over others, but who does not really believe that his powers can keep pace with his ambitions. Accordingly, we find that quick temper is often a man's weapon for making himself the last word, so to speak, of his environment and keeping his womenfolk and children (and probably his business colleagues and superiors as well) in permanent shock. He can do this with outbursts of anger, or perhaps the mere threat of one may be sufficient. He thus succeeds in breaking all opposition. For no means—neither reason or violence—can avail against his fuming and raging. The more senseless his conduct seems, and the more effusive his regrets afterward, the more successful an illusion of irresponsibility. Yet experience teaches us that, despite the storm and fury, the hot-tempered one knows well enough what he is doing, and contrives to adapt his behavior to his situation. An example will confirm this point.

A married couple were accustomed to drinking a cup of coffee together every morning and evening. They became devoted to this habit, and came to think a great deal of their individual coffee cups with their names inscribed on them. One day the man was ill and stayed in bed in the morning, so his wife served him his coffee in bed. By some means or other she managed to irritate him, and the husband, who was subject to "anger fits," went into a tantrum and threw his cup on the floor. The wife, who knew these "attacks" as of old and realized that it was best for her to keep calm, fetched the dustpan and broom and was sweeping up the pieces when she suddenly exclaimed, "That's my cup you broke! It wasn't even yours!" The man was peaceable enough once the attack was over, and he answered with a smile. "Do you think I'd have smashed the cup if I hadn't seen it was yours?" Now the cat was out of the bag. He had given himself away by admitting that he would most likely have controlled himself if it had been his cup instead of hers, and his wife made such adroit use of this confession that she actually succeeded in breaking her husband of his quick temper.

Like the effects of exhaustion and excitement, very complicated and lasting reactions to terror and anxiety cannot be considered physiological. They represent rather a psychic enlistment of these experiences in the service of personal aims.

Sexuality has always played a particular role—both aetiological and symptomatic—in the scientific studies of the problem of neurasthenia. At one time "sexual neurasthenia," first described by Bread-Rockwell, was regarded almost as a disease sui generis. But it was never made quite clear to what extent sexual disturbances are the causes, and to what extent the results, of the complaint. The following, as we said above, were generally considered the causes of sexual neurasthenia: masturbation, venereal excesses, abnormal intercourse, frustrated sexual excitement, coitus interruptus, and also sexual abstinence. Several of these are themselves the results of a disorder, and rarely occur in healthy individuals (e.g., excessive masturbation, abnormal sexual intercourse, etc.); and, as we know today, they all are the concomitants rather than the causes of the other "neurasthenic" disturbances of the sexual function, such as impotence, sexual weakness, distress following the act, etc. The view that all these derangements result from "exhaustion of the nerves" through mistaken behavior has been shown to be false.

This error reveals itself most strikingly in the untrue estimate of onanism (masturbation)—a mistake that is extraordinarily prevalent among the public, and the effects of which are catastrophic. The prevailing opinion is that onanism leads to a serious impairment of the general health, the "nerves," and especially the sexual powers. But not a single word of this is true. What, then, is the origin of this widespread delusion? It is true that fifty years ago similar views were expressed in scientific medical works, owing to the fact that the causes of tabes and paralysis were still unknown. Only after Wassermann had discovered his method of blood analysis were these diseases recognized as sequelae of syphilis. It was proved that neither tabes nor paralysis was possible without previous luetic infection. In former years it was also believed that other abuses and disorders could produce tabes and paralysis—such abuses, for instance, as excessive alcoholism and general loose living, but chiefly any sort of venereal disease, onanism, and the other sex habits mentioned above. The notion was then prevalent that neurasthenia was responsible for spinal injury; and this notion still troubles the minds of our neurasthenic patients.

Modern medical science has found this viewpoint to be patently false, but it persists nevertheless and continues to be spread among the public. We may state as a general truth that several decades must always elapse before the results of science can become common property and be widely disseminated through the medium of popular medicine. Scientists may change their views in the meanwhile, but we will find the earlier views still prevailing among the people through this lag-period. The so-called "doctor books" are one of the chief reasons for this lag in medical knowledge, since they pass on the old, false views unchanged through edition after edition, and seem to hold a special attraction for neurasthenic patients. And the lag in popular medicine has probably never produced such catastrophic results as with regard to masturbation. For the injurious effects of onanism are not too organic, but purely psychic; they are produced by a dread of the supposed consequences of the practice. All the assertions pointing to injurious organic effects of masturbation are wholly unfounded—including the formerly widespread assumption of an inflammation of the prostate and the posterior urethra (the colliculus seminalis) as the result of onanism.

Freud's psychoanalysis pointed out the importance of the sense of guilt resulting from onanism, and asserted that onanism can produce none of the neurasthenic symptoms unless a sense of guilt is present. However, the Freudian doctrine has served in recent years to bolster up the original contention that neurasthenia has an organic root, and hence has tended to heighten from another angle the difficulty of understanding the psychic problems involved. The old notions of nervous exhaustion and irritability—the notions pointing to a derangment of "the nerves"—have not been revived, it is true. But in their stead we have the theory of the somatic influence of sexual energy, the "libido." At first, Freud differentiated anxiety-neurosis from neurasthenia and termed both of these, together with hypochondria, the "real neuroses" (Aktualneurosen) as distinguished from the "psychoneuroses." The Aktualneurosen, according- to Freud, originate in disturbances of the libido economy, and have nothing to do with psychic functioning. A definite disturbance of libido-economy leads directly to definite pathological symptoms. Thus, according to this theory, true neurasthenia results from a spinal irritation produced whenever the adequate release of sexual tension is supplanted by an inadequate release of such tension—for example, in excessive masturbation and overfrequent pollutions. The cause of anxiety neurosis is somatic libido-repression—for instance, sexual abstinence, coitus interruptus, and frustrated sexual excitement. These symptoms, Freud claims, have no psychic significance, but are the direct somatic effects of sexual disturbances. Reich goes still farther and finds the pathogenic agency not only in the faulty discharge of venereal energy, but also in the absence of orgasm. He also creates the concept of chronic, hypochondriacal neurasthenia and distinguishes various types of neurasthenia, thus considerably complicating Freud's formulations, which (originally, at any rate) had at least the virtue of simplicity. Reich, too, probably considers acute neurasthenia as the result of libido-repression in consequence of abuses (in contrast with anxiety-neurosis, which results from abstinence), but he adds the factor of a continual increase in tension owing to the obstruction of orgastic discharge. The chronic type of neurasthenia he regards as mainly the result of a pre-genital form of sexual satisfaction that, like repression, interferes with orgasm. Corresponding to this view there is an alleged form of impotence, genital asthenia, in which the penis becomes the symbol of the female breast, and there results a trickling of semen and urine from the flaccid organ. The father-fixation is supposed to be lacking in such a case, and the mother-fixation is supposed to take its place. In neurasthenic hypochondria, Reich asserts, that due to damming up of the genital libido the entire body becomes, as it were, an erected genital. Freud, too, regards the hypochondriacal complaints as real somatic sensations produced by the overcharging of certain organs with narcistic-somatic libido. It is also claimed that the fear of castration assumes a definite form in neurasthenia. The neurasthenic patient feels that he is already castrated, and hence he has actual complaints, whereas the hysterical patient, for example, only fears that he will be castrated, and suffers only from apprehensions. A number of Freudian diagnosticians stress the "anality" of neurasthenic patients (their fixation on the anal stage of libido-development.) Reich attributes this mal-development in part to faulty education, and believes that parents who are themselves subject to anal-fixation strengthen this fixation in their children through an exaggerated attention to the anal functions.

Reich also takes a purely energetic view of the various neurasthenic symptoms. The sense of pressure on the head, nausea, and the disturbance of the rational powers are in part the result of the chronic physiological irritability of the sexual organs, but they are also connected with constipation. According to him a state of "mental constipation" is produced not only by the round about way of possible intoxication and increased blood pressure, but also by a shifting of sexuality to the upper part of the body (the mouth representing the anus.) The repression of the coprophilic tendencies results in nausea and loss of appetite. The conditions of excitement and exhaustion conform to the organic sensitization of the whole body, which functions as a genital. All this, Reich claims, is the real, physical effect of undischarged sexual tension.

We have had to present these views in considerable detail because psychoanalysis is the source of the strongest resistance to a psychological understanding of neurasthenia. Now we shall compare these views with the evidence of two case histories.

Case 1: 1.R; 33 years of age, city employee.

The patient suffers from insomnia, vertigo, asthma, palpitation of the heart, lumbago, sensations of burning on the skin. The symptoms have been present for half a year. He is engaged, and would marry if he were well. Has had no sexual intercourse for some time because of his fear of becoming weak. Had similar complaints a few years before, but other organs: stomach, heart, lungs. Objective symptoms: fluttering of the eyelids, hyper-reflexes, dermographism. Nothing else in particular.

The patient is an only child. A brother died before he was born. His mother was always greatly concerned about his health. She was always anxious about him, mainly because his brother had died. His father often found fault with him, and his mother took his part. His parents were fairly severe with him—for example, the patient was forced to eat everything on his plate. He always had a delicate stomach, and vomited frequently. He followed a regular diet when he was a child, and continued to do so until he was in the upper grades in school. After that he had no more trouble with his stomach. Suffered previously from lack of appetite, and refused to eat. Was always timid as a child. Had frequent nose-bleed, chiefly after running. Did not care to leave the house and his playthings to take walks, etc. His nurse was kept for him for years, and until he was ten he was never away from his mother. Someone always had to sit by his bed when he went to sleep, and a light had to be burning; and whenever he woke up in the night, a light had to be lit. He was often frightened out of sleep. When he was small he felt especially sorry for cripples. He was extremely sensitive, and was easily hurt, often without cause.

His early childhood recollections were the following: At four years of age he played with dolls and helped sew clothes. At five years his parents went to a restaurant, and he cried bitterly because he had to stay home with the maid; his parents consoled him by giving him a present. When he was six the maid was trying to put on the patient's shoes; she did something he did not like, so he took a shoe and threw it at her.

When he was five and a half, the patient had whooping cough, and vomited after every attack. Because of the whooping cough he took the work of the first two grades of school at home. His parents were afraid that he might contract other diseases at school. He enjoyed going to elementary school, but he did not like the upper grades so well. He was terribly afraid of examinations. But often when this fear of examinations was unusually strong, he would suddenly become quite calm. As early as his first year in elementary school he was told that he had a special talent for language and languages, and he was never afraid of the examinations in these subjects. He always had friends at school, and was generally a quiet, docile child. He showed no interest in girls while he was in school. In the fifth grade he was ill for several months with a lung-infection, and he took the year's work over. After the final examinations he wasted a year, and then entered the city employ. He had difficulties with his superiors on only one occasion. Up to the time of his illness he always liked to be in the office. He felt a desire to stay home only when he was ill.

At about the time of puberty he was extremely bashful and uneasy. But after the final examinations he attended a dancing school, and began to get over his bashfulness. His first Platonic love affair began there. At twenty, he had sexual intercourse for the first time with an acquaintance from the "park." And he says that he took the initiative himself. But after one repetition of the act he lost all interest in the girl. She was too uncultured to suit him. A half-year later he had intercourse twice with another girl, but then his interest again waned because, so he said, he knew that she went out with other men. For several years he had a Platonic affair with an acquaintance from the dancing class, and it seemed that he was expected to marry her. During this period he had no sexual intercourse at all. He began to imagine that he had spermatorrhoea, continually "felt sensations" in the penis, and suffered from spells of nervous anxiety, shortness of breath, and stomach disorders. So, because of his illness, he kept away from the girl for several months. He took a trip, and came home well.

Then he met the girl who became his fiancee. Their affair was serious from the beginning. He soon began to consider marriage. But then they had a quarrel. He was irritated by her caprices, which he could never understand. And then he took ill again. He felt indisposed after exertions or long periods of work; and when he tried to rest he found that rest did not agree with him either, and he began to be alarmed about his condition. There was a recurrence of his stomach disorders and shortness of breath. The break with his fiancee was not a matter of complete indifference to him, but he did not take it so very deeply to heart, for he knew that he could make it up at any time. It was really true that the girl was only waiting for him to make the first move toward a reconciliation. His illness served as the prime reason for not making the expected move. He had no desire to go out; the idea gave him no pleasure. And so the engagement was broken off.

When the patient was twenty-five his father died, and from then on he lived with his mother. The two of them got along very well together. Their only disagreements were over his fiancee. His mother opposed the marriage; she always insisted in general terms that he should marry, but actually she was against his marrying and wanted to keep the patient at home with her. He and his mother were very much attached to each other. She objected violently to his fiancee in particular, claiming that she was not the right girl for him. But this, the patient says, was only a pretext.

After his mother's death he was very despondent, and tried to lose himself in social activities. He began to see his fiancee again. About a year ago they renewed their engagement, and marriage was an immediate prospect. But then his illness intervened. First the genital organs, especially the testicles, were "over-irritated" and painful to the touch. He had ejaculatio praecox. For months he avoided sexual intercourse for fear of overstraining his nerves. Both his fiancee and his physician agreed that abstinence was best for him. After he took ill, his great love for the girl disappeared. He formerly liked her a great deal, and he is still glad to have her with him, and also has a very high opinion of her qualities. But, despite the fact that she showed him every attention while he was ill, he does not love her as he once did. She became impatient during his illness, and accused him of lacking energy. The result was a quarrel, in which her family also took part after their doctor had expressed the opinion that nothing was really wrong with the patient. In his opinion things had been handled badly and the patient had only been irritated.

Recently the patient has also had difficulties in his work. He left the department in which the disagreement occurred; and since his new chief shows him special consideration, he has very little to do. But only a few hours of work completely exhaust him, and he feels worse after resting. He suffers from shortness of breath, and has trouble with his heart. His stomach is continually out of order; he is always agitated and out-of-sorts, and sleeps poorly.

This patient presents a typical picture of neurasthenia. But this particular case also shows quite plainly how the individual was definitely prepared in childhood for his later symptoms. He not only had the misfortune to be an only child, but was further handicapped, before his birth, by the death of his brother, which made his parents especially solicitous for his welfare. They began a series of upbringing measures which were seemingly calculated to preserve his health, but in reality made him peculiarly unfit for the struggle for existence. He was forced to eat, and was over-impressed with the importance of his digestive tract. The child, spoiled and pampered as he was, developed his digestive tract into a weapon, with which he first opposed his parents' discipline, and later on contrived to evade all the dangers of life. He learned at an early age that his sickliness and timidity were apt means for subjugating his environment and gaining special indulgences. He would not tolerate being left alone at night, and was always permitted to stay at home with his mother (e.g., his first two school years.) It is apparent that this individual, who has never become aware of his own powers, must necessarily evince his lack of courage in every instance when a difficult problem confronts him. He was afraid of all examinations except those in which he felt quite sure of himself (languages). And, accordingly, he built up his "nervousness" as a safeguard against all the emergencies that might possibly bring him to defeat. He cultivated this condition from childhood on, and organic ailments served to aid him (whooping cough led to vomiting; inflammation of the lungs, to shortness of breath.) And we see that his complaints came promptly to the fore whenever any sort of difficult situation arose.

It is not mere chance that, apart from his trouble at the office, his chief difficulties arose from his love affairs. Even as a child he did not dare to take his stern father as a model. Rather he preferred to try the feminine role (playing with dolls, etc.) since he believed that this role would be easier and entail less responsibility. Subsequently, he avoided all contacts with girls at first, and when he finally began to take an interest in them, he was extremely diffident and continually making excuses for himself. The first time that his relations with a girl reached the serious stage and demanded a definite decision from him (he was expected to marry her), his illness set in with full force and gave him the required pretext for beating a retreat. The same situation repeated itself in the case of his fiancee but in this instance his anxious mother clearly abetted him. He could flee from the demands of life into the close bond of union with his mother. But when he was left alone after his mother's death, he turned again to the woman from whom he could expect a certain motherly attention. But, upon realizing that he would have to give as well as receive, he retreated again, under cover of his usual symptoms. Naturally he "suffers" from his complaint; but his aches and pains are only, so to speak, the indemnity that he must pay for having alienated himself from the logic of human society. They are, as Adler says, only the "war costs." They provide him with an alibi, and create the illusion that he cannot help himself—that his illness came against his will although it patently serves his purpose to guarantee himself against defeats and dangers, and paves the way for retreat. This is particularly true of the patient's love life, but it applies equally to his occupation and his social activity.

We will find much the same conditions in the following case.

Case 2: S. A., 54 years of age, cabinet maker.

The patient suffers from lumbago, sensations of dull heaviness in the head, insomnia, various pains throughout the body, numbness of the fingers, irritability, melancholy, distress after sexual intercourse, etc.

He was the third child, preceded by two girls, and followed, seven years later, by another boy. He got along with the elder sister, but poorly with the one nearer his own age. He liked his mother best, but had great respect for his father, who was very strict but made him, the first-born son, his special favorite. His father punished him less frequently than he did the girls, and discussed his future vocation with him when he was still quite young.

Earliest childhood recollections: He recalls that at three years of age his mother gave him a sugar-loaf for Christmas, and his sister was very jealous and angry. When he was four he and his sister were given new shoes. His pair had tassels, and again his sister was jealous of him. He also remembers playing with girls at this time. They played with each other's genitals, covering the girls' sexual organs with bits of stone and then scraping them off. Once, when he was four, he was at home alone with his mother when burglars broke in and stole a watch. His mother's only fear was that he might be strangled or kidnapped.

As a child, he suffered from inflammation of the eyes, and he was always very small for his age. He was superstitious, concerned about himself, and afraid of contracting every possible disease. He always clung to his mother's skirts, and hid behind her whenever anyone addressed him. He was timid and afraid of the dark. When his brother was born, he was annoyed at having to keep an eye on him, and later he was angry whenever the little fellow wanted to tag after him. Finally he was given a beating for failing to watch his little brother and letting him almost kill himself.

He was proud to go to school, and felt very grown-up. He learned readily, was very ambitious, and took rebuke to heart. His frequent absences were due only to his inflamed eyes. His school friends he chose among the respectable and well-bred, and they were mainly larger and stronger than he. He avoided fights and ignored insults. He says that he would have liked to associate with younger boys, but felt that this would be improper. He was everlastingly afraid of appearing ridiculous. While he was in the third grade he changed to another school, where the teacher favored the well-to-do children and slighted the poor ones. An undeserved punishment aroused his indignation. Thereafter he did poor work, and was not promoted. But the following year, when he returned to the old school, his work was as good as ever.

During his apprenticeship his honesty and diligence were highly commended. But he was humiliated by the fact that the workbench was too high for him and he had to stand on a block. His shortness made him the butt of ridicule, and prevented him from winning respect and recognition. But his work and conduct were always beyond reproach, and he attended special trade schools.

He could never get on at all with the younger of his two sisters. His behavior toward her was quite the opposite of his conduct at school. He was rude and slighted her, and they frequently engaged in scuffling matches. She was the stronger of the two, and treated him as her inferior. Once, when she scratched him, he swore never to speak to her again as long as he lived. Mentally, however, he was her superior, and missed no opportunity to trick and mystify her. For instance, whenever a train passed—they lived near the tracks—he apprised her of its destination; and this made a marvelous impression on her, although of course it was all a pure hoax. When he was eight, they and a number of other children frequented a shed, where they played "father and mother" (with each other's genitals). He was very fond of his oldest sister, although he did not see her very often, and she took a great interest in him. She had won his admiration on two occasions in particular—once when she carried a heavy sack of coke on her back, and again when she put to flight a group of boys who had been tormenting her. She, the eldest, was always in high spirits, but the other sister was morose and tearful.

At this time a companion "enlightened" him about the "facts of life," but he failed to show any special signs of sexual curiosity. During his apprenticeship he was abashed in the presence of girls, and avoided their company. And—he got more good out of his professional training than his colleagues because he did not waste his time on girls. Generally he stayed at home and puttered about in his spare time. He still retained his fear of seeming ridiculous. It was his constant desire to be larger and more impressive, and he continually dreaded appearing comical. Later, he avoided conversation with strangers, for fear of committing a faux pas; and until he was twenty-two, he never ventured to visit a restaurant alone, even when he had plenty of money, but always waited until he had someone to go with him.

When he was fifteen, his father died, and he assumed the role of father to the youngest child (who, by the way, was the mother's favorite.) And while he himself was learning a trade, he also took two fatherless apprentices under his wing. When he finally took employment, his diligence and proficiency continued to attract attention, and he ambitiously expected to be made foreman of the shop. He was hard hit when a curtailment of the payroll made this impossible. He could not stomach such injustice, and only the thought of his mother prevented him from giving up the job. He was disgruntled, and felt that he had been shabbily treated.

His first voluptuous sensations occurred when he was seven, after he had run to school and was afraid of being late; and he experienced them a second time under similar circumstances. When he was seventeen, a companion taught him to masturbate on the water-closet, but this practice was rendered difficult by a phimosis, which was gradually relieved by dilation. He discovered, however, that other young men had organs much larger than his. The attempts at onanism did not give him much pleasure, and he soon abandoned them. Later on, he was incessantly afraid that his appearance betrayed his sexual practices. He felt especially uneasy in the presence of his mother, and was humiliated when she discovered traces of pollutions on the bed linen.

Until his thirty-fifth year he lived with his mother. She was very self-centered. The patient always had to get home early because otherwise his mother could not sleep. No matter how good a time he was having, he had to leave the party; and finally he was so ridiculed for his devotion to his mother that he gave up society altogether. He was very fond of walking trips, and favored the steep climbing-paths (provided they had guard rails). But he always went out alone, to avoid having to accommodate himself to others; and so he never joined a hiking-club, for the others were always either too slow or too fast to suit him.

The other young men were successful with the girls, but he was so small that they laughed at him.

At the end of the period in which he was learning his trade he had sexual intercourse for the first time, with a public prostitute who got hold of him before he knew what it was all about. Afterwards he dreaded infection, and he never dared go to a prostitute again. His next intercourse was several years later, and was with a much younger girl (sixteen) and again one time was enough. She was capricious, he said, and he was afraid of pregnancy. Subsequently he paid no attention to girls for a while, and he was not so fortunate as to have someone fall in love with him and take matters into her own hands. Later he went for a half-year or more with a girl who refused to give herself unless they married. He really would have proposed, he believes now, if she had been willing to favor him beforehand. But as matters stood, she did not seem to be really in love with him. Before long he stopped seeing her, and from then on he had only passing acquaintanceships. He could never make the right sort of beginning by himself, but always needed the moral support of a group of companions. These brief affairs rarely went so far as intercourse. He had to be on the alert, for all the girls had their caps set for him (he had a good job); and so he never went out more than two or three times with the same girl, for fear of being tied down. He limited himself to a regular "Sunday spree." The precautions kept him from complete satisfaction in the sexual act. He had to practice coitus interruptus, since the erection subsided whenever he used a prophylactic cover. And his feelings about the act were never quite right, for he was never really in love. He did not like to be introduced to a girl's family. The well-to-do girls, he felt, were too good for him, but he always favored those who were well educated and intellectually superior to him. By and large, he focused his attention on retreat rather than conquest in all his relations with women. He no sooner got himself into an affair than he began to consider ways and means of getting out again. He acquired the notion that love is bestial since it robs a person of his self-control and enslaves him to the "animal instincts." He once dreamed that he took hold of the genitals of a fat girl, and when he withdrew his hand it was dirty. In this dream we can readily see his training to put distance between himself and women.

His mother continually tried to turn him against the girls with whom he associated. She never liked him to go out with them, and in every instance she claimed that the girl was not the right one for him. It was not until she grew old, and was no longer able to manage the housework, that she herself began to urge him to marry. But by this time he was, of course, afraid of marriage. He feared that he had had too little intercourse and would fail in the sexual act for want of practice. And, at this time, he really did fail in two attempts at coitus with a respectable girl. Then, for a long period, he lacked the courage to make any further advances, and excused himself on the grounds of his undernourishment and the cold rooms.

The girl whom he finally married was recommended to him by the relative who provided the family with food. And her praises were sung so loud and long that he swerved from his original intentions and began to consider her. She interested him not at all, but he visited her frequently, let her augment the food supply, and finally started a correspondence with her. He began to think more seriously than ever before of marriage; but, despite his mother's urging, he repeatedly decided against it. Gradually, however, he got accustomed to the girl, and began to admire her for her character—her quietness and respectability. He also realized that, financially, the match would be a good one. But he says now that the final decision was the hardest struggle in his life. He still did not love her. And, what was more, he failed consistently in his attempts at intercourse with other girls, ostensibly because of his long abstinence. His impotence, like the old trouble with his eyes, he attributed to a spinal complaint, but he did not consult a physician. Now he was all the more doubtful about marrying, but finally he did marry, despite his qualms. He was nervous and diffident; but, against all his expectations, the coitus was successful.

At first he could not acclimate himself to married life. He had to treat his wife with special consideration, inasmuch as they had few interests in common and were frequently at a loss for conversation. But she was a notable housewife, and he soon began to get on more comfortably with her, especially after the birth of a son. He came to realize that her poor education was not really a drawback. Previously he had shown a preference for girls who were sophisticated and superior to him—"they were more amusing, and a person could learn something from them." But his wife was a more serious matter. It was better for her to be as she was; he did not need to tax himself to be her superior. Now he even began to love a little. He felt well cared for. She was never irritating, but gave in to him at every point, and acted as a sedative influence. It was his intention from the outset to be the master of the household, and she completely subordinated herself to him. But sometimes he thought that, if he had known marriage would be so easy on the nerves, he would have married a very different sort of woman. His mother was always on his side, and often pointed out faults in his wife.

When his mother died, a few years ago, his trouble began. It started with insomnia, which continues to be his chief complaint, and bothers him particularly in the nights preceding Sundays and holidays. On these days he is totally exhausted and dejected. In consideration of his insomnia he completely shuns society; he never accepts evening invitations, never attends the theatre or the moving pictures, and becomes increasingly irritable and critical toward his wife. It vexes him that she can sleep so soundly, and that she remains composed when he loses control of himself and flies into a tantrum. Her apathy irritates him, and he claims that she does not show him the proper sympathy. She always has to go to bed first, in order to be asleep by the time he retires; and he wakes her up, not only whenever she snores, but whenever he looks at the clock or turns over. But she is not allowed to make any extra motion in bed. Sexual intercourse also has a bad effect on him; the next morning he is completely fagged out, and his wife has to rub his back with alcohol.

He feels that he has been slighted in his work since he was transferred to a new shop where his merits are not properly appreciated. He also is afraid of being laid off.

All his life the patient has been afraid of illness. Once, after he visited his brother at a sanatorium, he developed a throat irritation, began to cough and bleed at the nose, and became firmly convinced that he was tubercular. And another time, when a dog bit him, he read up in a "doctor book" and passed through all the stages of rabies; and since then, he claims, he cannot send his arm backward without pain. At the slightest sign of a cold he doses himself with milk and honey. He asserts that the only aid against his insomnia is a bandage application, but he adds that a cold in the head also helps to relieve it.

This patient, like the other, felt as a child that there was a close connection between his physical condition and the difficulties of his life. His eye trouble handicapped him in school; his short stature exposed him to ridicule. And all this was made more distressing by his bad start in life. We see from his earliest recollection that he felt he had to fight for his place against the younger of his two sisters in particular, and felt he could prevail over her only by intellectual means, since she was physically his superior. Then too, his dependence upon his mother could not increase his self-assurance, but simplified his flight from difficulties; when in difficulty he hid behind her skirts. From the time he was small she had taken especial pains to protect him from harm, as we see in her attitude at the time of the burglary. Whenever the sailing was easy, he was highly successful; but any sort of opposition moved him to despondency and failure. Note the occasion of successes and reversals at school. His entire mental life was dominated by precautionary measures against possible defeats, and when these occurred they were made all the more bitter by his great ambitions and his heroic struggle to overcompensate his supposed weakness. We can find no trace of a spirit of cooperation, or of any sympathy with others, in this individual. All his thoughts are directed toward the end of acquiring prestige for himself.

He was particularly afraid of the opposite sex. This fear of the female was developed not only from the personal humiliations that he suffered at the hands of the younger of his sisters; for as a child, he also experienced the superiority of women in less painful form—through his relationship with his oldest sister and mother. It was almost inevitable that his feeling of social insecurity and uncertainty should take an especially sharp effect in relation to girls. And so, from the very beginnings, he approached them warily, intent upon nothing so much as providing himself with a timely means of retreat from a too intimate relationship. At a very early age (4-8) he recognized the possibility of sexual connection in the sexual play with his sister. Thus he approximated what I have called the feminine type of sexual evasion, and was strengthened in this attitude by the phimosis, which renders all sexual excitement especially painful. Hence we can readily understand why he not only renounces women, as dreaded partners in the sexual act but even repudiates sexuality by and large; he regards it as "bestial," and trains himself in his attitude of rejecting sexuality by such dreams as the dream of the dirty genitals. With such views, it was natural that he should continually strive for superiority over girls, to prevent them from getting beyond his control.

He would certainly never have considered marriage if his mother had not urged him on, and if he had not needed a substitute for his mother's waning attentions. In this conflict he displays the typically neurotic indecision toward the inevitable problems of life. He wants to marry, but at that very moment he becomes impotent. As he says, this was "the hardest struggle of my life." Only when he saw that his wife would not really be "dangerous" to him and would not jeopardize his position of superiority—that he would not be tied down too much emotionally, and that her care of him might serve as a substitute for his mother's care—did he finally decide to marry. In his choice of a wife he seemed to have sufficiently protected his position of ascendancy and found an adequate safeguard against a possible defeat; particularly, as long as his mother was alive, he felt safe enough.

But when she died, he began to look for new guarantees of his position and found them in the same device that his mother had used to bind him more closely to her—insomnia. The fact that he was especially troubled the nights preceding Sundays and holidays, when he was alone with his wife, and the results which this had on his family life, show clearly that his insomnia was a weapon against his wife. By means of this weapon he reduced her more than before to the position of his personal servant, as he himself admits freely enough. His illness makes it possible for him to evade all the consideration due to his wife, and yet compel every consideration of his own needs at the same time that he neglects his wife and home and has the opportunity of shunning all his responsibilities to society and his friends. Thus he can reduce the scope of his life to his own four walls, where he has the best chance of gaining recognition and of exercising complete authority and is least likely to suffer defeats. The necessity of using illness to strengthen these safeguards also arose from his situation at the shop. Here, too, illness served as a sop to his vanity and made his meager success easier to bear. But if he were to lose his job, he would no longer be able to lord it at home in his accustomed manner. In case he should lose his job and his wife were called on to support them, her earning power might even prove greater than his own, and he would be in danger of losing his position of dominance over her. Of course he would guard against such an eventuality—so his complaints must not become severe enough to result in his losing his job. We can understand why his symptoms have become noticeably worse in recent days; and also why they have not been severe enough to make it necessary that he give up his job.

This patient also provides an excellent illustration of the relation between sexual intercourse and neurasthenia, and shows particularly the meaning and significance of coitus interruptus. He knew the supposed injurious effects of coitus interruptus from "doctor books," which neurasthenic patients almost always read to provide themselves with new weapons against their environment. Nevertheless, he did not give up the practice—supposedly because he could not do without it since he was determined to avoid a pregnancy and the erection subsided if he attempted to slip on a cover. When I spoke with him about it, and asked him whether he had tried having his wife put on the cover, he indignantly declared that he could not expect her to do such a thing, his wife being so terribly modest—so he claimed—that she would not even talk about such matters! But the wife, when I spoke with her personally, proved to be very intelligent and reasonable and not in the least prudish. She did refuse to apply a pessary, because of the common prejudice against it; but she declared herself willing to follow my instructions. And now the patient's behavior was very typical. He suddenly discovered that intercourse overtaxed his strength; that afterwards he slept more poorly than ever; and that, even if he did happen to sleep soundly after intercourse, he developed the same complaints as if he had not slept at all. Therefore, in the interest of his health, he said, he preferred to give up sexual intercourse altogether.

Thus we see that coitus interruptus in this case is clearly a device for evading complete surrender in the sexual act. For this, in the last analysis, is what all neurasthenic patients fear most, not only because of the exaggerated battle for personal prestige that these individuals wage with the opposite sex, but also because complete sexual surrender constitutes the most intimate possible union between two human beings.

This patient also shows how useful a seeming physical weakness—the so-called "neurasthenic predisposition"—can be in the struggle against assuming the responsibilities of living. Toward the end of the treatment—then the patient, because he understood the significance of his conduct, was already undertaking a revision of himself, and hence no longer needed the pretext insomnia—he still tried for a while to disparage the importance of the psychic factor in his recovery by attributing his improved sleeping to the use of a malt drink. Earlier he had attempted to prove the efficacy of certain other measures against sleeplessness. The application of bandages to his head, for example, never failed to protect him from the disadvantages of his methods of warfare. And it is very significant that he could always sleep soundly when he had a head cold. Since the cold guaranteed him the necessary concern and consideration on the part of his environment, he did not need his insomnia.

From the brief discussion of these two cases we can see that the complaints of the neurasthenic patient become meaningful and completely understandable when we know his secret aim. But the use of these expedients by a discouraged individual presupposes a definite training. This preparation is begun in childhood, when, because of an organic inferiority or a mistaken attitude on the part of the parents, the child becomes aware that he can use physical ailments as a means of achieving recognition or of evading the unpleasant responsibilities imposed by living in a community. The multiformity of the neurasthenic symptoms results from the variety of the training. The neurasthenic patient is usually a pampered child who does not ensure himself against a specific danger, but matches his physical weakness against all comers—against all the duties of life. Much the same is also true of the organic neuroses and the neuroses resulting from war experiences or after accidents.

Naturally the love-problem plays a significant role in the lives of all these discouraged individuals, chiefly because the complete surrender, without which true love is inconceivable, cannot be reconciled with their strong desire for "guarantees" and "safeguards." Disturbances in the sex life are always the result of a mistaken attitude toward life, and they are always inseparably bound up with a peculiar notion of the nature of love and the relation between the sexes. Only if we completely abandon the attempt to understand an individual's behavior for its own sake and fail to see his behavior as his way of relating himself to his social environment and his way of answering the problems with which life confronts him, can we bring ourselves to the point of assuming, as the psychoanalysts do in their conception of neurasthenia, the existence of some sort of special energies, "drives," or the like as causal factors. In point of fact, the condition alleged to be an anal fixation occurs very frequently in neurasthenics. It results from the utilization by children of natural biological processes in their struggle against their parents, whenever the parents—as Reich says, pay too much attention to the anal functions. But, under some conditions we may also find especial importance attached to the ingestion of food, as in our Case 1. Hence, so-called "anal fixation" is by no means a necessary integral part of neurasthenia. Likewise, it is by no means true that derangements of the sexual powers always assume the form that Reich describes as genital asthenia. There is a suggestion of this sort of disorder in our Case 1, it is true. But even when there are no symptoms of hysteria, of anxiety, or compulsion neurosis, we will find all varieties of sexual derangements present in neurasthenic patients. A sharp distinction between the different types of neurosis is possible only if we presuppose in each instance the existence of a distinct and definite type of disturbance in energy apportionment and consumption; and, if we do this, we deprive the symptoms of any sort of intelligible relationship. In following this procedure psychoanalysis has deserted the realm of psychological consideration. And this has shown itself to be a grave mistake. Instead of the vague notion of general human degeneration which dominated the earlier studies of neurasthenia, we have a new obscurity not much less mystical—the doctrine of human "drives" and the impeding of their development in childhood.

Here we can see one of the reasons why Individual Psychology meets with opposition. One might think that understanding of psychic connections would take a great load off people's minds. But experience has shown that no one really enjoys admitting to what a great extent his neurosis is evasion and alibi. Freud's doctrines met with great resistance at first, because people were actually ashamed of their sexual lives. But finally this sense of shame was broken down and unlocked from the dungeon in which sexuality had been imprisoned in the interests of the prevailing "masculine" order of society. Enlightenment in sexual matters was impossible unless women, too, were freed from ignorance. Today open admission of sexuality is often made, and sometimes even pride is taken in perversions and incestuous passions. (Cf. Our modern belletristric literature!) A theory which comfortably puts all responsibility on "drives" and suppressed instincts is often welcomed by the discouraged individual as a pat excuse for all the failures in his life. But Individual Psychology makes the individual responsible for what he does.

Our attempts to reduce the prejudices and superstitions attaching to the problems of neurasthenia and to understand the real nature of the problem will continue to encounter difficulties as long as people look upon their social obligation as a secondary consideration and their personal security, their struggle for prestige, as the prime concern. As long as this attitude is current, they will keep on hunting for some sort of fatality—something they themselves cannot do anything about, on which to place the blame for all the errors that hold them back from human cooperation and prevent them from finding proper places in human society. And the old notion of neurasthenia—the belief in a debility of the nerves as the physical basis of the complaint—or the newer notion, the theory of the somatic effect of repressed sexual energy, or libido—provides the best possible grounds for shirking the real issue.

See the section "Sexualneurasthenic" in Alfred Adler's *Das Problem der Homosexualität.* (2nd ed.), Leipzig: 1930, p. 78ff.

THE SOCIO-PSYCHOLOGICAL DYNAMICS OF PHYSICAL DISABILITY*

Since Alfred Adler first presented his theory of behavior based upon organ inferiority (1907), the terms "organ inferiority," "Inferiority feelings," "Inferiority Complex," and "Compensation" have been widely used. Many authors investigated the application of Adler's concepts to pathological conditions where inferiorities are an outstanding feature. No condition lent itself as readily to such investigation as physical disability. Here the inferiority is obvious; and it is only natural to seek a clarification of the impact of this inferiority on the development of the personality and on the process of social adjustment. Many authors explored Adler's theory, but their findings were extremely contradictory. It is the purpose of this paper to clarify the position of Alfred Adler and his co-workers and to show how and why so much disagreement is possible in regard to its validity, exactness and testability.

Most investigators, studying the psychological and social problems of the handicapped child and adult, use a statistical approach. A great variety of tests are applied and these are compared with the findings of their normal equivalent. The results of the various investigations contradict each other. Some investigators find the physically handicapped child shy, emotionally unstable, retarded or below normal intelligence (11, 18, 20, 22, 25), while others come to opposite conclusions (15, 17, 21, 26, 28).

* *Journal of Social Issues*, 1948, 4, 39-54.

Barker, et al, state in their excellent review of the latest research on this problem, that "personality tests of the inventory type have not differentiated between physically disabled and physically normal persons" and that "present day tests of the inventory variety are not suited to this problem."

Most investigation of the factors which may determine adjustment is of a rather mechanistic nature. A great variety of factors are mentioned as influencing the development of the handicapped child. Duration, severity, or changing degree of disability seem to have some correlation to maladjustment, although it cannot be considered as high (Barker). Many authors put the emphasis on the parental attitudes which are mainly described as over-protection or rejection. Allen and Pearson believe that the behavior difficulties of crippled children arise in response to faulty parental attitudes rather than as a reaction to physical disability as such. Kammerer expresses the mechanistic tendency clearly when he states that the occurrence of maladjustment seems to depend upon the number and severity of the problems with which the child is confronted. Barker puts his finger on the important point when he deplores that few investigators are concerned with the attitude toward their own disability.

This is the crucial point of departure between a mechanistic and a dynamic concept. Most prevalent descriptions of intrapsychic, psychosomatic and sociopsychological conflicts and relationships are based on mechanistic formulations. The genetic emphasis on hereditary factors is equally mechanistic as the behavioristic analysis of environmental influences. Even the efforts to describe the interrelationships between hereditary and environmental influences on the development of the personality structure result in a mechanistic picture of a struggle between antagonistic or supplementary forces. The present psychosomatic literature is full of such mechanistic formulations, describing the conflict of emotional, instinctual, and biological forces with each other or with the social demands pressing upon the individual. The influence of society and culture upon the individual is also mostly described in terms of a mechanistic interaction. A good example of such rigid thinking is given by

Allport: "Strong bodies, well-formed and socially approved, predispose people to develop extroverted, realistic, sociable traits; conversely, frail, malformed or markedly atypical physiques tend (in response to social and environmental standards) to produce introverted, intellectual or artistic personalities." Barker expressed a similar idea in a much more dynamic manner. "A person who lives in a culture where social distinctions are made upon the basis of age, sex, race, stature, beauty, or physical normality will behave, upon observing his own physique, in accordance with his evaluation of these criteria." The inclusion of the words "in accordance with his evaluation" makes this a dynamic statement. The individual is no longer regarded as a mere battlefield of forces within and around him, but as a decisive factor in the process of integration of physiological, psychological, and socio-cultural stimulation.

It is the contribution of Alfred Adler to have introduced to medical and applied psychology the dynamic concepts of the individual, who determines by himself what significance the forces have which affect him from within and from without. Adler developed his Individual Psychology (the psychology of the Individual, of the unit which is indivisible) in accordance with similar concepts of Gestalt-psychology and of Wilhelm Stern's Differential Psychology. All three emphasize the undivided totality of a person. For them, recognition of the entity of each individual provides the only basis for an understanding of his function and his problems. Adler's approach was less theoretical and general than the other two, because he was more concerned with the analysis and the therapy of individual patients. Consequently, he developed a concrete and applicable technique of psychological investigation and treatment.

Oddly enough, Adler's first psychological investigation attempted to demonstrate the organic factor in the development of neurosis and psychosis. Therefore, it was a mechanistic concept which evolved. In his study of organ inferiorities Adler says, "This work aims to refer all phenomena of neurosis and psychoneurosis back to organ inferiority, to the degree and nature of the not quite successful central compensation and to compensatory disturbances which enter into the matter." The psychic conflicts arising within the person or from the social environment are described as follows: "When the psychical impulse arising from physical needs—through insufficiency of the organs, or the pressure of life and culture—meets with more unserviceable brain material, when the compensatory activities only get half way, a condition of high psychic tension must arise from these psycho-physical relations, causing those persons . . . to be no longer capable of contending with any sort of heightened requirements." One must keep in mind at this time Adler was still under the influence of Freud's mechanistic and almost chemical formulation of libido-economy. Adler, too, spoke of "pleasure-seeking dispositions," and of the "satisfaction of the nutritive apparatus, restricted by the social organization." But there is already a slight indication of his later dynamic formulation: "The mastering of children's defects, and all the difficulties which arise from the inferior organ, point to compensatory activities in the superstructure. They really represent . . . lines of direction from life of the psyche and are signals which indicate the peripheral and central inferiority which has not yet been successfully overcome." This is an obvious reference to psychic life seeking its own directions.

Without realizing it at first, Adler departed with this investigation from Freud. With it he laid the foundation for a dynamic concept of the indivisible personality. In examining the outcome of inferiority feelings, he discovered the dialectic nature of compensation, which biologically is always an overcompensation. This book was a first groping. In his later works, Adler enlarged and clarified his position. Therefore, investigators who use this first book exclusively as their reference, cannot do justice to Adler's concept and contribution. They suffer from another source of misinformation, namely the poor translations which make Adler's early English books difficult to understand.

Organ Inferiority

Crookshank gives a comprehensive review of Adler's dynamic concept of organ inferiority. He says, "The individual may apprehend his inferiority (a) on the somatic level, (b) on the sympathetic level, (c) on the psychic level. In a child with a club foot, the other leg may, as it were, try to grow stronger to compensate. This is a somatic compensation and is hardly realized consciously by the patient. On the functional or sympathetic side, the body may assume a peculiar habit of walking; but on the psychical side the patient may be conscious of it and will deal with it as best he can." The essential statement, characteristic of Adlerian psychology and found in all publications by Adler and his co-workers, is "The personality is not determined by the inferiority, but by the reaction of the individual to the inferiority."

Adler constantly developed and enlarged his formulation of compensation. A few years after the "Study" he spoke of the compensation-ideals which "represent the directive and emotionally steeped preparations of the psychic life of the neurotic." The element of courage became for him the decisive factor in determining the outcome of any inferiority feeling. He states: "A good compensation will be made only where there are courage and a favorable situation." He clarified further the dialectic and not mechanical interrelationship between inferiority and compensation by stating, "By courage and training, disabilities may be so compensated that they even become great abilities. When correctly encountered—(note the conditional and not automatic result!)—a disability becomes a stimulus that impels towards a higher achievement . . . Those who have attained remarkable success in life have often been handicapped in the beginning with disabilities and with great feelings of inferiority. On the other hand we find that a person who believes himself to be the victim of inherited deficiencies and disabilities, lessens his efforts with a feeling of hopelessness, and his development is thus permanently retarded."

Adler considered organ inferiority first as a morphologic and/or functional disturbance of a physiological nature which, he assumed, exists in any case of personal maladjustment. Later he restricted the term organ inferiority to the more definite conditions of physiological weakness, but enlarged the concept of inferiority feelings to encompass more than merely organ deficiencies. The basic inferiority feeling became a social phenomenon as Adler recognized the desire to belong to the group as a prime motivation of human beings. Inferiority feelings are based on a correct or incorrect assumption of social inferiority, primarily in early childhood. The application of this principle to the problems of physical disability were often and clearly described by Adler. He stated:

"Physical defects, whether congenital or acquired, invariably cause feelings of inferiority, and we can generally trace a special effort to compensate for the specific defect." (4, p. 39) "Children with imperfect organs . . . are overburdened. They may become discouraged by comparing themselves with those around them and . . . their feelings of inferiority may be stressed by the pity, ridicule or avoidance of their fellows . . . they may consider themselves personally humiliated by the world."—"The responsibility for failure cannot be placed upon hereditary or physical conditions. No imperfection of organs compels a mistaken style of life. We can often see children who overcome these difficulties and who, in overcoming them, develop unusual faculties for usefulness."—"From the body we cannot judge whether the development of the mind will be bad or good. However, the greatest part of children who started with imperfect organs have not been trained in the right direction. Their difficulties have not been understood. For this reason we find such a great number of failures amongst those children who . . . were burdened with imperfect organs." (In all these statements the term "imperfect organs" refers to any organic deficiency, from a slight disfunction to a severe disability.)

In the same book Adler states, "Imperfect organs offer many handicaps, but those handicaps are by no means an inescapable fate. If the mind is active on its own part and trains hard to overcome the difficulties, the individual may very well succeed in being as successful as those who were originally less burdened. The handicap may be a stimulus to go further ahead. Thus an imperfect organ can turn out to be the source of great advantages; but only if the mind has found the right technique for overcoming difficulties." About this right technique he said, "Only a child who desires to contribute to the whole, whose interest is not centered in himself, can train successfully to compensate for defects. It is not the organic deficiency which is to blame for failure, but our method of education. If we used the right method, children with organic deficiencies would be interested in others as well as themselves. A child burdened with imperfect organs is only interested in himself alone if nobody is at his side to develop his interest in others."

This idea of interest in others was called by Adler "Gemeinschaftsgefuehl" and translated into English in many ways; the last term used by Adler was "social interest" or "social feeling." It became Adler's basic concept of human motivation. All maladjustment and psychopathological conditions appeared to him as consequences of restricted or inadequately developed social interest. Its restrictions are always based on an inferiority feeling, substituting the prime desire toward participation with a compensatory drive toward self-elevation. In his last book Adler discussed the relationship between organic defect and the development of social interest. "Organic inferiority . . . may have misled the child into forming his particular style of life and may have cramped the development of an adequate amount of social feeling."—"Early illnesses that impair the physical . . . development may also lead to more or less serious deformities . . . are most likely to do injury to the social feeling (if) the anxiety and care of the persons around the child give him a great sense of his personal worth without his contributing anything himself."

Adler's Basic Concepts

A great number of publications by Adlerians explain Adler's concepts in great detail. Only a few can be mentioned here, and only those published in English. We may distinguish in our further discussion four points: (1) The dynamic significance of organ inferiority and inferiority feelings; (2) the mechanism of compensation and over-compensation; (3) the concepts of "Inferiority," "Inferiority Feelings," and "Inferiority Complex," and, in line with the latter, (4) the goals to which a disability can be directed.

(1) Crookshank described the dynamics of organ inferiorities as follows: "Regarding the apprehension of the organ inferiority as a stimulus, there are three kinds of responses which the individual may make: 1) Courage leads to compensation, 2) Despair leads to retreat and degeneration, and 3) Wobbling leads to neurosis. The courageous response converts an organ inferiority into a blessing, the despairing response means retreat into disability, and the neurotic response says, 'How much better could I do if I had not this disability!' Wexberg stated, "A defect, harmless in itself, but troublesome or deforming, may severely shake the courage and self-confidence of the child, since he estimates the importance of the organ inferiority only by the outward defects there—of and by his own subjective impression."

The writer stated, "An organ inferiority is never static. It is not something that merely exists. Rather it operates dynamically through the final use to which it is put . . . The decision is simply a question of more or less courage, of whether the child allows the difficulties resulting from an organ inferiority to discourage him or not. On this depends the course he subsequently takes."

(2) The mechanism of compensation, as Adler described it, has been elaborated upon and clarified by many authors. We shall mention only a few. Shoobs stated, "Physical inferiorities may bring about not only physical compensation, but also a mental reaction or attitude towards this extra handicap in life. Neither body nor mind will tolerate an inferiority, a weakness or injury. An immediate compensation takes place to improve this unfavorable condition." He reiterates Adler's biological principle of compensation: "Nature responds to a deficiency or inferiority in three ways: 1) Successful overcoming or compensation, 2) Complete breakdown of the organ or part affected, 3) Exaggerated over-compensation."

Beran Wolfe specified some ways of compensation. "Compensation for defects, whether real or imagined, may be effected in the following ways:

1. By training the defective organ or faculties, in which case the function of the inferior organ may frequently become superior to that of a normal organ.
2. By substituting the function of another healthy organ for that of the inferior organ.
3. By the development of a situation in which the defective organ is advantageous.
4. By the construction of a 'psychic superstructure' of compensation in which the whole organism reacts in such a way that the extraordinary sensitivity of the inferior organ or function is translated into socially useful behavior.

Alexandra Adler stated, "Persons having a definite organic inferiority may be thus stimulated by their handicap, and in fighting to overcome the difficulty they frequently develop beyond the average, because they strive harder than the others .... In these individuals one can trace the process of compensation and of over-compensation to their initial handicap, leading to a successful solution of their problems."

(3) The term "Inferiority" presents serious semantic problems. The words "inferiority," "inferiority feelings," and "inferiority complex" are used in the literature without sufficient differentiation. A clarification of each term is imperative.

Inferiority can refer to any objective inadequacy in function or in status. But it does not necessarily produce an inferiority feeling. A person may be weak, deficient or of low status without any realization of inferiority. On the other hand, an inferiority feeling may exist without any real inferiority. The decisive factor in the dynamics of inferiority feelings is the person's assumption of being inferior, either physically, socially, or in comparison to his own goals and standards. This assumption may not always be expressed on a conscious or verbal level as the individual may not be fully aware of it. However, it can be easily detected in a psychiatric-psychological examinnation. Only the inferiority feeling can stimulate a compensation on the part of the individual. The situation is different in regard to biological inferiorities and organ deficiencies, because the whole organism takes them into consideration and may, therefore, prompt biological compensations and over-compensations, without any necessary awareness by the individual.

The term "Inferiority Complex" applies to an entirely different psychological mechanism. A discouraged individual may use a real or assumed deficiency for the purpose of special benefit, generally as an excuse or an alibi for nonparticipation and withdrawal, or as a means to get special services or consideration. This is the only type of inferiority of which the individual is fully aware, as he tries to impress others and his own conscience with the magnitude of his defects. The "Inferiority Complex" does not lead to any compensation. It is a deadlock for any further development.

Alexandra Adler clarified the difference between feeling of inferiority and inferiority complex. "We say that a person is suffering from 'an inferiority complex' when he reacts fatalistically to a crippling situation without attempting to correct or improve it. This should not be confused with the 'feeling of inferiority' which is present in everyone in certain situations, particularly in every child—a feeling which normally incites an individual to achieve future successful development."

The writer discussed the dynamics of the inferiority complex by describing as one of the four goals of the disturbing child his effort to "demonstrate his inadequacy"; "A child . . . may be discouraged to such an extent that he cannot hope for any significance whatsoever . . . Then he gives up in discouragement and refuses participation and functioning. There seems to be no sense in doing anything if it will bring only defeat and failure. This defeat, then, looms as the greatest danger, and the child tries his best to avoid it, by proving his inadequacy to himself and others. He uses his inability as a protection so that nothing should be required or expected of him. In this way he tries to avoid more humiliating and embarrassing experiences." (14) This point is later qualified: "It must be determined whether the child refuses participation in order to gain attention, to defy authority, to punish or hurt, or just because there is nothing to be hoped for. In the latter case the child seeks excuses and hides himself behind an inadequacy which may actually exist, but more frequently has been suggested to him by his environment. Sometimes the child assumes an inadequacy out of a wrong interpretation of certain experiences and succeeds in impressing others with it."

(4) We have already mentioned some of the purposes and goals which can be obtained through deficiencies and disabilities. Dukes, in discussing Adler's concept of organ inferiorities, stated "Physical defects and illnesses are not necessarily injurious. We begin to see that they fulfill a purpose and may have significance and value to the sufferer."

An Experiment

For example, of 80 severely crippled children, 36 were described by their teachers and housemothers as tending to use their disabilities deliberately, although not necessarily consciously. Twenty-four of them used it for attracting attention. A characteristic form of an inferiority complex was exhibited by the children who were described as using their disability for special help, making themselves appear more helpless than they really were. Ten children fell into this group. Five tried to get special sympathy by displaying their disability, and seven exaggerated their helplessness to avoid necessary tasks.

The applicability of the Adlerian concepts and techniques to the problem of physical disability can be best demonstrated in the discussion of individual cases. For this purpose three children were selected who had the same physical defect: all three had a congenital paraplegia with severe atrophy of the lower extremities, caused by spina bifida. One youngster was bitter, revengeful, expressing his hatred and unhappiness very openly. The second one was pleasant, apparently well adjusted, neither striving too hard nor avoiding tasks nor social relationships. The third was a go-getter, highly ambitious, who was determined to go through college despite the fact that she had no home, no money and had never been out of her wheel chair. Only a few striking facts, ascertained by reports and through interview, shall be presented here, omitting, out of necessity, many details and aspects of each case in short resume.

Case No. 1: Edward, age 19, responds readily, but in a curt way and not too frankly. He is most outspoken when he complains. And he complains easily, as he does not like anything around him. He does not like it at the hospital (although almost all the other children express enthusiasm). He says he has nothing to do, just sit around. He would like to listen to the radio, but finds fault with the one which is there. When asked about his relationship to the other children, he answered that he knows all the nurses. When asked about the food he replied, "The food here is slop." He felt that he had been pushed around and was now "shoved aside" and "stuck" in another institution—the report from the staff indicated that he uses the words "stinks" and "smells" frequently, when he wants to register dislike. He is quite opinionated and angered by those who take an opposite view. He shows a distaste for children who cannot use their hands, while he can use his. He gloats if others have to wait for help and he can get what he wants. He enjoys seeing people in uncomfortable and embarrassing situations. He is very much concerned with sex and was observed several times masturbating and in an act of exhibitionism. He wants a great deal of service. He had been at home until a few months ago when he came to the hospital. Asked about his future he indicated that he never gives it any thought.

Family Constellation: Edward has two older sisters, four and five years older, and a brother, two years older. His information about the members of his family is scanty, although he indicated that his oldest sister and brother are rather similar in character and temperament while the second sister was not very ambitious, quit school and did not amount to very much. He liked both parents—so he says; his father was the one who punished him. He never played with other children, was most of the time by himself. Father played with him a little when he was small, seldom one of the other siblings. He listened mostly to the radio and was taken out by one of his sisters in his wheel chair. He learned to read, but found no pleasure in it. The sisters read to him from time to time.

Earliest Recollections: It was difficult at first to solicit an early recollection, as the boy was not too commital in regard to personal information. Finally he told of an incident when he was four years old. He fell off a radiator when sitting and looking out of the window. He fell on one leg, burned it and got a scar.

Summary: Although the information about Edward's early childhood is very inadequate, a few important facts seem obvious. He was the baby of the family, and apparently did not have many opportunities to experience his own strength and to make any contribution. He depended entirely on the service of others for his social position. But he has not even learned to win others, as he can only demand and complain; therefore, he does not receive enough service and becomes necessarily disappointed. His earliest recollection demonstrates his outlook on life. He is an outsider, an onlooker, but even in this position he finds no safety. Left by himself he is lost and only gets hurt. His disability probably plays an important part in the development of his life style and of his exaggerated sense of helplessness, with which he can intensify his demands on others (inferiority complex). However, similar attitudes and concepts are not too rarely found in people without any disability. His handicap made his position in his family only more precarious, and facilitated his mistaken interpretation of life that one can receive things without doing anything. The important conclusion is that Edward did not develop much social interest, no courage and self-confidence. This is the basis for his social maladjustment.

Case No. 2: Frank, age 15, is well developed and rather mature looking for his age. He is frank in his answers and pleasant in his responses. He came to the hospital a short while ago. He was at home before he came here and had teachers visiting him for instruction. He had only a few friends as he could not go out. At the hospital he is happy, goes to school, participates in many activities, has many friends, and is liked by them. There is no complaint about him nor does he complain about anything or anybody.

Persons who do not have any practical experience with this type of examination may find it difficult to follow our conclusions. Briefly: the family constellation indicates the position of the child within the family set-up and the type of relationship which he established. The description of the personalities of brothers and sisters permits a comparison of the means by which the patient and other members in the family sought and found their social position in the group. The earliest recollections indicate the life style, the general outlook on life, as only those events are remembered which fit into this general outlook. From the family constellation and the earliest recollections one can deduct a person's attitude toward himself, towards the group and towards life.

Family Constellation: Frank has one sister, ten years older. The mother took care of him and played with him a great deal. He did not get along so well with his sister, who was in many ways unlike him. She was more persistent, trying to be independent. She argued with him at times, corrected him when he did something wrong, like making a mistake at the piano. Frank felt closer to his parents, even more so to his mother. When he was small he had curly hair and people thought he was a little girl. He always tried to please, but was stubborn at times.

Earliest Recollection: He remembers that, when he was not more than one or two years old, somebody said, "Isn't this little girl cute?" He neither minded nor enjoyed this remark. When he was eight years old he was sitting with his parents at the lunch table when a whistle blew. He asked what it was, and father told him that the war had started.

Summary: Frank is also the baby of the family, but he learned how to win service in a pleasant way. He had a friendly relationship with his mother, while his sister increased his feeling of smallness and weakness by her attempt to demonstrate to him her superiority. He in turn tried to please and to get his position through conformity. His acceptance of life is, however, not without inner reservation. The earliest recollections indicate on one side the charming little being, which obviously is the role which he still plays, although not as a man. The second recollection shows clearly his distinction between the hostile world outside and the protection within his own family circle. He can conform when he is with a person who is friendly to him, like mother, but is unable to cope with the situation where he has to contend with a stronger force, like his sister. He has sufficient social interest to permit an adequate social adjustment in a friendly and sympathetic group. However, his self-confidence and courage may not be great enough to bear up under adverse circumstances. His physical handicap might have added to his inability to assert himself against his older sister.

Case No. 3: Eva, age 18, is described by the staff as an extremely independent, ambitious, logical, brilliant and well-adjusted girl, except for a violent temper. During the interview she was very pleasant and answered easily and fully, without hesitation, mostly with a smile. She is a very pretty girl with a winning personality.

She was in another institution for six years before she came to the hospital. She did not like it there. She felt too restricted and was kept in bed all the time. Here she likes it very much. She feels that she gets a chance to do things and feels treated like a normal person. She graduated just recently from high school, now she is taking a college correspondence course, and expects to go to college as soon as crutches will be fitted for her. (It is not yet certain whether this will be possible.) She has many friends and feels liked by everybody. She does not want to get married as she is afraid of the hereditary danger to her children.

Family Constellation: She has a brother six years younger. Her grandmother took care of her because her mother was sickly. She died at the birth of her brother. Eva never felt close to her father. He remarried shortly after her mother's death, and Eva did not like her stepmother. She felt her resentment because she required so much care. She does not remember her mother. Father was a reserved person who permitted nobody to come close; he was strict and punished her by spanking with a razor strop. She admits that she was a problem child after her mother's death, refused food, threw up and was spanked for it. She does not remember much about her brother from whom she was separated after a few years. At the end of the interview she refused to be pushed in her wheel chair and insisted upon wheeling herself.

Earliest Recollection: She was three years old. It was Christmas Eve and she was sitting on a little chair in front of a tree, holding her teddy bear.

At the age of six, she went for the first time to school Grandmother took her in a wheel chair which she just got. The teacher put her in an "opportunity room" because she was crippled. Her grandmother did not like that. Eva realized that all the other children were retarded. (Within one year she finished third grade work!)

Summary: Eva was an only child until the age of six, apparently well treated and perhaps over-protected by mother and grandmother. Suddenly she was dethroned, not only by the birth of her brother, but even more by the loss of her mother. She was thrown out of her paradise. From then on she had a life full of hardship. She protested by becoming a problem, refusing to cooperate, and then becoming completely independent, standing on her own against a hostile world. Both recollections reflect this attitude. At the age of three, while she still was with mother and grandmother, she remembers only the situation when she was alone with her teddy bear under the Christmas tree. The picture of peace and pleasantness shows her all by herself, needing nobody else. Then again, when she enters school, she has to stand up for herself against a hostile world. She can show her own ability to those who are unfair to her. There is an obvious desire for superiority to make up for her deep feeling of insecurity within the social group. Her courage seems to be greater than her social interest. As long as she can excel, she might do well. However, a close relationship, especially on the basis of mutual equality, might be difficult for her.

An interesting detail is her reluctance to think in terms of future romance and marriage. Her reference to the hereditary danger is obviously a rationalization. Her pretended inadequacy to function as a woman is a typical inferiority complex. Her real reason for evading sex is her desire to be independent. Her real inferiority feeling is her distrust in close relationships and her assumption that she will be hurt or unfairly treated. Her handicap accentuated inferiority feelings in the outside world, exemplified by her teacher and stepmother. This relationship was in contrast to her early relationship to her mother. For this feeling of physical and social inferiority she compensated with her intellectual ambition. But sex does not fit into this life style.

We are now in a position to evaluate from our Adlerian point of view the subject of disability. The question of how a physical disability influences the personality development and affects the social adjustment cannot be answered through statistical investigation or through tests of the inventory type. Each individual formulates his own response to the experiences and difficulties which confront him and integrates the variety of experiences into one total outlook on life. In the three cases presented we have three individuals with almost identical physical handicaps. In Case No. 1 the disability added to the feeling of helplessness, discouragement and hopelessness and consequently led to social maladjustment. Neither courage nor social interest was adequately developed. In Case No. 2 an adequate compensation was achieved through sufficient development of social interest so that social adjustment was possible. In Case No. 3 the physical disability added to a compensatory drive resulted in extraordinary independence, self-reliance and intellectual ambition. We can see how the personality, the life style of each individual is not only influenced by the disability, but in turn determines the final effect of any physical handicap.

Certain statistical investigations may be of value, if they are not intended to prove values and qualities, but rather attitudes. Past and present attitudes of the individual, their courage or discouragement, their interpretation of themselves and of their condition, will prove to be most decisive in the correlation of disability and social adjustment.

Misinterpretations of Adler

Some confusion in the literature results from semantic difficulties. Barker reviewed the reports of 26 authors and found that feelings of inferiority were mentioned only six times, compensatory behavior five times. In line with our discussion on the term "inferiority feeling" we can assume the authors who referred to this term were impressed by an inferiority complex, not an inferiority feeling as described by Adler. One has to go deeper into the dynamics to recognize the basic inferiority feelings.

We find frequently in the literature references to the Adlerian concept. Many of them are misinterpretations of Adler's position. We shall discuss here some of the characteristic misunderstandings. Eisenson writes, "The Adlerian use of the term compensation differs from our use in that it presupposes the existence of an original weakness, which the individual overcomes by developing it into a strength. No substitute response is involved in the Adlerian concept of compensation." It seems obvious that this author is not familiar with the Adlerian literature. The development of weakness of one organ into strength of the same function is only one of many compensatory possibilities, described by Adler and his co-workers. The very examples which Eisenson gives for compensatory accomplishments are identical with those found in the Adlerian literature. Kammerer found compensatory behavior in 32% of the cases he studied. He reports that compensatory behavior occurred less frequently than timidity or evidences of inferiority feelings. From this he concludes that "There seems to be little support of the Adlerian conceptions." The findings of this author do neither support nor negate Adler's concept. Adler never made any statement about the frequency in which compensation occurs. Whether the individual compensates for his disability or increases his inferiority feeling depends on the conclusion which each individual draws, on his courage and social interest. The relative frequency of one or the other type of response in any incidental grouping of cases does neither prove nor disprove Adler's contentions.

Even authors who seem to agree with Adler often misunderstand him. McKinney for instance found that college students who were considered as poorly adjusted by their fraternity and house mates showed many more signs of physical weakness and bodily defects than those on top of the list as well adjusted students. He concludes from this that Adler's contention of the importance of organic inferiority seems to be supported. But this is only partly true, because Adler emphasized that organ inferiorities may also lead to overcompensation. For this reason the findings of similar defects in the lowest as well as in the top group would prove the ambivalent nature of organ inferiorities.

Barker, et al, recognized that only the early writings of Adler assumed "an unknown, direct, neurological connection between inferior organs and central nervous compensations, (while) in the later developments of this theory this organic basis became more and more tenuous. A purely psychological drive for mastery of protest against inferiority became the central figure, although the reference to the organic basis of inferiority feelings remain." This statement seems to be fairly accurate. But then Barker continues, "As developed by Adler, the theory was untestable inasmuch as criteria of organic inferiority or compensatory behavior were never established." We can agree: life style, courage, social interest, which are the most important factors determining the social adjustment of individuals with physical handicaps, cannot be "tested," at least not with the available method of testing. They require "examination" of each individual. This should not be too objectionable to Barker, who expressed his own doubts as to whether tests are suitable for our problem. The "criteria" of organic inferiority and compensation cannot be established in a general way, as the significance of both factors vary with each individual. The overt behavior and mental, psychological, and social abilities or deficiencies, observed at any one time, do not permit any conclusions about the original conditions and contributing factors without careful investigation of the dynamics of each individual, past and present. Adler's main contribution is the development of a technique which permits a clarification of the psychological dynamics in each case. Only through such an individual analysis can the role of a disability, the existence or absence of compensation, the person's attitude towards his disability, and all the other factors which influence his social adjustment, be established.

It occurs very often that authors argue with the Adlerian concept which they misunderstand, by presenting their own ideas which are really in line with Adler's. Meng is such an example when he says, "Organic inferiority does not have the etiological significance for the development of neurosis which Adler claims; but because of the frequent tendency to overprotect or to reject crippled children, inferiority feelings are common." He, like so many psychoanalysts, quotes only from the earliest works of Adler, ignoring the development of his ideas and theories. In this same way many analysts express Adlerian ideas, without knowing it, while at the same time quarreling with some early statements made by Adler.

We can fully agree with all the many authors who, like Allen and Pearson, Pintner, Lowman, Meng, mention as a fundamental factor in the socio-psychological dynamics of physical disability the effort of the individual to achieve social acceptance. Lowman gives a resumé of this situation with which we can fully agree. "Essential for good adjustment are a sense of security, acceptance by a group and successful achievement." We have to add that in our opinion the only bases for security are courage, self-confidence, and social interest.

Summary

Statistical approaches and inventory tests are insufficient to clarify the relationship between physical disability and personality development, social adjustment and achievements. Each handicapped individual formulates his own response to his disability in accordance with his life style, which can only be determined through dynamic psychological investigation. Alfred Adler developed a specific technique to determine the life style of each individual. This life style is developed in early childhood through the interpretation which the child makes of all the experiences and difficulties with which he is confronted. The disability is only one, although often an important factor. Not what the child has—in hereditary endowment and environment—but what he does with it, is all important. Courage and social interest, or the lack of them, determine whether a disability permits a good adjustment or leads to permanent failure. Any references to Adler's concepts are based on the misunderstandings caused either by knowledge restricted to early and poorly translated works, or by a semantic confusion about the terms "Inferiority Feelings" and "Compensation."

BIBLIOGRAPHY

1. Adler, Alexandra. *Guiding Human Misfits,* New York: MacMillan Company, 1938.
2. Adler, A. *A Study of Organ Inferiority and Its Psychical Compensation, New York:* Nervous and Mental Disease Publ. Co., 1917.
3. Adler, A. *The Practice and Theory of Individual Psychology,* Totowa, N.J: Littlefield, Adams & Co., 1962.
4. ————, *Problems of Neurosis,* New York: Harper & Row, 1964.
5. ————, *What Life Should Mean to You,* New York: Putnam, 1958.
6. ————. *Social Interest,* New York: Putnam, 1964.
7. Allen, F. H., and G. H. J. Pearson, The Emotional Problems of the Physically Handicapped Child, *British Journal of Medical Psychology,* 1938, 8.
8. Allport, G. W. *Personality,* New York: Henry Holt, 1937.
9. Barker R. G., Wright, Beatrice A., and Gonick, Mollie R. Adjustment to Physical Handicap and Illness, *Social Science Research Council Bulletin*, 55, 1946.
10. Brighouse, G., *The Physically Handicapped Worker in Industry,* California Institute of Technology, 1945, Bulletin 13.
11. Brockway, A. The Problem of the Spastic Child, *Journal of the American Medical Association*, 1936, 106.
12. Crookshank, F. G. Organ Inferiorities, *Individual Psychology Medical Pamphlet*, London: C. W. Daniel Company, 1936, No. 16.

13. Dreikurs, R. *Fundamentals of Individual Psychology,* Chicago: Alfred Adler Inst., 1953.

14. ————, *The Challenge of Parenthood,* New York: Hawthorn Books, 1948.

15. Dresdner, Irma, Ueber Koerperbehinderung und Seelische Entwicklung, *Zeitsch, f. Angew. Psych.,* 1933, 44.

16. Dukes, C. Adler's Contribution to the Study of Organ Inferiorities, *Individual Psychology Medical Pamphlet.* London: C. W. Daniel Company, 1938, No. 19.

17. Gates, Mary F. *A Comparative Study of Some Problems of Social, Emotional Adjustment of Crippled and Non-Crippled Girls and Boys,* Madison Wis.: University of Wisconsin, 1942.

18. Lee, J. J. Quoted by Barker (9)

19. McKinney, F. Concomitants of Adjustment and Maladjustment in College Students, *Journal of Abnormal and Social Psychology,* 1938, 31.

20. Malborg, J.N.A. Study of the Relations of Some Physical Defects to Achievement in the Elementary school, *Contributions to Education,* 9, 1922.

21. Meng. H. Zur Socialpsychologie der Koerperbeschaedigten, *Schweiz. Arch. F. Nevr., and Psych.,* 1938, 40.

22. Nilson, K. Certain Intelligence Aspects of a Group of Physically Disabled Pupils in the Minnesota Public Schools, *Journal of Educational Research,* 1933, 26.

23. Pintner, R., Eisenson, Jon, and Stanton, Mildred. *The Psychology of the Physically Handicapped,* New York: F. S. Crofts, 1941.

24. Shoobs, N. B., and Goldberg, G. *Corrective Treatment for Unadjusted Children,* New York: Harper and Brothers, 1942.

25. Strauss, F. The Initiative of the Crippled Child, *The Crippled Child,* 1936, 13.

26. Westenberger, E. J. *A Study of the Influence of Physical Defects Upon Intelligence and Achievement,* Washington, D.C.: Catholic University of America, 1957.

27. Wexberg, E. *Individual Psychology Treatment,* Chicago: Alfred Adler Inst., 1970.

28. Winkler, H. *Psychische Entwicklung and Krueppeltum,* Leipzig: L. Voss, 1931.

29. Wolfe, W. B. *How To Be Happy Though Human,* New York: Farrar Kroger (Ed.), Springfield: Charles Thomas, 1962, pp. 415-417.

This is a part of a research project by the writer under way at the Illinois Children's Hospital School, Chicago, to study the psychological dynamics in severely handicapped children. I am indebted to Mr. Richard Eddy, Superintendent, for his permission to study and publish the material, and to Miss Ruth Ryder, the educational director, for her assistance in compiling the material.

A CASE OF FUNCTIONAL DISTURBANCE OF THE DIGESTIVE SYSTEM*

I have observed that functional diseases of the digestive tract frequently disappear with astonishing rapidity in the course of psychotherapy. This happens in spite of the fact that we often deal with stubborn disease processes of many years standing, which have not otherwise yielded to the most varied treatments, including internal medicine.

The chronic suffering in these cases has generally continued with so little remission that physicians not trained in psychotherapy often get the impression of purely organic, instead of functional, disease.

But in psychotherapeutic treatment, one can recognize that the illness means an evasion of certain difficulties of life. One can only understand these difficulties and their evasions if one has comprehended the life-plan of the sufferer and its contradictions to the logic of human relationship. I reserve the detailed discussion of these connections for a larger work and wish here to give only one striking case.

The patient, in the late thirties, had been under the care of a physician for more than a year and a half, on account of a supposed "catarrh of the stomach and intestines." During that time, she did not digest normally, took medicine constantly, and when excited suffered pain as well. During the last twelve

---

* *International Journal of Individual Psychology*, **1935, 1, 57-62.**

months of this time, she lost a great deal of weight. According to the findings, achylia existed.

The neurological anamnesis showed a rather high grade disturbance of psychic balance. The patient was easily excited, irritable, and tremulous. Under excitement, she developed headache. She was troubled with insomnia intermittently, and had nervous anxiety states in which she imagined various horrors connected with her environment. She was lonely and lived as if on an island. She had been divorced for several years. Her relations with her relatives were not happy and she had no friends.

She threw herself into physical work in order to escape her thoughts and her longing for love and warmth. She was mistrustful, shy and reserved, and had already experienced many disillusionments concerning friends.

The circumstances under which the patient grew up were as follows: She was the last of five children. The eldest, a sister, died early. Of the two brothers who preceded her, the one next to her was three years older. The sister following was four years younger. The father was very strict and hot-tempered and preferred his sons to his daughters. She was afraid of him. He oppressed her mother, who during her lifetime was hurt and grieved by his conduct and often wept over it. The patient clung tenaciously to her mother although she believed that the somewhat older brother was the darling of her mother's heart.

The first childhood recollections are concerned with her mother. The first thing she remembers is that, at the death of her older sister, her mother was very much shaken, and took her to the cemetery with her. This she considered a mark of great distinction. She was delighted to be taken. The mother could not understand this joy of hers.

This recollection already shows that the patient probably considered the elder sister, who was up to that time the only girl in the family besides herself, more of a competitor than the brother immediately older than she.

We are led even more strongly to this assumption when we remember that she states that the father preferred the brothers. A still further confirmation, is the fact that the mother was annoyed because immediately after the death of the sister, the patient dressed by preference in trousers and wanted to be a boy. The behavior which arose out of the warfare of competition with the brothers will be discussed in greater detail later. Here we wish only to point out that apparently the mother was more concerned with the girls than with the boys. After the death of the older sister, she was especially concerned with our patient as the only remaining girl. Further childhood recollections of our patient confirm this.

She remembers that when she was watching her mother bake bread, she stumbled so that one foot went into a pot of boiling water. As the result of this injury, she was very much pampered. This recollection not only stresses the pampering, but her tendency to wish to be near her mother.

This tendency to wish to be near her mother shows still more clearly in the third childhood recollection. She remembered that her mother was in a sanitarium and that she (the patient) became ill—so it was said—out of longing for her mother.

The first childhood recollection needs no more comment. I can perhaps presume that it is known how childhood recollections contain those experiences which are employed to orient the life-plan.

As a small child, our patient was a tomboy. To her mother's anger, she teased her brothers. She was inordinately ambitious, and wanted to study continually. She was afraid of school for fear there would be something she did not know. For the same reason, she was afraid of her teacher and ashamed of giving incorrect answers.

In this conduct of the patient, we can see the tremendous urge upward. She battled against suppression and very early oriented her life to an ideal of perfection not commensurate with reality. A child who measures everything by such a goal of absolute perfection that she cannot endure giving one incorrect answer, cannot help being disillusioned and disappointed constantly. So from early childhood on, she was always disappointed, although others who did not understand her were at a loss to know why, and could give no reason for it.

She felt that her mother pushed her into the background in favor of her elder brother although really the mother was constantly on her side. Apparently she was in a battle of competition with this elder brother whose three years' advantage in age made him her superior in all accomplishments. But she was not only in competition with her brothers. Later, she was in danger of being slighted when her younger sister was born. This slight she was in time to feel most keenly. Besides these things, the patient suffered apparently from general over-estimation of the masculine role—an over-estimation which she made from the example of her elder brother, and still more from the tyrannical father who ruled the family. Her attempt to play a boy's role, expressed in her rowdyism and in her preference for boys' clothes, presents a protest against the seemingly inferior role of woman.

In general, she took a fighting attitude. This was evident not only in the fact that she teased her brothers, but in the difficulties she made about eating. Making herself a trouble to others was very agreeable to her. Like many other very ambitious school children, she refused to eat breakfast unless by so doing she enjoyed a triumph over her anxious family. It is thoroughly characteristic of the patient and especially important in understanding her, to know that later she was certain that never in her life had she made difficulties for anyone else. We can also understand that in spite of all the power and consideration for others which she enjoyed as a child, she was always unsatisfied with herself, and never valued herself too highly because, measured by her ideal of perfection, everything was valueless. From childhood on, she had sensed "the meaninglessness of life," as she put it. As early as her fifth year, she had the first thoughts of suicide. This was on the occasion of a quarrel between her parents, of which she was the innocent cause.

Later, this wish to die appeared again and again. Her inclination to feel herself wronged and limited was increased still more by a decisive experience. When she was eleven, her mother died. At that time, she received what was to her, perhaps, the strongest proof of her mother's love, and this made the loneliness which followed the more painful. Before her death, the mother told our patient that she was not worried about any of the other children, but only about her.

At the end, the mother told her that she should always think "about mother"; and in everything she did, should ask herself "what mother would think about it." In this way, the close connection with her mother, even beyond death, was fatally fixed. It is therefore comprehensible that from then on, the patient felt completely alone. The father took the part of the boys. When she asked him a question, he scolded and asked her how it was she did not know the answer herself.

Because of her feeling of smallness in comparison to her ideal of perfection, she did not appreciate that she was considered especially clever and a model for the other children.

The little sister tyrannized the governess and the father and was also aggressive toward our patient. She spoiled every pleasure for her and provoked frequent quarrels in which the governess sided with the younger, whom she favored.

At this time, the patient changed her behavior, which ever after kept the essential characteristics notable in that change. Out of her wild behavior came a particular, even a striking, calm. She sat continually with books. She read and studied a great deal. Her fighting attitude no longer appeared openly, but was nevertheless still present and easily discernible to the expert.

To help us understand her fear of a new relationship with a man, her fear of satisfying her craving for love and warmth which never left her after her mother's pampering, it should be pointed out briefly that, added to her bad preparation for living with other people in general, there was her great fear of sexuality. When she was ten, she asked her mother where children come from. The mother made her promise never to ask such questions again until she had some experience herself. The patient kept her promise. She was entirely unprepared for menstruation, knew nothing at all about it, and was very much upset when it occurred. At the age of seventeen, she fell in love with a strange man that she knew only by sight. She loved him only from a distance, but considered even this wrong and sinful. Her husband was the first to whom she gave a kiss and she therefore felt obliged to marry him.

We can well comprehend the life this patient had led so far. She could not get along with people. She felt herself worthless. She assumed a defensive attitude before defeat and disappointment, without knowing that she prepared this situation herself because of her inordinate expectations and deprecation of others. She did not recognize her own hostility. She considered, rather, that others were her enemies, and reacted with the maximum of defense to the slightest injustice done her. Not only herself and other people, but all of life seemed insignificant and unimportant to her, measured by her ideal of perfection. This led her to deprecate everything. Due to her strongly developed sense of justice, she marked every injustice in the world around her. These, too, she used for deprecation. She wanted to help everyone and was angry, disappointed, and disillusioned when her efforts failed. She could not understand that others were outraged by her assaults of will. Even among strangers she did this. A governess once said to her, justly, "You expect too much of people, give too little yourself, and then withdraw from others."

From what we now know, it is not to be wondered at that her marriage was a failure. It was only with great difficulty that she could free herself from her husband, who had turned away from her. One can concede to the patient with hesitation that her accusations about the faults and insufficiencies of others were correct, since no man could fulfill her demand that he be an angel. After this, the greatest defeat of her life, the nervous symptoms first appeared. After this, she did not trust herself to approach people. She withdrew into a narrow sphere of activity, thinking of her dead mother and turning away from living friends. Sharp differences arose even in the very narrow circle of her environment. This general feeling of unpleasantness, bitterness, joylessness was sensibly intensified by the stomach and intestinal symptoms which had appeared a year and a half earlier. Where then did these symptoms come from? Questioned as to the cause of this suffering, the patient answered that she had once injured her stomach and that since that time the discomfort had never stopped. But upon even more detailed questioning, the following came to light. Eighteen months earlier, some friends insisted that she try a health resort in the country. She went with the avowed intention of getting away from the narrowness of her life and finding some diversion and amusement. The first night at the resort, digestive troubles developed which were so bad that she had to go to bed. She left the place within the next few days. That she made no further attempt to get into contact with life after this experience can be well understood. Here too the meaning of this symptom can be seen. By means of it, the patient could carry on her meaningless, joyless, hermit existence in spite of all necessities, all advice—yes, even in spite of her insight and conscience. Considering her inability to discharge any sort of responsibilities (because of her recurring illness) a social life was not to be thought of.

In a strikingly short time, we succeeded in making these connections clear to the patient, who was extraordinarily intelligent. She came to understand that she owed more to the world than the world owed to her. She recognized that her digestive disturbances, as well as her other nervous symptoms, could not be looked upon as a blow from fate, but that they were safety devices; that they were her own active achievement. She took the trouble of correcting her mistakes, her faults of character, of which up to this time she had not the vaguest idea. She began to develop her social feeling and fellowship, which until now she had taken for granted. It is to be understood that this process of inner transformation was progressive, but what was noticeable immediately was the relief from pressure, the renewed joy of hope, and the first attempts to seek and to find again connection with her fellow men.

But perhaps the most striking thing of all was that suddenly the digestive system functioned normally. Once, some time later, the digestive symptoms reappeared, when the patient was burdened by some disagreeable circumstances in her environment and was again inclined to resume her old attitude toward life and people. As soon as she caught herself attempting to retreat and recognized her error, she gave it up. At once the symptoms disappeared.

In conclusion, I should like to point out that in dealing with functional disturbances of the digestive system, we are also dealing with disturbances of the vegetative system. But various observations point to the fact that it is just exactly these disturbances of balance in the vegetative system which are influenced decidedly through the psychic turning toward, or turning away from, the outer world. At any rate, according to my observations, this holds true of disturbances of the digestive tract, as can be seen from the foregoing case.

FRIGIDITY*

Discussion

The term frigidity implies a woman's inability to respond sexually, especially to reach a sexual climax, an orgasm. This condition may be chronic, or she may merely fail to be aroused by one specific partner, usually the husband. The causes for an apparent sexual inadequacy are almost as varied as the individual woman affected. Each case has to be understood on the basis of the specific dynamics of the personality and the situation. Some women, almost deliberately, refuse sexual excitement and gratification, while others may desire it, almost desperately, without ever being "able" to obtain it.

In the first category we find women who consider sex as dirty, shameful, only to be endured as part of a wifely duty. In some cultural groups women considered sex only for the purpose of propagation and to satisfy the male; any positive response on their part was considered sinful. These and similar considerations were prevalent in an autocratic society ruled by man. Frigidity was then almost considered as a "normal" feminine trait, as evidenced by some studies made at the turn of the century. (Dreikurs**) Only a woman not concerned with the satisfaction of her desire was able to accept the demands of her husband as a matter of fact; she was willing to serve, regardless of how much or little he demanded.

* In *Psychosomatic Obstetrics, Gynecology and Endocrinology.* W. S. Kroger (Ed.), Springfield: Charles Thomas, 1962, pp. 415-417.

** *The Challenge of Marriage.* New York: Duell, Sloan & Pearce, 1946.

As woman gained social equality with man, due to the democratic evolution, her demand for sexual gratification as part of her human rights increased. That, in turn, upset the sexual relationship. Previously, men demanded and the woman had merely to decide whether to submit or to deny; cooperation meant merely to be willing, to yield—the rest did not matter. Today, cooperation is much more complex and difficult. It is no longer the question of mere submission on the part of the woman; sexual activity needs her full participation. And this is difficult, since no two people can always want sex at the same time and to the same extent. As soon as one wants more —and it is by no means only the male who does—one feels rejection by the lack of equal desire, and the other imposed upon by the demand which is considered excessive. The disturbed cooperation in the sex may be a reflection of conflict between the partners in general; or, marital conflicts and tension may originate in the sexual relationship. In either case, the conjugal difficulty is the result of both partners operating in a new relationship of equals, where neither wants to be second or submissive.

In this situation, frigidity frequently expresses rebellion. This rebellion may be acceptance of the feminine role because of its assumed disadvantages and lower social status; or the rebellion may be directed against one special male who is rejected as a partner for whatever reason this may be.

Interestingly enough, frigidity may result from over-anxiety to reach a climax. Whoever is over-anxious, tends to defeat himself, since his anxiety usually expresses an underlying pessimism to attain what he desires. On the other hand, any thought during intercourse, not concerning the present enjoyment diminishes the sexual excitement and responsiveness. When a man or a woman begins to wonder about the ability to function, the interest wanders away from the sexual activity, and, therefore, produces exactly what is feared, namely the inability to function. A man then may become impotent, and a woman frigid. The harder one tries, the less one is able to perform sexually. The resultant diminished excitement then fortifies the initial doubt and confirms the existence of an "inability" although this exists only in the mind of the one who considers himself a failure.

Unfortunately, many men and women are so concerned with "perfect" sexual behavior that nothing but the ideal sexual interaction is acceptable to them; anything less is failure. This attitude is becoming most prevalent amongst women since they —in their striving to be equal to men—are becoming increasingly perfectionistic. In comparison to the idealistic picture of what sex should be, actual experiences may become disappointing and unsatisfactory to stimulate desire and gratification; frigidity may be the result.

Some women cannot find full satisfaction in intercourse because their first orgasmic experience during adolescence was of such nature that intercourse could not duplicate that specific sensation. One nymphomanic girl actually went from man to man seeking gratification without realizing that the thrill she experienced and still sought was that which she found while swinging on a swing. Naturally, no male could duplicate this kind of excitement.

Since any lack of full sexual participation can result in frigidity, many incidental factors may contribute to it. Once the assumption of a sexual weakness or deficiency has occurred, a vicious circle may ensue, giving an incidental occurrence of sexual coldness the aspect of an unavoidable permanency. Unfortunately, the fact that frigidity may be caused by such relatively "simple" mechanisms is not sufficiently known, since contemporary psychiatric theories assume in almost each case of frigidity deep-seated unconscious processes which then make any form of sexual deficiency appear as even more ominous. The fear of frigidity is still its most frequent cause.

THE FUNCTION OF EMOTIONS*

Emotions are not held in high esteem today; one can say that they are almost in ill repute. Describing a person as being "emotional" is generally not considered complimentary. Emotions are more or less distrusted. They seem to be irrational, provoking unwarranted actions, are difficult to "control," lead to faulty perspectives and misinterpretations. We witness a tendency to put the blame for any antisocial behavior on emotions. They are considered to represent the "lower" part of human nature, while intelligence is regarded as the higher human level. Emotions seem to pull man down, intelligence up.

A New Mysticism

How could such a universal picture, which is completely fallacious, develop? We can easily recognize a few factors which may have contributed to these concepts. It seems that human progress has been made mostly through the use of intelligence. Science and technique seem to represent strictly intellectual accomplishment. The underlying emotions which have generated such accomplishment are little noticed. Reason was a strong tool in man's struggle for his emancipation from the domination of natural and mystical forces, which previously were considered the masters of man and his fate. Rationalism became the opponent of mysticism, science the only trustworthy approach to the discovery of truth; objectivity became good, subjectivity evil.

---

* *Christian Register*, 1951, 130, 11-14, 24.

Such general cultural tendencies find strong "scientific" support today. Certain schools of thought, which obviously reflect more cultural prejudices than genuine factual evidence, describe man as being besieged by animalistic drives and urges which prevent him from adequate social functioning. A new mysticism, clad in scientific language and using mechanistic formulations, degrades man by assuming the existence of a cesspool within each individual containing all the repressed urges and drives—which then interfere with all good intentions and cause undue hostility and aggression. Little do these scientists realize that such premises would never permit man to gain full dignity, to become fully responsible for himself. Their findings are the more acceptable to the general public, as most people have not yet learned to deal with their own emotions effectively. However, this deficiency is not due to the nature of emotions which elude intelligent direction, but is rather the result of man's failure to understand the dynamics and the significance of emotions. The ideas which shall be expressed here are by no means new. But they contradict many assumptions prevalent in our era.

Epistemological Revolution

Emotions are an integral part of human nature. The total personality includes three main spheres of function, which are integrated and interrelated into one whole, the individual. He has a body and a mind. The latter provides him with the ability to think and to feel. Bodily functions, reason, and emotions are tools which mankind has developed in its struggle for survival. Full function is impossible without the use of all three.

We have a relatively full understanding about the significance of bodily functions; we know a great deal about muscular activity, physiological responses and mechanisms, the constitution and functions of organs and organ systems. And medicine is still progressing and is right now on the threshold of many new discoveries which will further clarify the physiology of the human organism.

The process of thinking presents greater problems. We assume generally that thinking serves merely for the preparation of actions. It is yet relatively little known that thinking can also be used as a substitute for action, producing ineffectiveness rather than stimulating action. The limitations of man's reasoning power became more discernible through new scientific developments in semantics, in physics (through the law of uncertainty), and other discoveries which actually led to a revolution in epistemology, the science of knowledge. But when it comes to the problem of emotions many people would be at a complete loss if asked about the purpose which emotions serve.

Action Requires Feeling

We may easily discover the purpose of emotions when we try to visualize a person who has no emotions. His thinking ability could provide him with much information. He could figure out what he should do, but never would be certain as to what is right and wrong in a complicated situation. He would not be able to take a definite stand, to act with force, with conviction, because complete objectivity is not inducive to forceful actions. This requires a strong personal bias, an elimination of certain factors which logically may contradict opposing factors. Such a person would be cold, almost inhuman. He could not experience any friendship and closeness. He would have to reject any association which would make him biased and one-sided in his perspectives. He could not want anything very much and could not go after it. In short, he would be completely ineffectual as a human being.

We can see now why we need emotions. They provide the fuel, the steam, so to speak, for our actions, the driving force without which we would be impotent. They come into play whenever we decide to do something forcefully. They make it possible for us to carry out our decisions. They permit us to take a stand, to develop definite attitudes, to form convictions. They are the only basis for strong personal relationships to others, for developing interests and for building alliances of interests with others. They make us appreciate and devaluate, accept and reject. They make it possible for us to enjoy and dislike. In short, they make us human beings instead of machines.

The Devil and the Id

It is not so difficult to recognize the benefit and purpose of emotions when we experience them as positive, constructive and helpful. The difficulty arises when we deal with disturbing emotions. Then we fail to see any purpose, any benefit in them. Then we begin to fight them because they seem to hinder us in what we want to do, or better, what we should do. This is the situation in which emotions seem to become uncontrollable. Then we dissociate ourselves from our emotions, as if we were not responsible for them. For this reason we are only too prone to accept theories which regard emotions as strange forces which overwhelm us. For this reason people believed once in the Devil, as they now believe in the Id.

Actually, disturbing emotions are not structurally different from positive and constructive emotions. They are not irrational, only their rationale is not recognized, particularly not by the individual himself. The person or group against which they are directed may have no difficulty in recognizing the purpose of such emotions. To be sure, they all have a purpose. Whatever a human being is doing is purposeful. He uses all his qualities, be they physical or psychological, to achieve goals which he has set for himself.

We Do What We Want

However, it becomes difficult to recognize our goals when they are in conflict with our conscience. We devote much time and energy to preserve the appearance of good intentions. Even if we accuse ourselves, often more than is justified, we try to demonstrate our high moral standards by criticizing ourselves. We have the ability to rationalize, to find good reasons for the worst purpose. This hinders us from taking full responsibility for all our actions. We blame emotions for our inadequate—or asocial actions, for our transgressions or omissions, while actually these denounced emotions are only the servants and tools of our real intentions. If our intentions are not in accordance with our obligations and our conscience, we use suitable emotions to "drive" us. We feel driven by them, while we actually create them. But we do not want to admit this to ourselves; so we set our emotions as masters when they actually are our slaves. A person who loses his temper is under the impression that he cannot control it, that it drives him to do things which he does not want to do. However, there is sufficient evidence that a person in rage can suddenly calm down when somebody enters the room to whom he does not want to display his temper. A closer analysis of temper outbursts reveals that they are usually used to impress someone into submission, to show power, to overwhelm others. But while these intentions are successfully carried out, the person pretends that he has no such intentions. He feels "overwhelmed" by the weakness of his "nerves."

Fallacious Dichotomy

Let us now examine the peculiar relationship which exists between emotions and reason. One generally assumes that there is a dichotomy between intellect and emotions, as if our intelligence would show us one direction and our emotions would drive us to the opposite. The appearance of a divergence between thoughts and emotions indicates always a so-called "rationalization," an assumption of reasons which we actually do not have. A derogatory attitude toward emotions led to the formulation of a distinction between "emotional and intellectual understanding." Such a distinction is nothing but a fallacy. A short story may illustrate this: A father took a walk with his small son. A dog came running after them, barking loudly. The boy ran away, hiding himself behind a tree. The father called to him, "Johnny, don't you know that dogs who bark don't bite?" Johnny, from a safe distance, shouted back, "I know it and you know it; but do I know whether the dog knows it?" This would be classified as a seeming difference between intellectual and emotional understanding. One could say that the boy has intellectual understanding of his father's dictum, but does not understand it "emotionally." The truth of the matter is that his behavior and his words make it quite clear that he surrenders outwardly to his father's opinion, but that he simply doesn't believe it. In other words, what we call "emotional understanding" is an expression of our real beliefs, our real convictions. They come into conflict with our "intellect" only if we do not want to display openly our convictions and beliefs.

We Don't Know Our Own Mind

We can distinguish, as Alfred Adler suggested, between our common sense and our "private logic." Our common sense includes all values, ideas, and concepts which we share with other members of our group; we all agree widely as to what constitutes right or wrong, good or bad, correct or incorrect behavior. But apart from these general principles we have our own ideas about what we can do and what we cannot do. A typical example of such an "inner conflict" is the ambivalence toward a certain duty. We may know very well that we should do it. But at the same time we may be afraid of failure, of proving to be inadequate, or of not getting the desired results and reactions. Therefore, we do not do what we know we should, often expressing our good intentions demonstratively in order to conceal, from others and from ourselves, our decision not to do what we know we should do. What we really think and believe is not illogical at all; but it may differ from what others think we should believe. The private logic is the only basis on which we act. We all act according to our own concepts, our own ideas and plans. They are by no means illogical, once we recognize them. But unfortunately, we do not know our own motivations, the purpose of our emotions.

"Know Thyself"

Our present system of education is predominantly moralistic. Children are taught what they should do and what not. Both at home and in school, emphasis is placed on the development of a conscience and of good intentions; emotional reactions are ignored. The child learns very soon that nothing infuriates the adults more than the open admission of bad intentions. As long as he can find good excuses which demonstrate his good intentions he is less liable to punishment for any misdemeanor which clearly expresses his defiance or other socially unacceptable intentions. Parents and teachers are yet far from understanding the goal of a child's misbehavior and deficiency. Therefore, they try to influence his actions, unsuccessfully in most cases, instead of helping the child to understand his intentions and to change them. We must learn to understand our private logic with its concurring emotions, our actual concepts of ourselves, of our place in the group, of the methods which we choose to gain status and to deal with social conflicts.

As we learn to take the full responsibility for what we feel and what we are doing, we become equipped to deal with our emotions. Realizing their purpose does not change emotions necessarily, although it sometimes does. But it enables us to reconsider our attitudes, our intentions. Once we do that, emotions change and destructive ones disappear. Man, entering the democratic phase of human society, must learn to recognize his own strength, his self-determination, his position as a master of his own fate.

This analysis of emotions demonstrates that reasoning and intellectual mechanism are not foreign to emotions, but rather at the root of them. An intelligent approach in education can change the private logic, the concepts and beliefs on which it is based. But it must be directed toward psychological factors and not limit itself to moralistic and intellectual generalizations. Whoever can change the concept of individuals or groups changes their actions. Any institution which concerns itself with helping human beings in improving their way of life must take this into consideration. This has far-reaching consequences for any liberal religious group.

Guidance—Not Condemnation

The orthodox forms of religion are inclined to limit their approaches to "preaching." They repeat their commands and put pressure on the actions of their followers: pressure of punishment, combined with the appeal of promises. This approach is characteristic for an authoritarian society which tries to impose its will upon its subjects. Rewards and punishment are perfect tools for keeping the subject in line with the demands of a powerful authority which has allied itself with a supernatural authority to enforce its demands. Such approaches fail in a democratic society. They fail in the community as they fail at home and in school. Different approaches must be found to stimulate people to change, to improve, to behave more constructively, to "feel" differently.

People need help and guidance, not criticism and condemnation. We know today that guilt feelings, evoked by such a procedure, are not conducive to improvement. On the contrary, the discouraging effect impedes reform. Guilt feelings, indicating discouragement, are merely a demonstration of good intentions without any change in attitude. Fear, which was so deliberately evoked in an authoritarian society to prevent transgression, is also recognized today as an impediment to courageous and cooperative behavior. Our contemporaries need encouragement, an understanding of themselves, of human motivations, of the psychological factors which motivate good and bad behavior.

For this reason it is encouraging to note that at the Portland Conference Unitarian ministers and lay delegates expressed on many occasions the opinion that a liberal church should make counseling services available to its congregation. This does not, naturally, mean to provide facilities for psychotherapy. But it takes cognizance of the fact that a knowledge of psychological dynamics is essential for us in our effort to become better human beings. Parents need counseling and guidance in dealing with their children; husbands and wives, in meeting the difficult task of a marriage between equals. Our family is permeated with the competitive strife characteristic of our cultural era, where man is pitched against his fellow man, each trying to get ahead of the next one, driven by fear of being found inferior and inadequate. We have to learn how to live in a democratic society as equals with equals, to solve problems by agreement instead of force. As long as we remain illiterate in these regards, unwarranted emotions will constantly interfere with our genuine desire to be good fellow citizens.

Group Therapy in Church

An important and encouraging experiment was made by Dr. J. Raymond Cope, minister of the Unitarian church in Berkeley, California, who introduced group dynamics and group therapy in his congregation. In a sense, every religious service is a form of group therapy, integrating each member, stimulating a feeling of belonging and providing spiritual and moral elevation. Scientifically oriented and planned group experiences can apparently supplement regular and traditional services. Group therapy seems to offer an unusual and vital opportunity to our contemporaries, who live in an emotional isolation, unable to let their hair down for fear of arousing ridicule or losing status. Both religious fellowship and group therapy break down the barriers in which our competitive social atmosphere keeps everyone.

But this is only one aspect of how a liberal religious fellowship can function in the community. The methods indicated so far are directed toward a change of the rational basis for emotional upheavals, for unhealthy emotional reactions, for social inadequacies of the members of the congregation. However, more should be done to keep the congregation together, to enlarge it and to make it a force within the community.

Sterility Without Emotions

In this regard emotions must be recognized and used as an effective approach toward influencing human motivations. Without strong emotions no strong acts are possible. We have seen that strong emotions are an indication of strong desires. And without strong desires nobody is going to do much about anything. We must arouse desires, arouse emotions which link one person with the other and all to the whole. In the past, liberal religion had a tendency to keep itself on a high intellectual level. While avoiding the moralistic generalization, it often substituted for it intellectual generalizations. And these leave people cold. Let us keep in mind that it is the function of emotion to make us forceful in our intentions and goals. Neglecting any deliberate emotional appeal produces sterility and weakness. The question then arises as to what kind of emotions we want to arouse and what methods we can use to this end.

Safety Is Not Enough

We have already indicated some of the main emotions which orthodox religion wanted to arouse and by what means it succeeded. The prime emotions were fear and guilt, the methods were exhortation and threat. Sure enough, there were also positive emotions on which religion played. It was the pomp and ceremony which created awe and stimulation; it was the promise of special protection; it was the safety under the will of a supreme power. All these stimulations of emotion are unusable today, at least for our effort to help man find his own strength, his own dignity, his own social satisfaction. We have to look for new symbols which can provoke emotions of the nature we consider desirable.

Before we can define the emotions which we want to arouse, we must be clear about the goals which they should reach. It seems that we are much more aware of our goals than of the emotions best suited for them. Seeking the truth; striving for liberty and freedom, the establishment of human equality, are some of our main objectives. But even those who agree with us on these principles use their private logic and their emotions mostly for other purposes, like elevating themselves over others, avoiding failure, having power or resisting power, excelling and being a success—in short doing the same as most of our contemporaries are doing. We distinguish ourselves from them perhaps through our intellectual platforms, through different rationalizations by which we seek personal glory and superiority.

Symbols Are Shortcuts

I am afraid that a great deal of our expressed beliefs are often contrary to our personal intentions. Consequently, our actions in our private lives may often not be very different from those of our contemporaries who belong to groups different from ours. True enough, we support different social issues, we take a different stand in questions of politics, national affairs, race relations, and labor rights. But our emotional lives might not show any significant difference when we deal with our families, our neighbors, our jobs. In many cases, belief in truth, in freedom, in equality of man is but lip service. It is questionable whether we Unitarians have amongst our friends and members significantly more people who apply our principles in their private lives than amongst Catholics, Baptists, Jews, or any other religious group on the American scene. Do we have in our rituals strong enough stimulations to motivate us to different attitudes? We do not know which symbols we actually should use. Every strong and forceful group has its symbols, which arouse strong emotions in their followers. Symbols are shortcuts, indicating thoughts, principles and issues through conditioned emotional reactions. The Christian religion has the Cross, standing for Salvation and Redemption; the Jews have the Torah, representing the Law and Social Order, and the Star of David, which is a national emblem, as each nation has its flag, signifying home, family, friends, childhood, language, and familiar customs. We have so far no anthem, no sign, nor anything else which could serve as a strong symbol.

I can see some of my friends shuddering at the thought that they should "lower themselves" to accept symbols. They may consider it childish. Perhaps they are typical intellectual snobs who are proud of being thoroughly rational beings. They prove by such an assumption what fools they are. It is not childish to have emotions—only human. Whoever wants to be superhuman is only less human. Symbols are necessary for any strong social cohesiveness. But symbols do not have to be concerned with anything supernatural, mystical or authoritarian. They could—or should—be concerned with man, standing for freedom, strength, and faith in man. Faith is belief, which means strong convictions. What distinguishes liberal from orthodox religion is the content of the belief. We believe in the dignity and the potential strength of man.

Fear Becomes Sin

It may require considerable thought and study to evolve approaches and methods for the stimulation of desirable emotions. So far, the main source of emotional stimulation in our groups has been a minister or group leader who could generate enthusiasm. This is important, but not enough. It seems that the crucial point on which our whole emotional structure hinges would be a strong emotion about one's self, about one's own value, one's own strength. Courage is an expression of such a positive attitude toward one's self. Deliberate stimulation of courage, of self-confidence, of self-respect, could be planned and executed. We know from psychiatric experience that fear, lack of self-confidence and inferiority feelings are the main reasons for socially detrimental attitudes. Fear must become identical with sin. The dignity of man must begin with the recognition of our own dignity. We must learn to have faith in ourselves before we can have faith in equals. A defeated and frightened creature looks for a superior power to compensate for his own weakness.

It it not the place here to go into more details. But we must offer emotional gratifications if we want to attract people.

The Use of Subjectivity

The function of religion throughout the ages was to unite people, to integrate each individual into one whole, to provide strong stimulations for each member in the group to live according to the social conventions characteristic of his cultural era. Neither of these two objectives was ever accomplished without the generation of emotions.

The recognition of the dynamics of emotions has another far-reaching implication for liberal religious groups. It is characteristic for them, as they are very much concerned with truth, that they stress objectivity as a most valuable human quality. We have already indicated that objectivity has its limitations. What makes us forceful as human beings is our own bias, which is the opposite of objectivity. Because we are all biased, we never can be completely objective. And it is even questionable how far we should be more objective and deplore our own subjectivity. The question is not whether we should or should not be subjective, but what use we make of our inevitable subjectivity. Here our concept of liberty and of the equality of man comes to a test. Do we use our own beliefs to justify or assume our superiority over others? This is the crucial point. If we are sincere in respecting the beliefs and convictions of our fellow men as we respect our own, then there is no danger that our personal bias will do any harm, either to ourselves or to others. The extent to which we are tolerant to others will be a testing ground for our principles. It will prove whether we have accepted these principles only "intellectually" or whether we really believe in them.

THE MEANING OF DREAMS*

Throughout civilization, as far as we know, dreams were considered with great interest. Their puzzling senselessness stimulated human imagination. Their fantastic symbolism made them appear tools of supernatural powers. Past attempts to use dreams for predicting the future and for similar unscientific, magic, and even monetary purposes have discredited dreams so that no serious and honest person would pay attention to them. Only recently has modern psychiatry recognized dreams as an extremely helpful way of exploring the inner life of a person. The analysis of dreams is indispensable in modern psychotherapy.

Dreams are thoughts put into action, mostly of visual nature, animated pictures created by the fantasy of the sleeper. During the deepest sleep the brain probably rests completely, with the exception of the centers of vegetative function. As the sleep becomes more shallow brain activities increase. Free of outside influences the thoughts take on any form which the personality wishes to give them. We dream every night, but we do not remember all of our dreams. Only if the dreams are more exciting or impressive are they remembered after reawakening. The dreams which are remembered occur most often shortly before awakening or in times of very shallow sleep, if the sleeper is half awake through physical irritation or strong outside stimulation. It is experimentally proven that the speed of thought, producing the impression of dreams, is extremely

* *Chicago Medical School Quarterly,* 1944, 3, 4-6, 25-26.

fast and not on the verbal level. Some of the confusion and bizarreness of dreams is due to the ability to have thoughts simultaneously on the non-verbal level. In their dreams, people think in symbols and create form, color and movement in an artistic way. Some people suppress their creative imagination to such a point that even their dreams become dull. Others reveal by the highly artistic symbolization of their dreams their general artistic ability. On the basis of this fact it was possible in some cases to discover special artistic abilities in persons who had not been aware of them before, and to direct their activities in a new field of endeavor.

In order to understand dreams one must be able to understand human thoughts. Normally, thoughts function to prepare action. Only under abnormal conditions can thoughts be used for substituting action as in obsessive ideas, indecisiveness, worries and similar symptoms of psychoneurotic disturbances. The preparation through thinking can again be on the verbal or the non-verbal level. Thinking can serve as deliberate planning of action by leading to conscious conclusions in regard to action and procedure; or the thoughts provoke attitudes and emotions in regard to the problem which has to be solved. It is very rare that dreams provide a logical and conscious answer to problems, even though examples for this are known (finding technical or mathematical solutions in dreams.) In most instances, however, the dream thoughts are not logical and cannot be understood with verbal logic. Nevertheless they are not senseless either, their psychological meaning is evident to anybody who understands the psychology of the dreamer. During sleep, in our dreams, we let our thoughts go and in this peculiar way of thinking-through we approach our problems not differently than we do in our awakened condition. Only while asleep we are completely free to let our thoughts wander, to visualize what we want to see and as we expect it to happen. We can create situations and arrange events without limitation, but in accordance with our attitude. Nobody can dream of anything he does not think of, nobody experiences in his dreams what he does not expect. Therefore, dreams reveal thoughts, expectations, and attitudes.

The attitude which the sleeper takes in his dream has repercussions for the immediate future. Through the picture of the dream a certain emotion is created which then is carried into the new day, regardless of whether the dreamer remembers the dream or not. The dream can be called the "factory of emotions" (Alfred Adler), because that is the function of the dream as a preparatory thought process. Even the most colorless dream has a certain emotional tone which is significant not only of the dream, but for the whole personality of the dreamer in a given situation of life. This emotional training through dreams is probably one of the reasons why dreams appear so "senseless." One cause for this apparent non-sense of a dream is the above mentioned lack of verbal logic. However, it can be proven this is not the only reason why dreams remain obscure. Even the best trained psychotherapist, who has little difficulty in "understanding" the dreams of his patients, fails to grasp the meaning of his own dreams. This reluctance to interpret correctly one's own dream is the consequence of the psychological function of the dream, namely to create certain emotions. All emotions serve the purpose of fortifying attitudes and actions. Their strength lies in the fact that their purpose is not recognized. If one realizes for what purpose one stimulates one's own emotion, let us say, of anger, of fear, of resentment, or even of elation or hate or love, if one would admit that all these emotions are self-created for a very definite purpose in each case—such admission would deprive the most violent emotion of its powerful drive. For this reason dreams must remain shrouded in mystery in order to be effective.

The meaning of dreams can be recognized by an objective and trained interpreter by looking for the purpose which the dream situation might have in the actual life situation of the dreamer. Without knowledge of the patient's problems and conflicts no dream can be accurately interpreted. The same dream might have completely different significance for each person. It is necessary to know what use a certain person could make of such a dream. Some psychiatrists are inclined to regard definite dream elements as standard symbols, which are supposed to have the same meaning always, supposedly of a sexual nature. Our observations do not confirm such assumptions. The dreams are symbolic, but not for each individual in the same way. However, certain generalizations are possible. Traveling in the dream reflects the direction of the dreamer's life; walking on a road or riding in a vehicle generally reflects the direction in which the dreamer moves at a certain time of his life. It is, therefore, significant whether the way goes upwards or downwards, what kind of obstacles have to be overcome and how they are met; whether the way is smooth or rough, beautiful or ugly, safe or dangerous. Flying dreams have different meanings, of course, whether the individual is actually concerned with airplanes or not. In the latter case it is generally an expression of the desire to be above the others, independent, of high position or exceptional ability. Again, the outcome of the flying is significant, whether it ends in a crash or not. Dreams of being examined generally indicate a life-situation in which the patient feels tested. Through the dream he fortifies either a cautious or confident attitude toward the test situation. To dream gives either a green or a red light for going ahead at work, in social contact or in regard to sex. Dreams which occur over a long period of time generally signify more than an immediate situation; they are characteristic for the general outlook of the person. Dreams which are remembered as having occurred during early childhood have the same meaning as early recollections. When a patient, for instance, remembers that as a child he dreamed he was alone in an otherwise empty house which suddenly began to collapse, then we recognize the desire of an only child to impress himself with the danger of being left alone, a concept which probably signifies the whole life style of this individual.

There are dreams which can be easily interpreted. They are so self-evident that everybody familiar with the structure of dreams can easily understand them, with the exception of the dreamer, of course. There are others whose significance is more hidden, where the connection between the content of the dreams and the life situation of the dreamer is not obvious. As a rule, the more the dreamer knows about dream psychology the more confused and complicated his dreams become. People who have not been exposed to psychotherapy or dynamic psychology in general have more obvious dreams. On the other hand, it is often easy to recognize a patient who has read psychoanalytic literature or has been under psychoanalytic treatment. His dreams reveal the characteristic symbolism of this school. During psychotherapy dreams are of special significance. Very often they reveal the attitude of the patient toward psychotherapy.

A patient relates the following dream. He is in a lifeboat with a man, looking for rescue. They see a merchant ship and they steer toward it. Then they see a Japanese warship coming from beyond the horizon to capture the merchant ship. They decide to steer away from the merchant ship to avoid being captured.

It is obvious that the patient sees some danger in being rescued. The discussion of the dream and the present life situation brings an admission from the patient that he is afraid of getting well. Then he would have to face the danger of life. Losing his symptoms would deprive him of an alibi to withdraw as soon as he felt exposed to situations where his prestige or his superiority was threatened. He preferred, at least at this particular moment, to sink, to drown, to go down in disaster, rather than to take a courageous stand in what he considered the battle of life.

The opposite stimulation in regard to therapy comes from the dream of a woman patient: She visits a girl friend who tells her husband of the patient's ailment, how sick she is, how much she suffers. The husband of the girl friend, however, makes a remark that the patient soon will get well. This dream marked the turning point in the treatment of this woman. She had been sick for many years since her husband deserted her, leaving her with a social disease. Without going any deeper in the case history, it may be said that she attributed her ailment and her misery in life to her husband. Previous to the dream she believed that she would never get well. It was for the first time that she envisaged the possibility of getting well —though it was only in her dream! It was highly significant that the statement "She will get well" came from a man because her neurosis was directed principally against men whom she distrusted and feared. Through being sick she avoided contact with men and especially the possibility of getting married again. She needed the strong defense of a neurosis as she felt lonesome and realized the need of finding a new haven. Confronted with the analysis of the dream she acknowledged the correctness of the interpretation by saying, "Yes, I am sick of being sick."

Those two dreams reflect directly the attitude of the patient toward therapy. A sudden inability of the patient to remember dreams is also significant. It might be either a protest against the therapist or against certain conclusions derived during the therapy. Sometimes the patient does not want to admit to himself what is going on in him. There are certain individuals who never remember dreams, others who even get furious if anybody mentions dreams. I had a patient who not only did not remember any dreams himself, but reported how angry he got when he overheard his two daughters relating dreams to each other. He could not understand how intelligent people could waste their time in paying attention to such silly and senseless experiences like dreams. What he did not realize was his reluctance to admit his inner problem to himself. He had developed an idea of himself which was in no way in accordance with his real opinion. A certain type of ambitious people, who are able to sell themselves and their environment the picture of being a strong man, refuse to admit to themselves their fears and their feeling of inadequacy. Their pride stands in their way to self-recognition. Once they become courageous enough to face themselves as they really are, they also remember their dreams which, then, often show the symbols of danger and threat. Those individuals are the same who often find it difficult to relate early recollections.

A typical example of such a type was a young man who could be considered highly successful. He had an influential position, was socially well liked and rather popular with men and women alike. He developed symptoms of impotence as soon as he considered getting married. It took him a long time to be convinced, after many unsuccessful attempts at medical and physical treatment of his impotence, that he needed psychiatric help. He was very slightly productive, did not have any dreams, nor did he remember anything of his early childhood. He denied any inferiority feelings and refused to recognize his impotence as a defense mechanism against getting married. Only after many consultations did he lose his defensiveness against the psychological approach to his problem. Then dreams appeared when he felt attacked or was confronted with a situation of helplessness. Only then did he remember an incident which occurred when he was three years old. He was standing in the garden on a lawn. On the other side of a small path of pebbles stood his uncle, a man who was regarded with great respect by the whole family. (He was an outstanding scientist of considerable fame.) Patient remembers seeing this uncle on the other side of the path and himself crying for help, because he was afraid of walking by himself over the pebbles. This situation shows what the patient, the only son of an over-protective mother, really thought of himself. He had tried all his life—and successfully—to hide from himself and others that he did not consider himself a real man. We can understand his masculine inferiority when we realize that he compared himself with his famous uncle. That was the incentive to his success, but also the cause of his retreat, when his ability to play the role of a man was really put to a test by the threatening marriage. His willingness to remember his earliest recollections, and thereby to admit to his inner feelings, was a prerequisite for remembering dreams.

The need to use dreams in psychotherapy emanates from their usefulness to indicate problems which might otherwise not come to the surface. A patient related several consecutive dreams in several weeks, in which he was attacked, chased or threatened by Negroes. The mere recognition of the emotional tone of those dreams was not sufficient. Patient had little contact with Negroes; did not have any special prejudice or fear in regard to Negroes and offered no solution why he constantly dreamed of Negroes. In such situations the technique of using free-associations in a limited sense is helpful. As a rule, we found it not necessary to use extensive free-associations which might explain all the details of the dreams of our patients. It is generally satisfactory and sufficient to know the general direction of the dream without wasting too much time and effort to discover from where the details of the dream-material came. This dream gives a good example for the use of—as it may be called—free-association. The patient was asked what came to his mind when he thought of Negroes. Then he remembered how not long ago they had a colored janitor. This man, who appeared to be a gentle, nice fellow, found his wife in bed with another man, whereupon, in rage, he took a knife and actually cut the man wide open. He was convicted for life for this murder. This association immediately revealed the significance of the dream. Patient was involved in a relationship with a woman and had just found out that she was married. He was in a conflict between giving up the woman he loved, or facing the consequences. With the dream he obviously stimulated himself in the direction of breaking up the relationship.

Dreams provide the most dramatic experience for patient and therapist alike when they reveal the changes which occur in the patient during therapy. One of my patients had a very peculiar type of dream. All his dreams were rather short and without any action. He did in his dreams what he did in life; he continuously figured out the best way of getting out of a problem, mostly without actually doing anything. He dreamed about difficult situations, figuring out what would happen if he acted in one or the other way, but even in his dreams nothing actually happened. When his dreams started to move and become active he started to move in his life, too.

A woman had the following dream: She had guests in her home. In the yard below her porch was a tramp behind a lilac bush. Her little daughter went out. Patient was afraid that the tramp would grab her, so she went out herself. There was a little cat instead of her little daughter. Patient took her in. It was a child and still a cat. Then she saw the tramp embracing a cat which leaped out between his arms. Patient lost her fear of the tramp and considered maybe he was harmless.

It is not so difficult to understand this dream when one knows that this woman felt strongly antagonistic against her little daughter, whom she blamed for her inability to enjoy and maintain social contact. (The identification of her little girl with a cat reveals the patient's attitude toward feminine tricks which were frequently used by her little daughter.) Patient is divorced from her husband and very much afraid of men who might bring new hardship upon her. But the tramp fondles the cat. Maybe her girl needs a father, and maybe it would be more advantageous than dangerous to contemplate marriage. The dream indicated the first shy attempt of patient to re-orientate herself toward men.

Another patient dreamed about picking candies which had colors inside. These candies signified prizes to be won. There was one big prize to be won—a watch. Thus patient picks the rest of the candies while another fellow gets one, too. Finally the patient gets the watch only to discover that it was second hand. He consoles himself that it is still a good watch, better than a cheap one. However, the proprietor asks patient to pay a second time and asked for too much money, but patient still considers the watch is worth it.

One can easily see in this dream how much concerned patient is with getting things as cheaply as possible. That actually was his life style: getting as much as possible for the least amount of effort. However, this dream signifies progress. Previously, only the best was good enough for him. He could not stand being cheated and he was unable to accept anything short of the best. He now tries to be satisfied with less. Recognizing his attitude after the dream was interpreted to him, helped greatly in speeding his adjustment.

In our culture, where we have to maintain the appearance of a social and civilized human being, without being sufficiently trained for cooperation and social participation, much of our inner life has to remain under the surface. Our conscience does not permit us to admit even to ourselves our attitudes and tendencies. The world of the dream is strictly and rigidly separated from the world of reality. Only those who do not keep a strict distinction between imagination and reality, act out their dreams. Here are the day-dreamers and the people who live in a dream world of poetry and fantasy. They often actually walk in their sleep, as they dream while walking. The emotions in the dream are capable of breaking down the barrier to conscious action by making the sleeper talk or move his body or limbs when the dream becomes too exciting. Similarly, overwhelming inner emotions might drive individuals, who are predisposed to losing contact with the logic of life, called reality, into dream-like actions. Schizophrenia and other psychoses are mental states which resemble very much the dream-life of the normal person. The content of hallucinations and delusions can be similarly interpreted as dreams. On the other hand, the dream-life of the normal person proves how much creative imagination is dormant in everybody and waits for rediscovery. Our dreams prove that we have not actually lost either the imaginative ability of our childhood or the creative imagination of our adolescence.

GUILT FEELINGS AS AN EXCUSE*

Guilt and social order are inevitably linked together; one is impossible without the other. A social order requires standards and values; any offense, breach, or neglect of accepted social conventions and prescriptions produces guilt. In this sense sin and guilt are synonymous. Sin, however, is applied mainly in the religious approach to the regulation of social behavior as one of the many symbols designed to create negative emotional attitudes toward breach of law, order, and convention. Shame, remorse, and regret are the resulting emotions, deliberately evoked by society and its representatives, such as lawmakers, priests, courts, educators and parents, to promote conformity. The threat of punishment is still another device to discourage misbehavior.

While the positive approach of stimulating proper conduct leads to the development of conscience, the negative threat of punishment and ostracism induces the development of fear and a sense of guilt. Every adequately adjusted person has a conscience; he knows what is right and wrong, good and bad, and accepts standard evaluations as correct. Although everyone occasionally acts contrary to his conscience, the average person is uncomfortable in doing so.

Realization of one's guilt does not follow on any particular offense, but may arise whenever one does something out of order in any sphere of social living. Since everybody transgresses occasionally, all have the occasion to develop guilt feelings.

---

* *Individual Psychology Bulletin,* 1950, 8, 12-21.

Recently, guilt feelings became a focus of scientific, primarily psychiatric, research. Despite intensive preoccupation with guilt feelings, their true significance is still little recognized. Exponents of traditional thought and old-fashioned concepts believe that guilt feelings are necessary to maintain order and proper conduct. They do not realize that the opposite is true, that guilt feelings seem rather to impede social conformity today.

More modern investigators realize that guilt feelings—and the correlated notion of sin—no longer stimulate conformity but express superimposed and ineffective pressure of moral concepts. However, many are inclined to the other extreme that mere removal of pressure will eliminate such detrimental emotional attitudes, and do not realize that guilt—or sin—will exist as long as social conventions exist, i.e., as long as man lives in a society. Advocates of the past order and those in favor of self-indulgence and license, contribute to great confusion as to the nature, dynamics, and significance of guilt feelings. A clarification of the fundamental issues involved is long overdue.

At the root of the confusion lies a semantic problem. Guilt has little to do with guilt feelings. One may be guilty and not suffer from guilt feelings; conversely, one may feel guilty without being so. We find the same confusion in regard to the correlation of inferiority and inferiority feelings. One is possible without the other, but the extent of one by no means indicates the extent of the other. While guilt is a necessary product of social standards, guilt feelings are not at all necessary for social living. They are merely a product of given cultural conditions in our present society, and can be removed when society permits improved social functioning in each of its members.

Guilt feelings are the expression of a particular social order, one which has prevailed for the last five to six thousand years, based on a human relationship of superiors versus inferiors. This relationship precludes a stable equilibrium, since it is contrary to the "logic of social living" (Alfred Adler.) Stable, social harmony is possible only among equals; otherwise the inferior one invariably rebels inwardly, and the superior one is obliged to rely on his simple force to keep the other one in line or under control.

The characteristic means for keeping an inferior person or group in place were—and still are—bribe and threat, and reward and punishment. Under these conditions true social adjustment and sincere conformity was and is impossible. Accompanying educational procedure, founded on religious and moral principles, was primarily concerned with development of a conscience to stimulate conformity. Conscience, knowledge of right and wrong, is undoubtedly necessary for proper behavior, but is in itself insufficient to assure it, since it guarantees only a limited, and often a superficial, conformity. The prevalence of such time-honored, but inadequate educational procedures may be responsible for the persistent social maladjustment of individuals and groups, one giving rise to the domestic, national and international frictions and conflicts so characteristic of our civilization, in which even murder is legalized under some conditions.

Since this method of indoctrination, reflecting the unstable structure of the whole society in an autocratic system, fails to induce in its members a willingness to respect social values and demands and to behave in accordance with them, individuals use various means to avoid the moral pressure applied to them. Some refuse altogether to accept social prescriptions; consequently, their consciences remain under-developed. Their utter disregard of moral, ethical, social, or legal prescriptions and conventions does not evoke moral pricks or guilt feelings. These are the openly anti-social criminals and psychopathic personalities.

In contrast, the average person has a well developed conscience, which does not prevent him from rebelling against obligations and social demands whenever they conflict with his personal goals, purpose, and interests. We all use innumerable tricks to appease our own consciences or to excuse and rationalize our behavior so that our actions do not contradict our conscience too strongly, thus permitting ourselves to maintain the semblance of good intentions. Children learn to avoid unpleasant consequences for their misdeeds by finding good excuses. This training enables them as adults always to find convincing alibis, to excuse themselves, no longer to their parents, but to their own consciences.

The arrangement of logical and ethical excuses for our actions is characteristic of all of us. It is one of the reasons we cannot see ourselves objectively and feel more or less justified in our behavior regardless of the protest and objections we evoke in our fellow men, the more so the closer our contact or the more discrepant our interests. When our actions become too obviously anti-social and conflict openly with our own good intentions or "better knowledge," we may take refuge in the assumption of being sick and develop symptoms to excuse us in avoiding responsibilities and obligations. Only then do we speak in clinical terms, like psychoneurosis, even though the entire psychodynamics on which we operate are neurotic.

A neurotic tendency is characteristic of our entire civilization, although it has never been as obvious and general as today. Our city population especially displays this neurotic tendency to an alarming degree, with its ensuing inability to live happily and harmoniously. The increase in domestic frictions, the almost "usual" marital troubles, the difficulties parents have with children, tensions within the the community, national and international conflicts, all are indisputable proofs of the neurotic maladjustment of our contemporaries. We all know how to behave, but do not act accordingly. The factors generating neurotic behavior in all of us are well known through analysis and therapy of individual cases. They are a sense of inadequacy, a doubt of one's own value with a compensatory effort mainly to consider one's own self-elevation, which restricts our social interest and willingness to co-operate unreservedly.

The unsettled and disturbed human and social relationships of our time are the result of increased competition and rapid changes in social, moral, economic and political conditions, characteristic of the present transitory period between two cultural phases of human society. In the past, we had a social order based on superior-inferior relationships; now we move toward a democratic society based on fundamental human equality. The process of equalization intensifies the conflicts between individuals and between groups, because the inferior one is no longer compelled to accept his inferiority, but rebels openly, and the superior one feels his power threatened. Mutual antagonism and suspicion result, increasing the neurotic tendency to seek alibis for ensuing anti-social attitudes and actions.

Guilt feelings play an important role in the symptomatology of many neuroses. While the sense of guilt seems to express a desire to be good and to behave properly, it is used as an effective scheme to defy order and obligation without admitting such defiance openly. Sometimes good intentions are all the neurotic has to maintain an appearance of decency, though he obviously acts against his conscience and common sense, shunning obligations, withdrawing from participation, passively or aggressively upsetting his relationships with others, and limiting his functioning within his social setting. With his guilt feelings he can demonstrate to himself and others his good intentions and high moral standards. Moral enhancement through guilt feelings is a frequent experience in childhood. Whatever the child may have committed, he can make a favorable impression by admitting his guilt, preferably with an ostentatious display of regret and remorse. No misdeed is really so bad when the child can convincingly demonstrate how sorry he feels. Accepting one's own guilt becomes, therefore, a sign of high moral standards. Just as he did as a child, the neurotic may rely on his guilt feelings as testimony to his high standards to offset his vague realization that he is not functioning properly. His frequently exaggerated moral qualms serve in this way to enhance his own moral comfort. By displaying them to others he can offset any possible accusation of being too little concerned with his obligations and the welfare and needs of others. Through an exhibition of his moral concern with his own shortcomings he may even indicate a certain moral superiority over those who do not stress the moral issue, but simply function adequately. By feeling guilty, he is not only better than his actions would indicate, but even better than those who do not share the high moral standards he expresses in his self-accusations.

Another misleading feature of guilt feelings fitting into the neurotic pattern, is the ensuing confusion between present and past obligations. While guilt feelings always occur when a person is confronted with present conflicts in the face of which he feels inadequate their content is always a misdeed of the past. It is possible to know that we are doing wrong right now, but what bothers us is always what we did yesterday or before. Any intense concern with either the future or the past disguises an antagonistic attitude toward the actual, present situation. We only use past events or future dangers to justify our unwillingness to function today. Nobody wastes much time in thinking about the past or future if he is engrossed in playing his part today. But if present problems appear too difficult, one can minimize their significance and importance by thinking about possible future dangers, or injustices, calamities and mistakes of the past.

The neurotic feels himself unable, and therefore unwilling to do his duty today; therein lies his guilt. But he is unwilling to recognize his present attitudes and shirking of responsibility, because recognition would prevent him from maintaining his moral integrity. Instead of reconsidering his present antagonistic attitude and anti-social intentions, which he could change if he wanted to do so, he refers to some past transgressions that cannot be changed. Such concern with past sins impedes him from functioning adequately in the present. Guilt feelings, consequently, are a clever scheme emphasizing actual or imagined past faulty actions for the purpose of justifying present mistaken attitudes. Anyone suffering from guilt feelings can easily realize that the same feeling of guilt does not prevail all the time. What makes them come and go? If he were willing to look, he could easily recognize that there are always some acute calamities which make him look back and feel ashamed of himself. It is always a present discouragement seeking proof in the past to justify a feeling of worthlessness or inadequacy.

Guilt feelings must, therefore, be deceptive, by the very nature of their functions. If we were to admit to ourselves their true meanings, they would become useless. Consequently, we should not be surprised to find a great variety of deceptive qualities in the structure of guilt feelings. One is the belief that one is really sorry for what one did, since one sincerely regrets one's actions or behavior. In most cases the fallacy of such an assumption is obvious. Realization of wrongdoing is not at all necessarily associated with deep regret. Everyone recognizes many of his transgressions, without being concerned for them. Those who feel sorry for what they have done do not necessarily refrain from misbehaving in the same way again. A person who is sincere in his regret does not develop guilt feelings, but tries to correct and amend what he has done.

Contrary to the subjective impression, guilt feelings appear only if one is unwilling to amend, and is still trying to maintain the assumption of his good intentions. As soon as sincere efforts are made to atone or amend, guilt feelings disappear. Instead of the "feeling of guilt" which prevents constructive action, a new interest in remedial efforts expresses the new "active remorse." As soon as guilt feelings appear, one can be reasonably sure that one has not the slightest intention to improve or amend. A person who "feels guilty" does not believe in himself or his courage to do something about his deficiency.

Guilt feelings, therefore, are not primarily concerned with a misdeed. One does not feel sorry for what he has done, but rather for what must be endured right now. One is not concerned with the moral issue being stressed, but with his own prestige and assumed lowered value. Actually one does not feel "guilty" at such moments, but "inferior." One is not concerned with the others, their rights and requirements, but only with himself, his status, prestige in himself, of course without renouncing his good intentions. On the contrary, guilt feelings and good resolutions which express an increase of good intentions belong together. Underneath lies doubt in one's "ability" to carry them out.

Sometimes, we find a semblance of "self-punishment" connected with guilt feelings, a mechanism greatly stressed by many investigators, which is equally deceptive and fallacious, as are all other rational aspects of guilt feelings. To understand this mechanism we must recognize first that the sequence of "guilt-punishment" is not as definite as we assume. Such assumption is based on an erroneous evaluation of educational, moral, and legal procedures. It is almost "wishful thinking" to assume that punishment can actually "enforce" law. A misdemeanor or transgression is more frequently not followed by any punishment or the unpleasant consequences, than we in our self-righteousness are ready to admit.

Punishment, as a sequence of guilt, depends on two restrictive prerequisites: first the culprit must be caught; and second, there must be somebody superior, stronger, or more forceful to impose the punishment. Despite all the fears we have instilled in children and adults alike for thousands of years, most people think that they can misbehave and get by with it, at least with the majority of their violations of rules and order. This attitude is so prevalent that it can be considered to be normal. There is no reason to assume that the knowledge of having committed a sin or misdeed leads automatically to expectation of punishment, and that punishment absolves the guilt. Only superficially it appears that a child who is punished for misbehavior or an adult who is sentenced for a crime has paid in full. Actually, the completion of the punishment does not absolve the crime, since the person is not restored to his good social status and does not reassume his previous good relationships. All that punishment eliminates is the immediate threat of an aggression by an offended authority. The "culprit" is not actually concerned with his misdeed, but with the antagonistic and dangerous power confronting him.

This combination of fear and defiance is characteristic of all our present human relationships in a society of superiors and inferiors. A peculiarly vicious circle develops in which sin and violations, which cause fear, are actually caused by fear of the authority opposed and defied by the misdemeanor. Punishment ends one cycle of contested authority and begins a new one. The conflict with authority, order, society, or whatever the symbol of the opposing force may be for the "sinner," continues after one round has been finished by punishment. The subjugated rebel then tries in a new round to see how far he can get by.

This structure of various phases in the fight with a dominant authority is essential for an understanding of the mechanics involved in the process of punishment. It would be a grave mistake to assume—as many do—that children, or anyone else, want to be punished, notwithstanding the fact that they obviously drive to this point. Closer analysis reveals the purpose of such an apparently paradoxical and nonsensical procedure involving pain and discomfort. Two elements are outstanding in the private logic which these children follow. They are both parts of the contest for power in which children and their parents are involved. One element is the child's desire to excite his parents, as part of his demonstration of his own power. He is willing to give in only when the defied authority goes to the extreme effort to end the battle.

The second factor is the child's effort to "have it out." He does not particularly cherish the tortures and uncomfortably violent phase of a power contest and wants to bring it to an end. Once he is severely punished, he is satisfied and willing to start all over again. He knows that there are many victories yet in store for him before the final showdown comes again. He knows that in the end he will lose out, since the opposing powers are too strong for him. But, in the meantime, he can retaliate, provoke, and defeat. For any point the parents may score by their punishment there are a hundred points on which the child scores. The same is true of a criminal who disregards the law. He knows that eventually he may be caught. In the meantime, he can score all his victories, and after he is caught—if he ever is—and gets his punishment over with, he can start his cycle again.

This clarification is necessary to understand the mechanism so frequently described in present psychiatric literature as "self-punishment." It is assumed that the guilt feelings lead to a kind of "expiation," particularly since, as these authors maintain, the guilt feeling refers to sexually sinful desires for which the neurotic tries to punish himself. We have found no evidence of such dynamics in our patients. But we do frequently find an effort to provoke unpleasant consequences, an effort which may easily be misconstrued as "seeking punishment."

Actually, the dynamics for such behavior is in line with the interpersonal conflicts just described existing between a child and his domineering and punitive parents, or between a criminal and the law. The patient, involved in a warfare with society, may feel cornered. He then may want "to get it over with" so that no further efforts on his part to solve his problems may be necessary. We can hear such desires openly expressed by patients who act in such a way, although they are vague as to what they expect will happen after "they get through with it." All they want is to get out of their present predicament, whatever may come of it. It is a declaration of bankruptcy, an acknowledgement of inevitable defeat which they expect anyhow. They are ready to admit they just are no good; now, let others take on responsibility for their lives.

Another factor should not be overlooked; after the opposing force, be it parent, law, or society, has meted out its punishment and inflicted the inevitable humiliation, the child, the criminal—or the neurotic—is more convinced than ever of the correctness of their hostile and punitive attitude and feels more justified in maintaining it.

The guilt feeling is an acknowledgement of his "badness," of the power of society, of the dangerous and precarious position in which the neurotic finds himself. His guilt feelings express his antagonism against the society where he does not expect to find understanding and acceptance. But he does not say so openly, because his conscience and his common sense do not permit him to do so. Thus, he pretends to agree with the authority which he defies. His feeling of guilt indicates merely that he is confronted with an unpleasant situation, with dangers of humiliation, loss of prestige, or unfavorable treatment by others. He may then attribute his predicament, his mistaken evaluation of his social position, to actual or imagined past transgressions. If he is dissatisfied with himself in his present functioning, he may also attribute his deficiency to previously committed sins. It is misleading, therefore, to take his rationalizations at their face value, instead of recognizing the dynamics in his present situation. The neurotic with no confidence in his ability to solve his problems may develop imaginary guilt feelings to rationalize his failure, and seek and escape into bankruptcy, since his approaches to remedy the situation are inadequate.

Summary

Guilt is unavoidable in a social order, but guilt feelings are not directly related to guilt. They are supposed to preserve conformity, but are mostly used to conceal defiance. The development of guilt feelings depends less on past transgressions than on present antagonistic intentions. They serve mainly as a proof of good intentions. They can be used to gain moral superiority. Their deceptive dynamics make them fit into the neurotic pattern. They are primarily a neurotic mechanism for maintaining good intentions in contrast to actual anti-social attitudes. They permit a shift of emphasis from the important present situation to the past, thereby providing relief from responsibility for present attitudes. They provoke unpleasant experiences which a discouraged individual anticipates. They prevent constructive action under the disguise of remorse. "The tendency to atonement and remorse betrays often a strongly antagonistic, intractable, and inimical note" (Alfred Adler).

COUNSELING FOR FAMILY ADJUSTMENT*

An increasing number of people need and seek counseling for their adjustment to family life. Many find it difficult to live harmoniously and to get along with each other. This is reflected by the rapidly increasing divorce rate, by the rise in juvenile delinquency and by the growing frustration of parents in rearing children.

However, while people require more help and assistance, they get less than ever before. In the past, the main source of guidance has been the church. Priests, ministers, and rabbis functioned as counselors and guides in all problems of life. The family doctor was in a position to be consulted in crisis and conflict situations. Today, fewer people depend on their church, and even many faithful church-goers do not bring their personal problems to their spiritual leader. The family doctor has been replaced in many instances by the specialist; most doctors know little about family relationships and the intimate life of their patients. Furthermore, the complexity of modern life makes it more difficult for them to give merely on the basis of common sense and good judgment. Probably the greatest amount of family counseling is furnished by well-meaning friends with good intentions who frequently contribute more friction and confusion than help.

We must face the fact that rarely do the individuals involved or the public at large realize the real nature of the problem. Many reasons are offered for the rise of divorce and

---

* *Individual Psychology Bulletin*, 1949, 4, 119-137.

juvenile delinquency, but very few see the real issues. Statistical evidence is completely inadequate. The reason for divorce presented in court is notoriously unreliable; but not less misleading are the reasons which are actually given for the conflicts within the family, and especially for the maladjustment of children. Many attribute their conflicts to in-laws, financial hardship, sexual incompatibility, or difference of temperament and interests. All these should, however, not be regarded as the cause of the friction, but rather as the consequence of a disturbed human relationship. A faulty equilibrium between the members of the family is the real basis of family maladjustment and conflict. However, most persons involved are unaware of the nature of their relationship with their close relatives. And, most of all, very few realize the part which they themselves play.

A mother who asks for help with her child, or a husband or wife who complains about the partner or the mother-in-law, present the same picture: their opponent seems to be utterly unreasonable and uncooperative; and we cannot blame our client if he does not know what to do, and is unable to understand the other one's behavior. The report of each is like a recitation of a dialogue in which the lines of one actor are omitted. Take any dialogue in a play and read only one part and it will make no sense. But when you add the other part, each word and action becomes meaningful and sensible. The report of our client omits one part—that one which he plays. We all know what the other one is doing, but not what we ourselves contribute to the situation. The mother sees only the misbehavior of the child, the husband the faults of his wife, and neither of them sees his or her part in the game. Harmony or friction describe a relationship to which both parties contribute equally. Both behave either adequately or provocatively, both have their own faults and shortcomings. But no fault or misbehavior creates any conflict as long as the partner does not respond destructively, as long as the human relationship between them does not become affected and disturbed. Two people generally have the same faults and shortcomings when they fall in love and get married as when they get a divorce; what had changed was only the relationship. As a rule, they knew their faults when they got married, but accepted each other as they were. The disturbance in their relationship is generally not caused by their faults; these are rather used as a justification for a wrong attitude of the person who complains about his mate. (If such faults really appeared first after marriage, they may have been provoked by the complaining partner.) A typical example is the relationship between a drunkard and his wife. Often enough, she knew that he was drinking, which did not prevent her from marrying him; on the contrary, many women like to marry men to reform them. If the husband started drinking after marriage, nobody, including the wife herself, realized the role which she played in his addiction. Everybody sympathizes with the poor noble soul who takes on all responsibilities, makes all the sacrifices until she no longer can take it. The husband is obviously wrong—and he knows it himself. Unfortunately for him, he was the loser in a contest with this wonderful person, his wife, who made him feel like a heel—and act as such. Actually, the disturbing factor in this marriage is often the indulgence and protectiveness of the wife, her moral superiority and her high expectations which the husband could not match nor meet. His drinking or his "weak character" are not so much cause as consequence. We find often the wife of a drunkard to be such a superior holy female, who has all the virtues on her side and therefore leaves only the faults to the husband with which to fight back.

The disturbed human relationship within the family can only be understood fully if we recognize the cultural and social conditions in which we live. The same factors seem to be responsible for the increase in family maladjustment as well as for the increased tension in our whole society. There is a striking similarity between the conflicts within the family and those on the national and international scene, between management and labor, between the white and the colored people, between Gentiles and the Jews, between America and Russia. What was said before about husband and wife, about mother and child, is equally true here: everybody knows only what his opponent does wrong, how unreasonable and uncooperative he is but none knows how he provokes such a disturbing behavior. We have reason to assume that this prevalent pattern of conflict and friction has some common ground which can be found in the particular predicament of our present civilization. Our time seems to be especially chaotic, full of danger and insecurity, wrought with threat of impending doom of our whole civilization, perhaps even of our whole earth.

Many reasons have been promulgated for this precarious state of our culture. Some blame the weakening of religious faith for the present confusion, others the loosening of morals, still others again the industrialization, the accelerated and disproportionate development of technical sciences, others the increasing materialism. They all may have a point. But again, they seem to confuse the symptom with the cause. All these above mentioned factors would not cause friction and conflict on this wide scale were it not for the change in human relationships underlying all these spiritual, ethical, economic and technical changes. We are moving towards a reorganization of our human society, characterized by the establishment of democracy. This democracy is based on the assumption of fundamental human equality and of equal human rights. Never in the past has such a pattern of a relationship between equals existed, although the need for it has been recognized and has been expressed throughout the ages, since the beginning of our civilization. The Greek Stoics, the late Roman lawyers, the early Christians, not only dreamed about this human equality, but also urged its realization. The French Revolution established the idea of democracy as the guiding principle of political and social development, the American and the Russian Revolutions tried to put it into practice. Right now we are in the process of making democracy work. But we have not succeeded as yet. So far, human equality exists only on paper. The existing human relationships are still patterned after the principle of superiority-inferiority, which has been the basis of all human relationships in the past. Our present problems and conflicts are part of the struggle to overcome the previous pattern and to establish a new one. We cannot turn back the wheel of time; the evolution of mankind now moves toward actual equality, which alone is the basis for harmonious and stable relationships, in line with what Alfred Adler called "the ironclad logic of living together."

In this light, the problems with which we struggle, individually or in groups, take on a new significance. We all want to live in peace and harmony, but we have not learned to regard our fellow man as an equal. On the contrary, today more than ever we have the tendency to push everybody down. Today, man has actually become man's enemy, regardless of any closeness by interests or blood. This is due to our present social organization which has—at least partly—destroyed Feudalism. Under Feudalism, group superiority and inferiority were rigidly maintained. It was progress when these limitations were removed and the way was open for everybody to go ahead. But when the static structure of society changed into a dynamic one, everybody with his unlimited chances had to contend with everybody else. This led to the intense competition of today. If we speak of equality today we mean usually that everybody should have an equal chance. That in itself is a fallacy, because nobody actually has really the same chances to go ahead. What is worse, this concept of equality certainly does not imply equality in fact. In order not to be inferior to you, I must try to be superior to you. Such an attitude does not permit stable relationships and harmony.

As we approach equality, the friction between individuals and groups becomes more violent. Those who are in a superior position are afraid of losing it, and those who feel inferior or are considered so are no longer willing to accept their fate. The result of this relationship is increasing mutual suspicion and fear, anxiety and hostility which destroys the only basis for human cooperation, namely, the feeling of belonging. This general pattern of neurotic attitudes prevails in our society and penetrates into the life of each family. It is the prevalent pattern between husband and wife, between parents and children, and between brothers and sisters.

Our cultural atmosphere affects the present day family in more specific ways also. There is first a new equilibrium between men and women. It changes rapidly towards equality.

Equality between the sexes never existed previously in all human history. We have not yet reached equality, but have more of it than mankind ever knew before. But while masculine superiority diminishes constantly, the friction between the sexes increases. The "masculine protest" (Adler) affects men and women alike. Women no longer accept the position of the second sex, and men who still feel obliged to live up to a masculine pattern of the past, find it increasingly difficult to prove their superiority and become suspicious of and antagonistic to each other, despite their best intentions, despite their love and affection and their sincere desire for peace and harmony. This fear of losing out in the competition, of being dominated or defeated, abused or humiliated, creeps into their relationship, almost unnoticeably in the beginning, and not fully recognized even in the stages of full-blown warfare. In an atmosphere of violent competition no agreement is possible, not even in the most simple matters. They cannot decide whether to go to the movies or to stay home because either decision makes one the winner and the other the loser. In this struggle for prestige every little incident serves as a welcome opportunity to seek a short-lived victory. As they cannot agree on anything they might finally agree to get a divorce. But even then they may not get anywhere because they cannot agree on the terms, as many court cases prove.

The very essence of the male-female relationship, namely sex, becomes a pawn in this struggle for superiority. It is hardly possible that both mates are always equally interested in sex. As soon as one desires more, the other feels imposed upon and the first one rejected. Sexual incompatibility is the result rather than the cause of personal disagreement. Prevalent concepts of the nature of human sex tend to confuse the issue. Human sex is not merely a biological urge, but a function which can be used according to the individual's intentions. Unlike an animal, it is independent of glandular activity. Impotence and frigidity as well as perversion express an antagonistic attitude toward the opposite sex.

The increase in sexual maladjustment is clearly connected with the precarious equilibrium between men and women. It is true that sex has always puzzled and confused mankind. However, that is not due to any intrinsic antagonism between sex and social living, as some are inclined to believe. Sex, linking two individuals in the most intimate union, had to be perplexing as long as man was unable to establish this union on the basis of the logic of social living, i.e., on mutual equality. As long as such equality did not exist between man and woman, and it never existed in the past, sex which bound them together remained full of inner antagonisms. Love, desire and affection could not serve as means of true unification; sex was used primarily in the interest of the superior gender. The double standards for men and women throughout the ages prevented full sexual harmony. Monogamy was required through religious and legal precepts; but it was never practiced, as society granted the superior sex special prerogatives.

While it is true that sex was always confusing and disturbing, today the situation is even worse. Women were always inhibited in their sexual function through rigid regulations and restrictions. As long as women had no sexual rights, their sexual response did not matter and did not cause any sexual maladjustment. Few were the women who could break the strict code and become sexual problems for men. Today the situation is radically changed. Man is no longer sure of himself. At a time when society guaranteed man his social status and backed his sexual demands, he had little difficulty in performing sexually. Impotence and homosexuality became widespread only in times of increased feminine emancipation as it occurred during certain phases of Greek and Roman history as well as in modern times. Our sexual education has not caught up yet with the social changes and our children are not yet prepared to accept their sexual role without fear and resentment.

The difficulties in establishing family relationships in accord with the new democratic principles affect not only the relationship between husband and wife, but especially our parents. They are confused in their efforts to bring up children. Educational techniques always reflected existing social patterns. It always has been mentioned that in the past human relationship was based on the principle of superiority-inferiority. Order meant the ability of the superior one to keep the inferior one in line. This was done by means of bribe and threat, reward and punishment. Many parents still adhere to this principle and cannot imagine that order in the family could be maintained without it. But their children, growing up in the democratic atmosphere of our country, no longer accept such treatment, and, backed by the revolting spirit of their peers, retaliate by applying the same methods in subjugating their parents. Some other parents start out with the idea of a new order. They want to respect the needs of their children and wish to let them "express themselves." They think that this is democracy, while it actually means only laissez faire. They confuse freedom with license and democracy with anarchy. Consequently, the children get out of hand and demand more than the parents can give. In their despair the parents revert to the old scheme and try to suppress the misbehaving child. Most contemporary parents vacillate between over-indulgence and suppression. They either neglect the respect for the child by belittling him, by nagging, scolding and punishing, or they disregard the necessary respect for themselves by yielding, by permitting the child to impose his whims upon them and to put them into his service. Most parents are ignorant of methods of child training which do not require punishment or reward. Fathers and mothers share this predicament with the rest of the contemporary civilized world; we all believe in democracy, but have not yet learned to put it into practice. We profess our willingness to respect the rights of others but are too much concerned with our prestige. The present system of small families makes the position of parents even more precarious. It is small wonder that our parents, confused and inefficient as they are, become defensive, feel frustrated and inadequate.

We can see now why the problems which are often blamed for causing family maladjustment are not really the causes of the conflict. We may now identify the commonly known reasons for family strife, like in-laws, financial hardships, sexual maladjustment and misbehaviors of children, as test situations. They merely test the solidity of the existing relationship between husband and wife, between parents and children. They may stimulate strife and conflict only if the courage and morale, the feeling of belonging between all the family members has been weakened. Economic hardships can as well break up the harmony between husband and wife as solidify it. The decisive factor is their relationship. If one blames the other for his failure or shortcomings, then the resulting warfare between the mates makes any task unsolvable. On the other hand, if their relationship is based on mutual respect and confidence, and they are willing to help each other without fear of being imposed upon or slighted, then hardships may unite them even stronger.

The same is true for in-law problems. In-laws can break up a marriage if husband and wife fail to recognize them as their common problem. As soon as one blames his mate for friction with his relatives, the relationship loses the necessary resistance to ward off the danger. Furthermore, the disturbing in-laws themselves, let us say a mother-in-law, can be a problem only if the couple fails in its effort to maintain a proper relationship with her. People who disturb rarely do it out of sheer meanness. They are generally motivated by fear of losing their social status. Then they may become over-demanding, domineering, aggressive and hostile. If one recognizes their need for appreciation, reassurance, and estimation, one can deal with them more adequately. This is never accomplished by either yielding or fighting; but most people, confronted with in-law problems, do exactly this.

Difference of cultural, religious and educational background can endanger a marriage only if they are used by one mate to look down upon the other one. The same is true for any difference of interests or temperament. Such differences add color and breadth to a marriage, as long as any evaluation of superior-inferior is avoided and neither partner feels ignored, neglected, or humiliated. If one assumes superiority and belittles the other's achievements, even strong common interests and activities can easily deteriorate.

We can see now that all family conflicts, frictions and maladjustments which may require counseling are not so much caused by any objective predicament or hardship as by the effect which this particular condition has upon the relationship between the members of the family. The gravity and destructiveness of a problem does not depend on the nature of the actual adversity, but on the attitude of the individual toward it.

Effective family counseling must recognize these facts in their full significance. They indicate clearly which methods of counseling can be expected to be effective; they also explain why others are limited in their value, although they have been widely used. We are witnessing some fundamental changes in counseling techniques in line with the new insight in human motivations and a new understanding of human behavior.

When a person asks for help and assistance, he naturally wants to know what he should do. It is equally natural for a counselor to fall for this temptation and to give advice. Today we realize the ineffectualness of such procedure. As each person behaves in accordance with his attitude, it helps little to tell him what he should do. With the proper attitude he would find for himself the right answer to his problem; with his present faulty attitude he is in no position to carry out the best advice. There are a few situations where good advice may be helpful. This may be the case when the client actually is not aware that simple solutions exist. However, such occasions are rare in family conflicts. Here the problems are generally complicated and do not permit an easy solution.

A counselor who tries to give advice in a family situation usually appeals either to the conscience or to the common sense of the client. This approach has its unquestionable historic value. We must keep in mind that moral teaching and good sense was the basis for all education in the past. Conscience and good intentions were the main objectives of educational efforts until psychiatric research demonstrated their limitations. What could not be reached through reasoning and preaching was considered unapproachable. Many still believe that the development of conscience is the prime objective in the training of children; consequently, they regard all actions, behavior patterns and motivations, which do not correspond or conform with such prescription, as irrational, evil, unreasonable, or uncivilized. Today we know better. We need conscience, the knowledge of good and bad, but this is not enough. Conscience, or as one may call it, "common sense," is only part of our reasoning. If we do not act according to our conscience, we are by no means bad or irrational. We merely act on the basis of another reasoning, which Alfred Adler called our "private logic." We know what we ought to do, which is in line with social, religious, and moral conventions; but we may have personal goals and intentions which cannot be attained with socially accepted methods. In our evaluation of a given situation, non-accepted behavior patterns may seem more efficient. We do not necessarily give up intentions which are not acceptable to our conscience; but we learn to conceal them from ourselves. Our attitudes, supported by our emotions, are the result of our personal evaluation, whether we are aware of our reasoning or not. For this reason, emphasis of our moral obligation or our better judgment is of little avail when we have decided not to take a stand despite of them. We know most of the time what we should do; but we do not always like doing it, we cannot get ourselves to act according to our "better knowledge." Further appeal to it increases only the feeling of frustration or the feeling of guilt; neither of them is conducive toward a more adequate attitude.

As the futility of such counseling becomes obvious, some suggested that the best counseling is non-directive. They assume that the good sense of the client is sufficient to lead him to proper solutions if his reasoning power is stimulated by questions. Such procedure may be helpful in many cases. However, one can doubt whether complete objectivity on the part of the counselor is really possible, and whether he can abstain from directing the client, even though his part in the counseling might be restricted to asking questions. The forcefulness of innocently sounding questions has best been demonstrated by Socrates. Freud had gone to the extreme in demanding complete passivity on the part of the therapist, who should only listen and refrain even from asking questions, thereby stimulating the patient to solve his inner conflicts by himself. Freud's fatal mistake, as we know today, was the assumption that "free association" is actually free and provides a reliable basis for discovering the emotional forces which struggle within the individual. No, there is no chance in any human cooperation to be truly non-directive. We influence each other merely by being together. There are a thousand subtle ways for communicating ideas, expectations, and opinions. Whether the therapist asks questions with a poker face, or the analyst sits in back of the patient, in each case the patient is aware of the reaction, the attitude and the direction of his therapist.

The technique I found most helpful is that of interpreting the patient to himself, based on Alfred Adler's concept of goal-directed behavior and life-style. It is possible to show the patient a picture of himself, and let him draw his own conclusions. Nobody knows himself completely. What he knows are his wishes, desires and intentions as far as they are reconcilable with his conscience. He does not realize his fundamental attitude toward life, his life style, nor is he always aware of his true intentions, his real attitudes toward others in the given situation. As our approach is based primarily on the revelation of attitudes it could most adequately be called Attitude Psychology. It can be used on various levels. On the most superficial level, general negative attitudes can be disclosed and positive attitudes stimulated through interpretation. On a deeper level, the specific attitude toward the present situation can be disclosed while the most profound level is the discussion of the patient's fundamental attitude toward life, his life style.

Destructive attitudes are always based on the client's wrong evaluation of himself. We are all conditioned to succumb to inferiority feelings, partly as members of the human race, but particularly through our childhood experiences. Feeling to be less than others in a group prevents cooperation and constructive action and limits the development of social interest, of the feeling of belonging. Inferiority feelings stimulate fear and resentment, as the feeling of belonging and self-confidence leads to courage and acceptance. A discussion of the client's concepts, evaluation and interpretations of himself and of the existing problem can demonstrate his errors and mistakes in judgment and stimulate a new attitude. General Semantics uses similar approaches.

A few cases will demonstrate our point.

A couple came for consultation with the following problem: the husband had taken one of his employees out for lunch to discuss with her some business matter. The wife became jealous and demanded that he refrain in the future from such practice. He objected to her request because he felt justified in arranging his work as he saw fit. Why should he not use the lunch hour if he did not have any other time for the necessary discussion? They had long arguments and asked me to decide who was right. The wife did not suspect any personal interest of the husband in the employee, but still felt that his behavior was not correct. Was she right? There was no answer to this question on the logical or moral level. Both parties seemed to have some justification, and both were wrong at the same time. She had no "right" to interfere with his working habits nor was he correct in ignoring her "feelings." An investigation of her attitude provided a completely new slant on the situation. They had recently moved into a suburb, and his work had increased considerably. Prior to that time he had spent much more time with her, had seen her several times during the day, and they often had lunch together. Now she was alone all day long, he came home late, and—due to pressure of his increased work—often took work home with him. And even if he did not spend the evening working, he was often preoccupied with work. She felt neglected, without having any good reason to complain, as she realized that under the circumstances he could not act differently. Once she had considered lunching with a male acquaintance but had refrained in consideration of good taste. The incident of her husband's luncheon engagement gave her the first opportunity to voice her resentment openly, to justify her antagonisms against her present life situation, which she was no longer willing to accept. This disclosure changed immediately the attitude of both parties. Neither of them had been aware before of the wife's predicament. Recognizing it, the husband no longer resented her complaint, and she for the first time could express her resentment openly without resorting to his assumed misconduct. As they became aware of the real nature of the problem, they came to the logical conclusion by themselves, deciding to move back to Chicago as soon as possible. Having made this decision, she lost her feeling of frustration and her resentment.

This is one of the rare cases where a couple came for consultation early in the game, when the wrong attitude of one partner had not yet disturbed their relationship, and a simple interpretation could solve the problem. As a rule, people are caught in a vicious circle. One party feels slighted and frustrated, and in his ensuing effort to compensate for it, he instills the same feeling in the other. The result is the well-known picture of mutual retaliation. In the above case this vicious circle was interrupted right at the beginning. It is only in premarital consultation that one has frequently a chance to see a couple before the wrong attitude of one partner disturbed the whole relationship.

A young couple intended to be married in a few weeks, when the bridegroom suddenly got "cold feet." He suddenly doubted whether he really was in love and whether he should go through with the marriage. The girl was puzzled and felt hurt, but was willing to accept any decision of the psychiatrist. Of course, I did not intend to make any decision, but tried to find out what was going on. The young man was utterly confused. Most of the time he was sure of his love. But he got spells of despair, of depression, where he wanted to run away from everything. A short discussion revealed that he was the son of very ambitious parents. He constantly tried to live up to the highest expectations. He was a fine and successful young man who operated on the mistaken belief that he must please everybody. If he could not do so, he gave up and ran away. As a rule, he had managed pretty well on that basis, But now, for the first time he was confronted with a situation where he tried to satisfy antagonistic interests. The needs of the bride conflicted with certain requests of the parents; her family had certain ideas about the wedding date and arrangements, and his family had others. As it was impossible to please all parties concerned, he felt utterly inadequate and defeated. He was not sure whether he could ever make a good husband, without knowing that the real reason for his doubts was his exaggerated desire to please. Our interpretation cleared the air immediately. The girl recognized that his difficulties were not directed against her. She no longer felt humiliated; on the contrary, as he suddenly understood his problem, she wanted to stand by and help him. He on his part realized for the first time what bothered him. He smiled happily as his puzzling confusion cleared up. He now knew that he just had to learn to take a stand, not to depend on the approval of everybody. He may require psychotherapy later on, but he was sure he could go through with his marriage. This case is typical for the problem of many premarital indecision. Such last minute hesitations can often be dissipated by one interview if the real reason can be uncovered.

Most counseling is not restricted to the clarification of one person's attitude, but must take into consideration the existing equilibrium, i.e., the attitudes of both. It is not always necessary to see both parties, although this is desirable. In many instances it suffices to make one party aware of his own and also of his partner's attitude, which he had not realized before either.

A young girl came into my office just to make an appointment for her mother, who was depressed and suicidal. She gave me this initial information: her mother, a woman with high standards, raised in a conservative tradition, could not bear the breakup of her marriage. Divorce seemed inevitable. The father no longer showed any interest in his family, spending his time with his young secretary upon whom he showered gifts and money. At home he was irascible, either criticizing and quarreling or sullenly silent. They tried in vain to pacify him. Now all were against him. The girls had been his favorite and previously got along well with him. Now she was disgusted with her father and sided with her mother, quarreling with him as much as the others. Without any intention to go deeper into the problem at that time, I just mentioned some possible reasons for his behavior. Perhaps he felt the need to assert his masculine superiority at the time when he got older and when the children became more independent and less submissive to his leadership. Perhaps his young secretary gave him the desired recognition while the growing criticism of wife and children had demonstrated to him that at home he no longer was the "big shot" and could not hope for admiration and respect. So he lost interest in his family and got deeply involved in his outside activities. The daughter admitted that at home nobody had a nice word for him, and he must have felt that all were his enemies. We discussed her attitude and that of her mother and sisters. She considered the possibility of changing her tactics. Maybe she could sometimes ask her father's advice and appreciate his opinion and judgment. Maybe she, his previous favorite, could be the person to re-establish the old relationship where the father was the recognized master and leader. We agreed that her mother would make an appointment in the immediate future. But I never heard from the family again, until years later when the daughter wrote that after her interview she was able to influence the family situation, and now mother and father lived peacefully together in another state. It is only rarely that one can alter a situation so rapidly. As a rule, well-established patterns of relationship require time for reorganization; people don't change their attitudes so easily. It takes time and effort.

We can distinguish four steps for counseling. The first is the establishment of a proper relationship between counselor and client. Many misunderstandings exist as to what "proper relationship" means. Some see it in a strong emotional attachment of the client (transference). Others consider absolute and impersonal objectivity as the criterion. Some others, influenced by patterns of the past, believe that the counselor should be impressive, that his power and superiority are the most important factors in counseling. As we understand it, proper relationship is mutual confidence and respect. This requires a certain warmth and personal interest on the part of the counselor, without any attempt to impress with his own capacity, but also without disdain. A counselor who distrusts or frowns upon the client does not fulfill the first requirement. One should not go further with any counseling before having established a proper relationship; and during the whole counseling procedure the relationship must be watched carefully and immediately re-established if any disturbance occurs.

The next step is to understand the client and his problems. This requires an investigation of the client's attitudes, of his relationship with others and of the attitudes of his opponents. The cultural factors must be recognized in their influence upon the reasoning of the participants, which in turn affects their attitudes. As all problems are interpersonal problems, we prefer to work with all parties involved simultaneously. Such procedure is at variance with a present trend of having different counselors or therapists assigned to each person. This trend is based upon the assumption that human conflicts are intrapersonal, meaning that each person has his own problems, independent of those of his opponent. We find no evidence for each assumption. On the contrary; the problem situation, the existing disturbed relationship is exactly what they have in common and what they should change together.

After the counselor understands the client's problems, i.e., after he has made the diagnosis, he must help the client to understand himself. This requires generally more time than either of the first two phases. But "insight" is not sufficient. Knowing his attitude does not necessarily induce the client to change it. Insight is only a prerequisite to the fourth step.

This fourth step consists of re-orientation. In the process of thinking the problem through together, the client may become aware of the mistakes in his concepts and ideas and correct them. It is a mistake to suggest that the client should change his behavior. Actions depend on judgment and evaluation. As long as the client maintains his outlook, he cannot act differently. His evaluation must change not only in regard to his situation and to his opponent, but first of all in regard to himself. Most mistakes—and the most disastrous ones—are in our own evaluation, are the doubts in our position, our power, ability and our value. For this reason, encouragement is the most effective tool in adjustment. As most people do not realize their own contribution to the present situation, so they fail to recognize their own power and ability to produce a change.

The same four steps characterize psychotherapy. But counseling is not psychotherapy. It is necessary to distinguish between both. The main difference seems to be the objective. Counseling is concerned mainly with the acute situation and the solution of immediate problems. Psychotherapy, on the other hand, is designated to affect the whole personality and to stimulate the individual to a complete re-organization of his life. For this reason, psychotherapy implies more intensive and extensive work and requires a lengthy procedure. Opinions differ on the indication for psychotherapy. Certain guidance agencies do not accept children unless the mother undergoes psychotherapy. Our own experience does not substantiate that counseling for adjustment always requires psychotherapy. The majority of persons who come for consultation in family affairs, especially those who have difficulty with children, do not require extensive psychotherapy. A clarification of the immediate situation is often sufficient, although it takes six to ten interviews to produce insight and reorientation. Only if the patient or client is unable to adjust himself in this way must one proceed to uncover his whole life style and to correct his entire outlook on life. Some knowledge of the client's life style is necessary for every counselor. But in counseling the immediate situation remains in the foreground, and any reference to the life style is either completely omitted or only incidentally touched upon; while in psychotherapy the emphasis is placed on the patient's life style and the present situation is regarded as a neurotic symptom and only used as an illustration and example.

This is the case of a man who was deeply upset about his marriage. He became involved with another woman, but did not have the courage to break up his marriage. He had been married for twelve years but became increasingly disappointed, when he finally fell in love with the other woman. While he wanted to marry her, he hesitated because of his seven-year-old child and his concern about the reaction of his friends. He also felt responsible for the despair of his wife, who broke down completely. He always had accepted his responsibility to his family and had tried very hard to stick it out; but he no longer felt capable of managing the situation, especially since he now felt responsible for the other woman, who had left her husband for him. He could not understand how he, who always had such high standards in life, could get in such a dilemma. He wanted to know what he could and should do. There was no answer on the common sense level nor on moral grounds. He knew all the possible answers, but could neither see a chance of reconciling himself with his wife nor the possibility to break away from her. We tried first to understand the present situation in the light of his personality. We found that he was the third son who got ahead of his older brothers by being always so good. He found his social position within the family by being exceptionally good and considerate, by taking on responsibility, in contrast to one brother who was aggressive, selfish, and unreliable. He married a girl who was just "right." Both had very high standards and everybody approved of this perfect match of two wonderful people. However, these high standards became their downfall. He could not live up to her demands. As soon as she began to criticize him, their difficulties began. This is what he called his "disappointment." The quarrels started when his sense of obligation outside of the family came in conflict with the domestic needs. Step by step he lost his position as the "good husband." Despite all the quarrels which disgusted him and which he hardly could stand, no idea of breaking up his marriage entered his mind. Then he found a woman who looked up to him as a god. We can assume that this was not a mere coincidence—but he did not realize that. The deep love which overwhelmed him, permitted him for the first time to reject his family obligations, his sense of loyalty shifted slowly from wife and child to the other woman who had sacrificed everything for him. At this point of our investigation it became obvious that mere counseling was not enough in this case. There was no solution to his dilemma, either in renouncing his love nor in breaking up his marriage. In either case his troubles would continue. He could not function successfully with his life style either in his present marriage, nor if he married the other woman. He considered disconnecting himself from wife and child and also from his friends who would disapprove of a divorce. But even in a new environment, in a new social setting which he planned far away from his present field of operation, he would not be able to maintain his desired position of a "wonderful man." It is different to play "God" to a woman whom one sees only on rare occasions in an outburst of mutual desire, than to a wife with whom one lives in daily contact. As he needed to be so good, he would run into the same conflict in any marriage; and if he changed his attitude and learned to function on a different level, he no longer would need somebody to admire and venerate him and, therefore, could function adequately in his present marriage. This patient needed psychotherapy. His present situation was only a symptom of a mistaken attitude toward life.

The problems of counseling are somewhat different in child guidance. While counseling parents and children follows the procedure of family counseling in making both parties aware of their disturbed relationship and of their faulty attitudes, the approach to the problem is different here. Counseling the child is actually psychotherapy, as the child's immediate goals are identical with his life style. We see the child, especially the younger one, in his formative years when his attitude toward parents and siblings becomes the basis of his attitude toward life in general. The family constellation, for example, which in the psychotherapy of adults must be carefully reconstructed, is here a forceful reality. Changes in the present family relationship imply for the child not merely a better adjustment to the existing problem situation, but to life itself. On the other hand, the discussion with the parents is entirely on a counseling basis because it is restricted to the immediate problem situation, without any reference to the parent's personality and life style. What they need is only an understanding of their own attitudes toward the child and a re-orientation, based on the recognition of the child's attitudes and goals. Only if parents cannot respond to this procedure are they referred for psychotherapy. Most parents, however, do respond. Their emotional distress, their feeling of frustration, their antagonism for the child, which is often mistakenly called "rejection," disappears when they learn to understand the child and discover adequate methods to handle the situation.

As neither parent nor child realizes the child's immediate goals, mutual disclosures are necessary. We found four goals of children's misbehavior. They either want to get attention, to show their superiority and power, to get even and seek revenge, or to avoid obvious defeat by demonstrating their inadequacy. The child responds to an accurate interpretation of his goal with immediate understanding, evidenced by his "Recognition Reflex." The child is accessible to psychological interpretations at an early age, as soon as he understands the meaning of the words. It is more difficult for the parents to accept an interpretation of the situation, of the child's schemes and of their own part in the existing conflict.

In child guidance we deviate on one point from our general counseling practice: we give advice to the parents. We feel justified in doing so, because the parents actually do not know what they could do, and because the advice is of a simple nature. However, all our education recommendations have as their main objective a change in the parent-child relationship.

Counseling for family adjustment will become an important part in our cultural setup as the need becomes recognized. At the present time we suffer from an extreme lack of facilities. If we intend to alleviate much unnecessary suffering and to prevent marital failures and juvenile delinquency, we will have to move fast. Our efforts must go in two directions.

First, we must increase the number of agencies for adequate counseling. Such agencies are marital consultation centers and child guidance clinics, which we prefer to call Guidance Centers for Parents and Children. Such centers should be decentralized. each serving its immediate community.

Second, we must provide adequate training for sufficient personnel. At the present time, the services are provided by a team of psychiatrists, social workers and psychologists. Such an arrangement is possible only if the service is centralized, intended for a large area. If the needs of the public are to be met, and each small community to have its own guidance center, the structure of the service will have to be changed. There are not sufficient psychiatrists available now, and probably will not be available in the future, to serve all small communities. For this reason psychiatrists should be employed only in a supervisory capacity, and all the detailed work be placed in the hands of specially trained technicians. This applies not only to counseling but also to psychotherapy.

Psychotherapy is a time-consuming procedure, and the number of persons needing it is increasing steadily. For this reason, adequate facilities will be available only if psychotherapy will be practiced by non-medical technicians. We have witnessed a similar development in occupational therapy and in physiotherapy. The development is clogged by a difference of opinion. We have no agreement, as yet, whether or not psychotherapy should be the prerogative of psychiatrists exclusively; and those who are in favor of non-medical therapists have not agreed as to which group should be entrusted with psychotherapy. At this time we witness a race between the psychiatric social workers and the psychologists for recognition as qualified psychotherapists. The outcome of this controversy will greatly affect the counseling services in this country. All counselors, be they psychologists, social workers or teachers, will require some training in psychotherapeutic procedures. A closer cooperation between their groups and psychiatry is necessary. This lecture is not only an indication, but the result of the present tendency to get psychiatrists and counselors together.

COMMUNICATION WITHIN THE FAMILY*

Communication in the contemporary American family has not broken down; it exists, but not always for beneficial purposes. Communication and cooperation are also indispensable for hostile interaction. Wherever two people have anything to do with each other, they communicate and cooperate fully, although it may be in their agreement to fight each other. Non-verbal communication is far more extensive and intensive than communication on the verbal level. Words are often used to conceal the meaning of actions, and in the case of conflicts, they become means of warfare. The democratic evolution with its concomitant process of equalization increases conflicts within the family; consequently, communication within the family consists to a large extent in mutual indications of the means best suited to defeat each other.

The purpose of my assignment is to discuss the breakdown of communication in the contemporary American family, its characteristics and its causes. The inability to communicate with each other, to understand each other and to make oneself understood, has frequently been described as an indication of a disturbed relationship. (1) The breakdown in communication is considered an early sign of warfare, long before it erupts openly in overt acts of hostility. For this reason, attempts have been made to re-establish communication and mutual understanding as a means of reconciliation, of settling conflicts and avoiding more violent conflagrations. It is assumed that being able to make people see eye to eye, to understand each other and to perceive the point of view of an opponent, means re-establishing the disrupted communication and moving toward cooperation and harmony. (2)

---

* Central States Speech Journal, 1959, XI, 1.

Consequently, the need to give serious consideration to what appears as a breakdown in communication between members of the family, and particularly between parents and children, became more keenly felt. In many American families, communication seems almost lost or at least greatly restricted. Frequently parents and children do not see eye to eye, particularly so in cases of adolescents. Ever so often, the parents fail to impart to the children their ideas about the need to conform, to behave properly, to take on responsibilities. Whatever they say does not bring the desired results: the children either do not respond, or do not listen. And what *they* may have to say makes as little impression on their parents, so that they, the children, feel equally misunderstood. (3)

This lack of communication exists also between the siblings and very often equally between the parents. Endless arguments ensue about the simplest task or endeavor. Getting the children out of bed in the morning and to bed in the evening, inducing them to put their things away or to eat, not to mention to eat properly, poses an almost unsolvable assignment in which parent is pitched against parent, and either or both fighting a hopeless battle with their children. Even in the most harmonious families, some areas of limited communication are evident.

Under these circumstances it is surprising that family life still exists and continues, that the breakdown of communication within the family has not succeeded in breaking up the family altogether. Whatever breakup occurs usually comes as separation of the parents. How is it possible that the close relationships, inherent in family living, continue despite an often almost complete lack of communication? Every close relationship requires cooperation, and this is impossible without constant communication. The question arises: If the members of the family fight with and oppose each other, have they really ceased to cooperate and to communicate?

The answer to this question can solve the puzzle of a family without apparent communication. The situation will appear in a new light if we stop using the terms "communication" and "cooperation" in the narrow sense in which they are usually understood. By general concensus, these terms are limited to an interaction which is positive, constructive, and beneficial. However, there is no justification for such limitation, since both terms relate to social mechanisms which are equally existent in a disturbed relationship. The disregard of the extent to which cooperation and communication exists and are necessary in warfare is greatly responsible for our incapacity to understand disturbed relationships and hostilities and to find ways and means to resolve them.

We fail to recognize the same mechanisms in both positive and negative relationships because of a tendency to attribute each, the positive and the negative, to different qualities, attitudes, emotions, and personality traits. It was Adler (4) who suggested that a switch from the useful to the useless side can be made without a change in direction, (wanting to be first, special, catered to). Nevertheless, most people, including psychologists and educators, cannot perceive the same intent if it is no longer expressed in a socially acceptable manner; if destructive means are used, the constancy of goals is no longer recognized.

Let us take an example: Ambition. We speak usually about an ambitious child only when he tries hard to get ahead through studying, applying himself, trying to improve himself and his status. When he becomes discouraged, he gives up constructive means of achieving prominence and switches to the useless side. His ambition continues, but it remains unnoticed by the average adult, parent or teacher. Little do they recognize that he may want to be the worst if he cannot be the best; or how proud he is of defeating all and causing trouble.

Many of our so-called juvenile delinquents suffer from a perverted sense of ambition. They want to be important, big, impressive, and do not know how to achieve these ends with constructive means. Even the child who gives up altogether the effort to study or to apply himself may be prompted to do so by his over-ambition; if he can't be the first, then there is no sense in trying at all. The same over-ambition is found in all the various forms of behavior; but it is not recognized. Therefore, few speak of ambition in children unless it is evidenced in a positive way. Obviously, this limited use of the term is inadequate, no, even dangerous, since it precludes the recognition of the basic motivation behind destructive or deficient behavior.

A similar situation exists in regard to communication and cooperation. They are recognized only if they occur in a positive sense, as beneficial and helpful forms of interaction; they are usually not perceived as indispensable for hostile interaction as well. I have previously pointed out (5) that cooperation has to be understood in a much broader sense. When we look carefully, we can see that all people cooperate fully with each other. Every relationship, regardless of its kind and pattern, requires such cooperation. Unless two people agree about the way in which they intend to treat each other, they could not deal with each other. Any real divergence of intentions can only be shortlived. Before long, they must agree on something—even if it is to disagree. Otherwise, they would only agree to avoid each other, which is the only open path in a relationship where mutual consent has not been established. Whatever happens between them is the result of their decision about their relationship. Their agreement may not be useful to either of them or to anyone else; and they may not be aware of such decision, which is usually the case.

We are accustomed to call cooperation only an agreement of mutual help and support that we are blinded to the extent to which cooperation is also necessary when we want to fight, to hurt, to be right and prove the other wrong, to dominate or to take advantage. No one could do so without the full voluntary consent of his partner, at least in our democratic setting. There are few exceptions where physical force still can be used successfully to subdue and coerce, although Ghandi's non-violent resistance opens the door for dealing effectively even with tyrants. Today, every victim is so by his own consent, although he is usually utterly unaware of his decision to play this role under existing conditions.

This is an extremely important fact which is rather difficult to perceive. It implies that nobody really can blame anyone else for what he does, but has to recognize fully his own responsibility. This is one of the most distasteful obligations which free men have to accept. Therefore, they prefer to attribute their own circumstances to others rather than seeing their participation in the dirty games in which they become involved. No relationship can continue in kind if one refuses to play his corresponding role. Consequently, the term cooperation would require considerable reconsideration and redefinition. Cooperation is the basis of *all* human relationships, be they positive or negative, friendly or hostile.

The same is true for communication. Wherever two people have anything to do with each other, they communicate fully! (This is not entirely true for psychotics.) This communication takes place, however, only to a small extent on the verbal level. Non-verbal communication (6) is by far more extensive and intensive than that conveyed through words. And the logical and factual content of words is far less significant than other aspects of speech: intonation, inflection, volume, speed and other characteristics of the spoken word and sentence. They usually convey more information than the content.

It is at this point that the significance of communication is usually misunderstood. Many concern themselves primarily with the meaning of words. Actually, words are not always used to communicate the meaning as defined in dictionaries. Speech does not always have the purpose of communicating the meaning which the words imply. But rarely does any verbal or non-verbal expression fail to reveal its meaning; therefore, it usually constitutes *effective* communication. Whatever we do or say expresses our attitude and intent and is, to a large extent, perceived and understood as such by those around us, often without realizing it. Misunderstandings are possible, of course. But the consequence of a misunderstanding depends on the existing relationship. If it is friendly, then efforts will be made to clarify the difference. In the case of hostility and antagonism, misunderstandings will serve well to increase both.

Words are as often used to conceal the meaning of our action as to convey it. No clarification of the "meaning" of the words can explain or change the purpose for which they are used. In order to understand another, one has to perceive the other as a whole person and not merely listen to what he says. The true meaning of his actions and approaches can be understood only within the total field of action, when we sense the "private logic" on which he operates, and not merely hear the logic of his spoken words.

This ability to "listen with the third ear" (7) or the ability to "read between the lines" is a prerequisite for understanding each other. We all need this ability to get along, although we are not always as fortunate as Siegfried in Wagner's opera of the same name. In a remarkable scene the deceptive use of words is demonstrated. Mime, the dwarf, reared Siegfried so that he could use him to kill the dragon who protected the hoard (the treasure he had collected). After Siegfried killed the dragon he licked the blood from his finger. This enabled him to understand what man usually cannot, such as the voices of the birds. And this special sense of perception made him realize what Mime really meant when he offered him a drink with sweet words. While Mime sings in the most endearing way, apparently using innocuous, friendly words, Siegfried understands that he wants to put him to sleep with the drink in order to kill him. When Siegfried expresses surprise at such intention, Mime is offended. How could he be so "misunderstood?" And he continues in the sweetest way, apparently expressing his deepest devotion. However, Siegfried perceives that he wants to cut his head off. Naturally, Siegfried refuses the drink.

If we do not limit our concepts of communication to the logical meaning of words, and it seems we are obliged not to do so, then it is obvious that a "breakdown of communication" is impossible. We impress each other constantly with our intentions, be it with words, without them, or despite the literal meaning of our words. For this reason, the real understanding between people is based on the apperception of each one's goals and intentions. (This teleo-analytic approach is characteristic of Adlerian Psychology which understands behavior as purposive.) (8) Words, in this sense, have to be analyzed from the viewpoint of the purpose which they serve. Similarly, confusion and misunderstandings can be recognized as meaningful, in no way hindering communication but rather serving some negative purpose which is well communicated and, therefore, usually highly effective. Naturally, the effect does not promote harmony, but justifies and intensifies conflict.

We are now prepared to analyze the kind of communication which takes place in our families when they outwardly give the appearance of a breakdown in communication. It is obvious that such apparent breakdown is not the cause of the conflict but rather an essential part of it. From where do the conflicts arise which plague the modern family, particularly in the United States? It has been far too little realized that they are the consequence of a democratic evolution, which deprives adults of their traditional power over children. (9) Democratic evolution means increasing equality. As other heretofore dominant groups (nobility, whites, management, etc.) lost their power over the previously subjugated counter-part, so men lost their power over women and adults over children. Women and children gained a degree of equality and self-determination which they have never before enjoyed in all known history. They no longer are willing to submit, but are always afraid of being forced to do so. As a consequence, the eternal war between the sexes and the war between the generations, which resulted from the inequality in the relationship between them, broke into the open. The ensuing struggle for power and status penetrates our families. Neither men and women, nor parents and children, have the skill and knowledge to live with each other as equals, since our autocratic tradition has not prepared them for such a task, nor provides them with any guide post for solving conflicts on the basis of equality, i.e.; of mutual respect. (10)

The conflicts within our families reflect this war between the sexes and between the generations. Our competitive atmosphere intensifies the struggle of each member of the family for status, if possible through some form of superiority and power. Each one is afraid that the other may take advantage of him or, what is even worse, appear superior. One can well understand the goals which each one sets for himself in this situation.

The strongest influence in each family is usually exerted by the mother. Taking care of the family is *her* responsibility as a rule. At the same time, American women are determined not to be inferior to men, although they still like to look up to a superior male—a sad inner contradiction, on which many marriages are wrecked. In many instances, mothers try to prove how right they are, feeling victimized by insensitive husbands and irresponsible children. The fathers, in turn, want to save whatever masculine superiority they can muster, either by withdrawing into business, sports, or politics, or merely behind a newspaper. The children, in turn, accept gleefully mother's sense of responsibility by refusing to take on any for themselves. They use mother's determination to make a success of her marriage and of her motherhood, by putting her in their service. In case the parents have any notion that they can subdue the child and make him conform, behave, study, or contribute, the child is well prepared to involve the parents in a power contest in which he has the greater resources. This is the characteristic conflict situation in our families. The children use a great variety of means to get power, revenge, or to withdraw. In this way they can defeat the parents who assume that they should be able to compel the child to behave or learn or contribute.

One can easily imagine what kind of communication ensues with the various protagonists within the family pursuing their own goals and manipulating all the other members of the family to "cooperate" with them in such pursuit. It is actually a sign of human ingenuity that each can achieve so much agreement in a most intricate pattern of interactions without really being aware of what he is doing, and nevertheless can accomplish his end with extreme efficiency. Examples can be found on almost any average day in any average American family, beginning early in the morning and ending when the children finally are quiet in bed, unless they choose to use the night as an additional area of interaction.

A typical instance of this is the so-called dependent child. He plays weak and helpless in order to get constant attention from his mother. She in turn is more than willing to do for him what he could do for himself, because this gives her an opportunity to impress the child and herself with her importance, and at the same time, with his deficiency. He is satisfying her needs for importance and superiority and she his desire for service.

During one day's time they give each other innumerable signals to move into action in their well-defined and assigned roles. The child gives his mother a chance to show how good and responsible she is, and she in turn, gives him the attention and service he wants. Each one knows very well the signs to which the other one responds, and neither misses any cue. Let us give an example which—in innumerable variations—can be found in almost any family.

It was a quiet street in a suburb, on a sunny noon. A little girl played alone on the sidewalk, when the observer, a woman passing by, approached. At that moment a third floor window opened and a woman called, "Mary, come up, lunch is ready." Nothing happened. The observer stopped, intrigued by this incident, and decided to watch and see what would happen. Shortly afterwards, the woman appeared again at the window and again called, "Mary, come up, lunch is ready." Again, nothing happened. So the observer waited, even more intrigued. A third time the woman appeared at the window, calling Mary to come up for lunch. When nothing happened again, the observer approached the little girl and asked her whether her name was Mary. The girl looked up, without interrupting her play and said, "Yes ma'am." "And was that your Mother?" "Yes ma'am." "Didn't you hear what she said?" "Oh yes ma'am." "And why did you not go up?" "Oh, Mommy hasn't yelled yet."

Now let us examine this episode. Was there communication between mother and child or not? From outside appearance it was lacking. Mary did not pay any attention to what Mother said; the meaning of her words was utterly lost. It seemed that mother could not make herself understood in her desire to have Mary come up. Therefore, we can speak about a breakdown of communication if we merely adhere to the meaning of the words which was lost in the interaction. Actually, however, it was a perfect example of well-understood communication. Mother did not really expect Mary to come up before she yelled; she probably never comes after the first call. And Mary understood very well that Mother was not expecting her yet. It would have been quite possible for Mother to communicate to her child, even without yelling, that she meant it when she called first. And Mary would have understood if Mother had changed her customary approach, calling her in a different way, indicating she had better come up or else, (implying punishment if Mother is not familiar with modern approaches, or logical consequences if she is.) As it was, both had apparently agreed that the first few calls were meaningless, some kind of forewarning which was not to be taken seriously. Of course, Mother was utterly unaware of such an "agreement," although she acted according to it.

The real issue was not the lunch, nor the coming up for lunch. It was the attention Mary demanded and Mother was willing to provide. The interaction between mother and child can only be understood when one realizes the role which each plays. The child is not willing to do anything unless she gets considerable amount of service and attention. She must be called several times, understanding very well what Mother says, but waiting for more attention on her part. And mother, being good and considerate, is willing to spend time and effort in giving the attention. She communicates to the child exactly how far she is willing to go. The yelling indicates the termination of the game to which the child is perfectly willing to consent. Therefore, there is no lack of communication whatsoever to be found in this interaction, if we for a moment forget the meaning of the spoken word and merely consider its function.

It is as difficult to stop a child from doing mischief in order to get mother's attention as it is to stop her from falling for his provocations. The words spoken by either are insignificant; they are merely props to stimulate the other one in his anticipated endeavors. A child in a power contest is honor-bound to do what he is told *not* to do, and to refuse to do what is asked. Everyone can clearly see that, if he is willing. It is not surprising that the parents usually do not see it, because if they did, they could no longer participate in the game. Therefore, they continue to tell him what he should do, every day newly surprised that he does not do it. Or they may ask him to stop what he is doing, knowing very well that he won't. If either would change the customary behavior, the game of fencing, of trying to overpower and defeat each other, would come to an end. Then they would be obliged to establish a new relationship. This they cannot do by themselves without help and instruction. First of all, they would not know what else to do. The child who would obey would feel utterly lost, and the parents who would stop trying to overpower him would also lose face and their sense of worth and usefulness. Each one keeps the other going in the direction which he has chosen for himself and each fulfills the other's demands in a complementary partnership.

It is a mistake to assume that parents are entirely responsible for the children's behavior. This would give them credit where they do not deserve it. It is probable that the children, in their mistaken ideas about themselves and their chances to find a place in the group, often induce the parents to react as they do. One can assume that in any relationship both parties work together to reach the final pattern of interactions. It is done by trial and error. Since neither party is aware of what he is doing to the other, neither is in a position to choose his approach "deliberately." Each manages very well however, to signal his expectations to the other.

The communication system usually functions to an unbelievable degree of accuracy. Children are particularly well equipped to size up the adults with one glance and to know what to expect from them. If the adult, parent or teacher, makes up his mind to respond in a different way, the child often instantaneously perceives such a change of mind and adjusts his approach. Again, this does not occur with full awareness. We respond impulsively to each other, fulfilling the expectations of those to whom we are exposed. Children exhibit greater vitality, ingenuity, spontaneity, and cleverness and therefore succeed much faster and more efficiently in inducing the adults to behave as they expect. However, in fairness to the adults one must admit that they succeed more often than it seems because their verbally expressed expectations of the child are often not identical with their *actual* expectations. They may believe in their sincerity if they tell their child they expect him to succeed; they would like to expect success, but actually do not anticipate it. And it is this anticipation of a child's failure which often induces it. In this sense, then, parents do communicate their expectations to the child more frequently than they know.

The accuracy of the communication which exists between a misbehaving child and the adult is startling. We can distinguish four goals of a disturbing or deficient normal child. Every child tries to belong; but if he becomes discouraged, as all our children do, he develops wrong ideas about his possibilities to find his place. Then he (1) either tries to get attention and service, finding his place through what he can get; or, (2) he tries to demonstrate his own power if the parents attempt to stop forcefully his demand for attention. If he feels completely beaten down and disliked, then he may try (3) to get even, to hurt as he feels hurt, as his only means to make himself count. If he is utterly discouraged and expects nothing but failure, then he (4) may flaunt real or assumed deficiencies in order to be left alone, thereby avoiding more painful evidence of his worthlessness.

The children are not aware of the purpose in their misbehavior; nevertheless they are very systematic in achieving their end. The adults are also completely unaware, in most cases, of the child's purpose in misbehaving, and consequently succumb to the child's provocation. The child does not appeal to their logic, but to their emotions; and this appeal is usually done skillfully and effectively. It is the evoked emotion in the adult which corresponds to the child's goal and makes the adult such an easy victim. When the parent feels annoyed, he is inclined to communicate this annoyance either by scolding, advising, admonishing, or coaxing. Little does he realize that in doing so, he is merely following the child's direction and demands, namely to give special attention. On the other hand, when the parent is provoked, feeling that he cannot let the child "do that to him," then he not only invites the child to show him that he can, but also becomes inveigled in a power contest in which the child is usually not the loser.

When the parent feels deeply hurt and cannot understand how anyone could be so mean, then he only responds to the child's intentions, namely to be hurt. And, as a rule, he retaliates and thereby provokes the child to hurt even further. And when the adult, parent or teacher, feels like throwing up his arms in despair because he does not know what to do with the child, then he merely responds to the child's desire to be left alone. Many children convince the adults that they are incapable, and induce them to treat them in such a way that both become more convinced of their inability.

Each relationship is a closed system, in which the responses to one stimulus are the stimuli to the next response of the same kind. There is no corrective feedback possible since both parties have agreed on the premises of their interaction, on the purpose of each individual act, fitting into the pattern of their definite, although unconscious, agreement.

The most important question concerns possible solutions. While our families can well continue with the established patterns of relationships, giving each member victories and defeats, satisfaction and frustrations, this kind of equilibrium is naturally too expensive, both for the individuals concerned and for society as a whole. Families fail to develop the qualities in children which they need for healthy and satisfactory living. Suffering is the price which all pay for their inability to live peacefully with each other in a democratic setting of mutual respect. It is mandatory that parents learn to use methods of raising children which have been proven effective. Without familiarity with new approaches, they are no match for their children and in no position to guide them, since they have lost the position of power and authority.

An essential part of the retraining of parents consists of extricating them from the undue demands of their children. Only after they have stopped providing unnecessary and harmful services, ceased taking on responsibility which the children should discharge but impose on them, refused to involve themselves in a power contest and being defeated in it, only then can the parents exert constructive influences and take effective steps in dealing with their children. This implies in fact a temporary *disruption of communication.* The signals from the children, which succeeded in provoking ill-advised reactions in the parents, must first be rendered ineffective. Then the way is open to re-establish communication for different purposes.

There are ways to establish a better and more productive "understanding" between all members of the family. They can be made aware of their present form of detrimental cooperation through counseling. They also can get together in a "family council" to discuss their common problems. The atmosphere in many families is not conducive to open and frank discussion. The greatest obstacle is the reluctance of everyone to listen to the others. This reluctance is quite meaningful and understandable if the relationship is devoted to struggle and mutual defeat. Seeing the point of view of the opponent would weaken one's own determination to win, to make the other do what one wants. The mere fact of listening to each other without arguing affects the relationship—because now they are willing to work together toward a real understanding of each other instead of using each other as sparring partners. The beneficial effects of a frank talk lies not so much in the growing realization about how the others feel, but in the willingness to sit down together to find solutions. Naturally, everyone engulfed in the subtle or open struggles which family life so often provides, wants a solution, would like to live in peace. But each one thinks only about what the others should do, considering himself a victim and not an active participant in the creation of the difficulties.

This brings us to the final point, the significance of talk within our present family structure. A large portion of all verbal communications are not devoted to any constructive purpose. Words are used to accuse and to defend, to criticize and to strike back. What is said is usually offensive and provocative; how it is said reflects the purpose. Talk as a means to convey ideas can only be used outside of a conflicting situation.

It presupposes that the other is willing to listen, which is usually not the case in a fight. To reestablish language as a means of communication within the family would require the avoidance of talk whenever conflicts arise. This is a difficult lesson to learn for everyone, particularly for mothers. It is an essential lesson, however, if words are to be instruments of positive and constructive communication in the service of harmony and peaceful living.

BIBLIOGRAPHY

1. Alfred Korzybski, *Science and Sanity,* Lancaster, Pa: Science Press Printing Company, 1933.
2. S. I. Hayakawa, *Language in Thought and Action,* New York: Harcourt, Brace, and Co., 1939.
3. Henry Clay Lindgren, *Mental Health in Education,* New York: Henry Holt & Co., 1954.
4. Alfred Adler, *Understanding Human Nature,* Greenwich, Conn: Fawcett Publ., 1954.
5. Rudolf Dreikurs, "Adlerian Analysis of Interaction," *Group Psychotherapy,* 1955, Vol. III.
6. A. Barbara Dominick. "The Value of Non-Verbal Communication in Personality Understanding," *Journal of Nervous and Mental Disorders,* 1956, Vol. 123.
7. Theodore Reik, *Listening with the Third Ear,* New York: Ferrar, Straus and Company, 1948.
8. Heinz & Rowena Ansbacher, *The Individual Psychology of Alfred Adler,* New York: Basic Books, 1956.
9. Rudolf Dreikurs, *The Challenge of Parenthood,* New York: Hawthorn Books, 1948. (Rev. Ed. 1958).
10. Rudolf Dreikurs, *The Challenge of Marriage,* New York: Hawthorn Books, 1946.

Index